DOOLEY

DOOLEY
MY 40 YEARS AT GEORGIA

Vincent J. Dooley

with

Tony Barnhart

TRIUMPH
BOOKS
CHICAGO

Library of Congress Cataloging-in-Publication Data

Dooley, Vince, 1932–
    Dooley : my 40 years at Georgia / Vincent J. Dooley with Tony Barnhart.
       p. cm.
    ISBN-13: 978-1-57243-755-5
    ISBN-10: 1-57243-755-3
       1. Dooley, Vince, 1932– 2. Football coaches—United States—Biography.
3. Georgia Bulldogs (Football team)—History. 4. University of Georgia—
Football—History. I. Barnhart, Tony. II. Title.

GV939.D662A3 2005
796.332'092—dc22
[B]

                                           2005048636

This book is available in quantity at special discounts for your group or organization. For further information, contact:

Triumph Books
542 South Dearborn Street
Suite 750
Chicago, Illinois 60605
(312) 939-3330
Fax (312) 663-3557

Printed in U.S.A.
ISBN-13: 978-1-57243-755-5
ISBN-10: 1-57243-755-3
Design by Sue Knopf
Photos courtesy of the University of Georgia Sports Information Department unless indicated otherwise.

Contents

Foreword by Barbara Dooley
vii

Acknowledgments
xiii

Introduction by Tony Barnhart
xv

CHAPTER 1
Regrets? Too Few to Mention
1

CHAPTER 2
The Players: From Peter Anderson to Ben Zambiasi
11

CHAPTER 3
The Assistants: Brother Billy, Hootie, and Erk
39

CHAPTER 4
The Characters: Bear, Shug, Woody, and Assorted Others
53

CHAPTER 5
Glory, Glory Days: Champions and
Those Who Walked with Champions
75

CHAPTER 6
The Last Waltz: 25 Years Seemed Like a Good Number
107

CHAPTER 7
Temptations: Why I Never Left Georgia
115

CHAPTER 8
A Series of Crises: From Chest Pains to Jan Kemp
125

CHAPTER 9
New York, New York: Next Stop, the College Football Hall of Fame
143

CHAPTER 10
Back on Top: SEC Football Championship Fills a Void
153

CHAPTER 11
President Michael Adams: The Controversy from My Perspective
163

CHAPTER 12
Still So Much to Do
193

APPENDIX I
Chronology
209

APPENDIX II
Vince Dooley's Top 10 Wins at Georgia
215

APPENDIX III
Vince Dooley's All-SEC Players and All-Americans
219

APPENDIX IV
Year-by-Year Scores
229

INDEX
243

Foreword

On March 19, 1960, I married Vincent Joseph Dooley. I was 19 years old and so much in love that I couldn't see straight.

He was an assistant football coach at Auburn and I knew he had ambitions of being a head coach some day. I had no idea what that would mean. I was so young that I just thought we would have a normal life. You get married. You have children. You go to work. You come home.

You know. Normal.

That was 45 years ago and you know what? Our life has *never* been normal. But it has been wonderful. Today we have four children, 11 grandchildren, and a million precious memories. We have been truly blessed because, in a profession where people have to move just to survive, we have been in the same home in Athens for 41 years!

When Vincent became the head coach at Georgia in December 1963, I had no idea what the job entailed. All I knew was that in the spring of 1964 at the SEC meetings I suddenly found myself in the same room with Bear Bryant, Shug Jordan (for whom Vincent played and coached), Johnny Vaught, Ray Graves, Charlie McClendon, and all of their wives. These people were legends whom I had heard my daddy talk about. I really didn't know how I was supposed to act, so I did what I always did—I just sort of made it up as I went along.

When Vincent was offered the job at Georgia, I told him that if he took it, I would never again complain about life as a coach's wife. Needless to say, I didn't keep that promise.

In fact, I only made it to New Year's Eve, 1963. I thought that the Georgia job was a really big deal and that when we arrived in Athens there would be a brass band and a bunch of people there to greet us. But when we got to the Holiday Inn there was no band. There was no parade. There were no people. There was just a lot of ice and snow.

Not long after we checked into the hotel the lights went out. Deanna, our oldest, was about two, Daniel was just a baby, and I was pregnant with Denise. Daniel was screaming, and we couldn't warm his bottle because there was no power. I cried all night because all of our Auburn friends were at the Orange Bowl in Miami where it was nice and warm. Vince, as he is known to do, took Deanna and got out of there, and he treated her to a candlelight dinner at the Holiday Inn.

That night was as bad as it got. And of course, things got a lot better.

When we moved to Athens, Vincent told me not to get too comfortable because you never know when they are going to kick you out. And I believed him.

In May 1964 we moved into our home on Milledge Circle. The place has undergone a lot of changes over the past 41 years but we're still there. Our children never lived in another home. They have had the same friends since nursery school. That is a blessing, and we know it. Only a handful of us in the coaching profession—like Joe and Sue Paterno at Penn State—have been able to stay in one place for our entire careers. We realize how lucky we are.

But it is not all luck. For 41 years Vincent has served the University of Georgia well and has become one of the most respected people in the history of his profession. This does not happen by accident.

This book is the story of his life, and that also makes it the story of our life together here at Georgia. I want to tell you a few things that maybe some people do not know about this extraordinary man. One of the things that made him successful for such a long period of time is that he has always been willing to change. When so many coaches back in the sixties fought integration, I watched Vince go out there and work on it. He knew it was the right thing to do, regardless of how others might have felt.

I remember huge arguments over the role of women's athletics and the passage of Title IX. He never balked. He just got into it and incorporated a bigger commitment to women at Georgia. Today Georgia has one of the best women's athletic departments in the country. It happened because Vincent worked to make it happen.

Vincent's integrity is impeccable. If he looks you in the eye and tells you something, you know he's going to do it. He treats people fairly and treats everybody with dignity, regardless of their situation. He has never been the type of person who has been full of himself. For all that he has accomplished in his life, he is a very humble person.

But he is also very naïve when it comes to people. He doesn't think badly of anybody unless it is blatantly in front of him. I think I can see the flaws in people pretty quickly. He always looks for the good in people first and gives them the benefit of the doubt. It is a wonderful trait to have, but sometimes he has been hurt by it.

People ask me all the time how we have made it work for 45 years. He's a strong personality, but I'm a strong personality too. The only way that we have been able to make it work is that from the first day of our marriage, he has been willing to let me have my wings. He has never once tried to hold me back from anything I've wanted to do. And I have wanted to do a lot of things, from charity work to public speaking to politics, and now I'm giving real estate a try. He has always supported me 100 percent.

By the same token I feel like I have supported him as he pursued his goals and dreams. Sometimes it was hard because of all the time it took him away from his family. The trick is that neither one of us tried to control the other. Of course I tried from time to time to control him when he was at home, but I wasn't successful.

There are some wonderful things about staying in one place for a long time. I think the closest we ever came to leaving Georgia was when Auburn, our alma mater, offered Vincent the chance to come back and be head football coach and athletic director in 1980. I really thought we were going. We had been here 17 years, but we still had a lot of friends back at Auburn, and, of course, they wanted us to come because Auburn's program was really struggling. Vincent felt pulled emotionally, especially considering that his college roommate Fob James, who was then the governor of Alabama, was trying to recruit him.

I will never forget Vincent walking through our home one day and looking at a wall that contained pictures of all of his All-Conference players and team captains at Georgia. He said, "You know, it's hard to leave when you've raised that many kids." In addition, all four of our biological children had been raised Bulldogs, and it was too much to ask them to change.

At that moment I knew we weren't going anywhere.

Maybe if we hadn't been playing for the national championship, Vincent would have been able to leave. But he just couldn't and I understood. He has never regretted it and neither have I.

I have to say that I really never thought it would end for Vincent at Georgia because of a president. We tried to have a good relationship with Michael Adams, just as we did with all of the previous presidents at Georgia. But I think Michael Adams came to the Georgia job (in 1997) with the idea of getting rid of Vincent. He was not Adams' only intended victim but certainly his most challenging. Adams was finally successful in June 2003 when he decided not to extend Vincent's contract. When all was said and done, all Vince wanted was just a few more years, and he would have settled for just one for the good of the university.

Vincent has handled the way he has been treated a lot better than I have. What I still don't understand is that with all the love the Georgia people have for Vincent, nobody in a position of authority stood up for him. The Board of Regents was silent, though I understood that publicly they all had to support the president's right to make the decision, however bad it was. The governor (Sonny Perdue), who was a walk-on football player for Vince on his first full freshman team, did nothing. I really thought somebody out there would step up to the plate. I just found that curious.

I was hurt and angry that they would do that to him because I know all of the family dinners he missed working to help the University of Georgia. I know he missed the church confirmation of his own child so that he could be in Rome, Georgia, to attend a church service with a top recruit (who played the organ) and his family. I know how much family time this man gave up and how much time he did not have with his own children as they grew up because of this university.

Vince has been a tireless fund-raiser for the university. In addition to raising several million dollars for athletics *and* academics, he has personally given approximately $600,000 of his own money—often against my wishes. It just doesn't seem right that he was not able to end his career on his own terms. He had earned it many times over.

But we will be fine. And I can promise you this: he may no longer be working for the University of Georgia, but you have not heard the last of Vince Dooley. At the age of 72, he has an energy that I just can't explain. We have a number of young guys who come in and help in his garden, and he will outwork all of them. Some of them quit because they couldn't keep up with him.

He is the most determined person I have ever known, and he will continue to find a way to make a contribution. I'm not sure exactly what he's going to do, but I do know this: he will be busy.

The past 41 years at Georgia have been a wonderful journey for both of us. I'm glad that Vincent has taken the time to share it with you.

—Barbara Dooley
Athens, Georgia

Barbara Dooley is the author of *Put Me In, Coach: Confessions of a Football Wife*. She and Vince Dooley were married on March 19, 1960. They have four children and 11 grandchildren.

Acknowledgments

On a project like this there are so many people to thank. Here are just a few to whom I am deeply indebted.

Claude Felton, Georgia's Hall of Fame sports information director, has always been a good friend and supportive of my career. He provided encouragement and plenty of access to the vast resources of his office. Karen Huff, Claude's administrative assistant, was always willing to help with one last photograph.

Becky Stevens, coach Dooley's administrative assistant when this project began, remained in that capacity until he retired as athletic director on June 30, 2004. She put up with all my phone calls and requests, even when the whole world was trying to get access to Vince Dooley.

Jennifer Kilcrease became coach Dooley's administrative assistant for one year in his new capacity as a fund-raiser and consultant at Georgia. Without her help scheduling interviews, I never could have completed this project on time. Thanks for making it easy.

Loran Smith set the standard for books about Vince Dooley and Georgia football. He has always been encouraging and supportive and for that I want to thank him.

Barbara Dooley. Behind every great man there is a great woman, and Barbara, you are the greatest.

And finally, to coach Vince Dooley. Working on this book was both a labor of love and a privilege. Thanks for your time and your patience. You invested a lot of both into the finished project.

Introduction

In more than 50 years as a player, coach, and administrator in college athletics, Georgia's Vince Dooley has seen it all and lived it all. And it has been a remarkable journey.

Dooley grew up on the tough side of Mobile, Alabama, with a quick temper and a wandering personality that was desperately looking for direction. He found that sense of direction in athletics, which would turn his life around and set him on a very successful path. He would go on to earn a football scholarship and become a successful quarterback at Auburn University.

On December 4, 1963, Vince Dooley was named the head football coach at the University of Georgia. He was only 31 years old. He was such an unknown commodity that when it came time to introduce Dooley at a press conference in Athens, Georgia president O. C. Aderhold could not remember his name. He simply introduced Dooley as "that bright young coach."

Before he was done, that bright young coach would win 201 games, six SEC championships, and one national championship. Just six years after his retirement as coach in 1988, Vince Dooley had his ticket punched for the College Football Hall of Fame.

When Dooley retired as football coach, some Georgia fans were ready to put him out to pasture, but he fooled them, putting together an ultra-successful third act in his life. As Georgia's athletic director, Dooley built a program that became the model for the rest of the nation.

On June 30, 2004, Dooley completed his 41st year as either coach or athletic director at Georgia. Today, after serving for a year as a consultant and fund-raiser, for the first time since December 1963 he is not an employee of the University of Georgia. The normally reserved Dooley is finally ready to talk in detail about an extraordinary life spent in the hot spotlight of college athletics. It is quite a story and I am very proud to have the opportunity to help him tell it.

This is a book I knew I would someday get the opportunity to write. Why? Because almost 40 years ago some cosmic force determined that Vince Dooley's life and career would become intertwined with my own.

I was only 12 years old when I became hooked on college football. It was Vince Dooley's fault. For me, the Vince Dooley story began on September 18, 1965, when Georgia met Alabama, the defending national champions, in a televised game played in Athens. In those days I wasn't a college football fan. I loved baseball and, like most of the boys in that day, I was a Yankees fan. But that day I watched a college football game that would change my life.

Georgia won the game 18–17 on a miracle flea flicker play from Kirby Moore to Pat Hodgson to Bob Taylor followed by a two-point conversion. I went nuts and ran screaming through the house. My mother thought I had lost my mind. In reality, I was about to lose my heart.

A week later I attended my first college football game in person when Georgia hosted Vanderbilt in Athens (some 30 miles from my hometown of Union Point). Georgia won the game 24–10, but that's not what I remember best. I remember the colors, the smells, the cool fall breeze, the bands, and all the pretty girls.

Not long after that, I met Vince Dooley and nervously asked for his autograph. Little did I know that our paths would cross many, many times over the next 40 years.

In high school I was a huge Georgia fan, which meant I was also a Vince Dooley fan. Billy and Mary Jean Ashley, the parents of my best friend Eric, took me on as another son and let me tag along on their game-day trips to Athens. That's where I began to build a reservoir of priceless memories. I can never repay Momma Jean and the rest of the Ashley family for that kindness.

I would later attend the University of Georgia, and in 1975 I became the sports editor of the *Red and Black*, the student newspaper. One of the perks of that job was traveling with the team on road games.

I don't think I brought coach Dooley much luck that fall. My first trip with the team was a 28–13 loss at Ole Miss on October 11, 1975. Later I went with the team to the Cotton Bowl, and Georgia lost 31–10 to Arkansas. In the other games Georgia was 9–1 that season. If coach Dooley ever blamed me, he never said anything.

I graduated from Georgia in June 1976 and went to work for a small newspaper in Union, South Carolina. While my work there focused on Clemson, South Carolina, and the local high schools, Georgia football and Vince Dooley were never far from my mind. On October 2, 1976, I came back to Athens for one of the greatest days ever at Georgia, when the Bulldogs knocked off Alabama 21–0 on the way to coach Dooley's third SEC championship. Traffic around town was tied up for hours, and the party did not stop until the wee hours of Sunday morning.

I moved on to Greensboro, North Carolina, in 1977 and stayed there for seven years. Because there was no Internet, and because very few games were on television back then, keeping up with coach Dooley and the Bulldogs became harder to do. But I usually found a way.

I remember calling home one Saturday and asking my mother, Sara, to place the phone near her radio so that I could hear Larry Munson call the action. My mother did it, of course, but secretly wondered when her oldest son would grow out of this kind of behavior.

Sometimes when the games were played at night, I could pick up WSB radio out of Atlanta, the flagship station for Georgia football. With the signal going in and out, I was listening that night in 1978 when Georgia drove the length of the field in the final moments and Rex Robinson kicked a 29-yard field goal with three seconds left to beat Kentucky 17–16. I can still hear Munson screaming, "Yeah, yeah, yeah, yeah," as Robinson's field goal split the uprights.

I can remember sitting in an EconoLodge in Tallahassee, Florida, on November 8, 1980, watching the Georgia-Florida game being played only a few hours away in Jacksonville. I was *so* tempted to make the drive over to Jacksonville, but I knew I would have had problems getting back to my assignment that night. So I nervously paced up and down in my hotel room when Georgia fell behind 21–20 with only 1:35 left. What was my reaction when Buck Belue hit Lindsay Scott for a 93-yard touchdown pass and a miracle 26–21 win? Let's just say that there is a lamp in the Tallahassee EconoLodge that will never be the same.

I can still remember the day in 1981 when I became the first person in my neighborhood to buy a VCR. I got it at Sears for the unheard-of sum of $800. A blank video tape (Beta format) was 20 bucks! The neighbors wanted to know what I was up to. Well, I informed them, I sure as heck wasn't going to shell out that kind of cash just to watch movies! The Georgia-Florida game, also known as "the World's Largest Outdoor Cocktail Party," was going to be on television that Saturday. I was going to be covering Duke at Wake Forest for my newspaper. I had to tape it so that I could watch the game later that night.

In case you're wondering, Georgia drove the length of the field behind Herschel Walker and scored late to win 26–21. It was worth every penny I paid for that VCR, and today I still have a copy of that tape.

In 1984 I realized my lifelong dream as a sportswriter when I came back to Georgia to work for the *Atlanta Journal-Constitution*. My assignment: to be the beat writer covering the University of Georgia Bulldogs. I was 31 years old. How could it possibly get any better than that?

That year I spoke to coach Dooley on a daily basis, and from him I learned much, much more than football. I learned why he has been a success in everything he has done. Without knowing it, Vince Dooley taught me one of the most important lessons of my life: it always helps to have talent, but talent is nothing without discipline, organization, and hard work. It is a lesson that has never left me.

I stayed on the Georgia beat only a year, but Vince Dooley and I would always stay in touch. I was in Jacksonville, Florida, on January 1, 1989, when he coached his last game. Prior to the Gator Bowl against Michigan State, I had a chance to visit with him in his hotel room and catch up on old times. I was 11 years old when he coached his first game for Georgia. Now here I was, 25 years later, sharing some meaningful time with Vince Dooley as he prepared to coach his last game for the Bulldogs.

I also had the honor to be at the Waldorf-Astoria Hotel in New York on December 6, 1994, when he became the first coach in Georgia history to be inducted into the College Football Hall of Fame.

As he began to put the finishing touches on his remarkable career as a player, coach, and administrator, I was given the opportunity to help him write this book. For a little country boy from Union Point, Georgia, this is all pretty heady stuff.

So writing this book with coach Dooley is both an honor and a privilege. It is the story of his life, but in it, I have found my life as well.

In February 2003 the NCAA convened a summit meeting of top officials from around the country in an effort to improve the overall level of sportsmanship in college athletics. The chairman of the summit was Vincent J. Dooley, the athletic director of the University of Georgia. When asked why they chose Dooley to head this meeting of the best and brightest in the profession, one of the organizers responded, "It's simple. When coach Dooley talks, *everybody* listens."

In this book Vince Dooley has finally decided to talk candidly about his extraordinary life and career. We would all do well to listen.

—Tony Barnhart
Atlanta, Georgia

1

Regrets?
Too Few to Mention

Where in the world have the past 41 years gone?

Barbara and I find ourselves saying that a lot these days. On March 19, 2005, we celebrated our 45th wedding anniversary.

Our daughter, Deanna, was just two and a half years old when we came to Georgia in December of 1963. Now she is 43 years old. How is that possible?

And you just wonder again: where has all of that time gone?

It was snowing and sleeting when I brought Barbara to Athens for the first time in 1963. I blinked a couple of times, and now all four of our children are grown and we have 11 grandchildren.

It just goes by too fast . . . way too fast.

But here we are, nearing the end of an incredible journey that began when we were both incredibly young. I was 31 years old when I became the head football coach at the University of Georgia. Barbara was 24—a head coach's wife and a child bride for sure. I signed my first contract for the princely sum of $12,500 per year. A housing allowance and a television deal (which I negotiated myself) bumped that total all the way to $15,000 per year. Needless to say, coaching—and coaching salaries—have changed a little bit since then.

And little did Barbara and I know that 41 years later we would still be living in the same house on Milledge Circle. Well, not exactly the same house, considering there have been nine major additions, but we've had the same address since we moved in six months after our arrival in Athens. Every time a kid would leave, Barbara would want to add a room. It didn't make sense then, but it does now. They do multiply!

In that span I can now say that we accomplished most of the things that we set out to do:

- In 25 years as Georgia's head football coach (1964–1988), we were able to win 201 games, six SEC championships, and one national championship.

- In 26 years as Georgia's athletic director (1979–2004), we went from a budget of around $15 million to one of almost $60 million. Three times in my final five years as athletic director we finished among the nation's top overall departments. In 1999 our athletic program won four national championships and finished second only to Stanford as the nation's best program.

- In my 40 years as football coach and athletic director, I saw the stadium grow by some 50,000 seats—from 43,000 to almost 93,000, with 77 sky suites. In that same period of time the contributions for ticket priority (money that fans pay to reserve their tickets) went from $75,000 to $22 million. Not only was our department fiscally sound (we always finished in the black), but I believe we did it while maintaining the highest of standards, both ethically and academically. Yes, we did have a problem from time to time, but each time we faced a crisis, we used it to make our program stronger.

What is interesting is that when you reach this point in your life and your career, the victories and the championships still mean a lot. But what means even more are the lives you touched, and how the lives of others have touched you.

I've always said that the great thing about being a teacher or a coach is that you continue to enjoy it for the rest of your life through your players and students. All the memories of competition don't become less important, but what becomes increasingly *more* important are the players who come back and say two simple words: "Thanks, Coach."

Some thank me for teaching them the simple lessons of discipline. Or they are grateful because I taught them to win—and to lose—with dignity and class. Or I taught them the work ethic that they would take with them and use for the rest of their lives. Or I taught them how to work through adversity in order to achieve their goals.

That's because the teachers you always remember are the ones who were the most demanding. When you're young you might not like to be in a class where the teachers are demanding, but to this day I still remember Mrs. McCloud, an English teacher who taught a course called Business and Professional Writing at Auburn. She was a tough son of a gun, but when it was all over I realized she had pushed me further than I knew I could go. Those are the teachers who mean the most to you later in your life.

I have been so fortunate in that regard, as my former players have gone on to be doctors, lawyers, teachers, businessmen, and ministers. We even had three professional wrestlers! When someone like Billy Payne, who has accomplished so much since his days at Georgia, expresses his appreciation, that is something I just can't put a value on.

The demands of being a head football coach and an athletic director at this level are great. I've been asked many times if I have any regrets about the path I chose and the sacrifices my family and I had to make to be successful. There are absolutely no regrets. From an athletic standpoint and an administrative standpoint, there is nothing quite like being around a university. Georgia is a very special place, and my family and I know that we have been blessed to have a relationship with the same university that has lasted more than four decades.

Are there some things I wish I had a chance to address in a different way? Of course! In this job you make decisions constantly, and you would love the chance to go back and revisit some of them.

I have told the story many times about playing Pittsburgh in the Sugar Bowl after the 1981 season. We went ahead of them late, but then Pittsburgh came flying down the field behind Dan Marino. It was fourth down, they were on the 33-yard line, and there were about 20 seconds left. We called time-out and had to make a decision on what to do. So we went with the blitz and sent the linebackers after Marino.

We went after Marino, but their halfbacks picked the linebackers up. I mean they literally put their arms around them and picked them up. That gave Marino an extra second, he threw the ball right into the receiver's hands for a touchdown, and they beat us.

So people asked me right after the game . . . and five days later . . . and even now: If you had it to do all over again, would you do it the same? And I say, "Heck no!" I know how that decision turned out. I would certainly do it a different way if I was given a chance.

But you don't get that chance, so you make the best decisions you can and live with the consequences. Decisions are always made in the best interests of the program and the team, so naturally some individuals will be hurt for the good of the whole. I always feel for those who were individually hurt in the decision-making process. The hope is that over the long haul you make many more good decisions than bad ones. I believe we did that.

Like I said, I was only 31 years old when I came to Georgia, and I believe that I was able to grow into the job. I learned over the course of time how to better handle individuals and how to coach a season. I was a much better coach in the eighties than when I started. There were times I wished I could start over, but I learned that you have to grow in the position or you won't be in the job very long.

Leadership Principles

One thing I learned early in my career is that while you grow professionally, you must always keep in mind that there are some basic principles that never change. We must constantly remind ourselves of these principles and reinforce them as we go through our careers.

In 1922 the great John Heisman wrote a book titled *The Principles of Football*. The intangible traits that made successful football teams, players, and professionals back then still ring true today. Here are just a few of his axioms:

- You can't make the team if you don't understand teamwork.

- You can't do yourself justice without getting—and staying—in shape.

- Never give up.

- Never play less than your hardest.

As coaches and educators, we employ—whether we know it or not—the basic, fundamental teaching philosophies expounded by two of the greatest presidents this country has ever known: Thomas Jefferson and Andrew Jackson. The Jeffersonian philosophy of teaching is "to give scope to ability." Translated into coaching, that means providing extraordinarily gifted players an environment in which they can utilize and exploit their superb talents. But the reality is that there are only a few of these kinds of athletes on any given team. The vast majority of a team is made up of players with average skills. Thus, we also employ the Jacksonian philosophy of education, which is "to raise the average." That philosophy challenges us to utilize all of our coaching and teaching tools to produce players who overachieve and rise above their limited talents.

As coaches and teachers, we implement these two philosophies by first making sure our athletes have learned the fundamentals of the game—because only by first mastering the fundamentals can someone maximize their ability.

Secondly, we must be both enthusiastic and demanding. The teachers we all remember were those who loved what they taught and demanded the best of us. The best teachers are those who push us beyond what we think our limits are.

Finally, if we have mastered teaching the game of football to our students but have failed to emphasize the values that the game brings to their personal lives, we have shortchanged ourselves and our athletes. We have, in essence, fallen short in providing one of the greatest services to our profession: teaching and reinforcing fundamental values to young people in a society that has recently proven to be declining in ethics, character, and morality.

We'll talk more about this later, but one of the things I'm most proud of is that when we were faced with a crisis, we addressed it in the right way and ultimately used it to make our program better. We finally learned that we should not spend all of our time defending what went wrong. We knew that even if we got a black eye, if the program was strong we would survive, and every time we survived, our program would grow stronger.

Part of growing in the job is learning how to be flexible. My core principles didn't change, but the way I handle people did. I learned to be a little more understanding. I learned to say no in a nicer way. I learned to be a little more outgoing instead of maintaining my reputation as a staunch Marine (which was the case early in my career). I don't mean to imply that I changed the core values of my Marine training, which have been a tremendous help to me; rather, I tried to be a little more flexible and outgoing.

I have to say that Barbara has been very helpful to me in that regard. I am not naturally an outgoing person. But she taught me that you can work at being a more open person, a more congenial person, a kinder, gentler individual. It came very naturally to Barbara, but as I have grown, it is a lot more natural to me now.

I would like to believe that I was as competitive at the end of my coaching career as I was at the beginning. But I think what moved me to retire at a relatively young age (56) was that I had done just about everything I wanted to do in coaching. You always want to win one more SEC championship, but we did win six. And, of course, I would really have loved to have won more than one national championship, but you get to the point where you wonder if that's all there is. There is always one more game to win, one more championship to pursue. Where does it stop?

The truth is, I had other interests in my life. I thought about running for public office—I gave that a lot of thought. But ultimately I discovered this: service in politics was something I wanted in my mind, but in my heart and gut I realized that I really didn't. In my heart I enjoyed athletics and being around a university campus, so that's why I ultimately took on the challenge of being an athletic administrator, which is something I found to be incredibly rewarding.

Obviously none of what I have accomplished over the past 41 years would have been possible without my family. It was tough being away from home so much, especially when the children were young, but

Barbara was great. She was the ideal coach's wife. She was a great mother . . . and still is. She was a great part-time father, too, which she had to be on many occasions. She was great with the children and great at being able to fill the void. Without her, there was no way I could have balanced the responsibilities of succeeding in coaching and being a good father. Our current coach, Mark Richt, manages this balance better than I ever did, and I have great respect for him.

Back when I started there were absolutely no restrictions on when you could recruit. I remember several times being on vacation and, about five days into it, things would just start to bother me. That was because I knew there was another coach out there talking to recruits while I was on vacation. So I would tell Barbara that I had to take off for a day. I would go visit three or four recruits and then I would come back to vacation feeling a lot better.

Barbara had to make sacrifices, and I know, to a certain extent, my children did too. In that regard, Barbara and I did have one running disagreement. She would go the extra mile so the kids could enjoy some of the extra opportunities that come with being the family of the head coach and/or the athletic director. I would tend to be more conservative. I didn't want them to get "perks" because of my position.

I believe that when you run an organization, you don't want your children to have more privileges than the children of the other members of the organization. I didn't want my children to be spoiled that way. Barbara and I would argue about that all the time. She tells some good stories about it. There were some disadvantages for my children, and they had many advantages. I just didn't want them to have *too* many.

These days I get asked all the time how I feel about the way, after all this time, my career ended at Georgia. In March 2003 I asked for an extension on my contract because there was still so much I wanted to get done at Georgia. I felt good, and the athletic department was in great shape—financially and competitively. But Dr. Michael Adams, Georgia's president, denied my request, which was certainly his right to do. That decision, unfortunately, created a lot of ill will among the Georgia people, and I'm afraid it still exists today.

People ask me if I'm mad or bitter about the decision. I tell them that once a decision is made, even if it isn't the way I want it to be, I pretty well accept it and move on to the next thing. I do not let myself have this type of regret. I do not let myself get upset, bitter, disturbed, angry . . . whatever. It might be that I didn't have the opportunity to script the last two or three years exactly as I wanted them to be, but I didn't let those negative feelings consume me.

While I have accepted the decision, I still believe that Adams made the wrong decision and that something other than good common sense entered into the process. In addition, he was never willing to accept a compromise that I suggested on two different occasions. I will always believe that if the president had compromised in some way, it would have gone a long way toward healing some of the wounds and bringing the Georgia people back together in the best interests of the university.

I didn't want to stay at Georgia because of my own ego; there were just a few more things that I wanted to do. I really felt that it was in the best interests of the athletic department that I stay there another two to three years to finish the capital campaign fund-raising that had gotten off to such a great start. The campaign is necessary for both academics and athletics and was something that I wanted to see through. I thought the fund-raising campaign would be better if I were around to help.

Once it was decided that my continued tenure was not what Adams had in mind, I adjusted to it. I have plenty to be proud of, so I'm not going to let a decision made by one person affect the way I feel for this university and the greatest number of people in it.

The following pages are simply my account of the past 40 years at Georgia: the good and the bad, the happy and the sad. There is the thrill of victory and the agony of defeat. I tried not to pull any punches. If we made a mistake—and there were some—I wanted to admit it. If I disagreed with the decisions of others—as was the case with Michael Adams—I have been as honest as I can be. History, I believe, will always be the final judge.

Regardless of the circumstances that ended my career at Georgia, it was an incredible journey, and retelling it here for you has been a pleasure.

They say that in any meaningful relationship, you always receive much more than you give. That's the way that I feel about my relationship with the University of Georgia and its people. Yes, I have given the balance of my adult life to Georgia, and I can say with great confidence that I worked just as hard on my last day for the university as I did on the first. I also know that my relationship with Georgia has enriched me and my entire family in more ways than I could ever count. Regardless of what happens to me in the future, I can promise that those feelings will never change.

2

The Players:
From Peter Anderson
to Ben Zambiasi

I've been asked what kind of players we tried to recruit to Georgia during my 25 years as head coach. Obviously, talent was important, but I believe if you're going to win on a consistent basis, you have to look beyond just talent.

I always wanted to have players who were willing to lay everything on the line. We looked for players who were absolutely relentless and had high standards both on and off the field. We wanted men who really overachieved as players as well as in the classroom. I just thought that was the ideal combination—if you could find it.

Even though we took some high-risk athletes, we hoped that they would become overachievers as well. And even if they weren't all things to all people, a player needed to have some of those qualities if he was going to succeed. As long as they tried, I wanted them. As long as they would lay it out there every day, there was a place for them in our program.

Whatever our players chose to do professionally after football— become doctors, lawyers, ministers, teachers, even professional wrestlers—as long as they did it well, I wanted to follow them. I feel a sense of pride as I see them grow into men. At the same time, I always feel a sense of disappointment for those who don't do so well. It often nags at me and I think I could have helped a little more. Regardless of how they turn out, they are all part of the family.

I always felt like we recruited well. We didn't have as many first-round draft choices as some people wanted, but for the most part our teams were overachievers. If you talked to the coaches of teams we played, they would tell you that you better buckle your chinstrap when you play Georgia. They are going to play you for 60 minutes. That was the one thing I thought was more important than anything else—that you gain that kind of reputation—and I think for the most part we did.

We always felt that it was our job as coaches to get each player to maximize his God-given talents. For some that may mean being All-American or All-Conference, for others that meant just finding a way to play on the special teams, or even just make the team. The standard for Herschel Walker is going to be different from the standard for "Little" Jimmy Denney.

Jimmy Denney (1964–1965) was an overachieving right guard when we came to Georgia. He wasn't particularly big or fast. What he had was two quick steps so he could get right on you, and once he got on you, he wouldn't let go. He was relentless. We would try to move somebody in who was bigger or faster or clearly more talented to take over that position, but we couldn't get him out of there because in every game he graded out the best. He always knew who to block and he could get on him. He was about 195 pounds.

We had a lot of players like that at Georgia. We also had a lot of All-Americans and All-Conference players. You need them all if you're going to be successful.

Here are some special memories of just a few of the players we coached over 25 years. I wish I could list them all because everyone who put on a Georgia uniform contributed to our success. I will always be grateful to all of them.

Peter Anderson, Center, 1983–1985

Peter came to Georgia from New Jersey with some raw skills and a desire to be good. By the time he left, he had become the bell cow of our offensive line. He had to learn the ways of team discipline, but once he made the conversion, all of his good qualities came out. I remember a team meeting with the seniors in the middle of the 1985 season. I sent Peter out of the room, and he looked like he thought he was in trouble. I brought him back in and told him that he had been named team captain! It was the first time we had ever done it in the middle of a season. Peter went on to become one of the best leaders we've ever had at Georgia. Today he lives in Jacksonville and has a very respectable construction job. I'm really proud of him.

Buck Belue, Quarterback, 1978–1981

We started recruiting Buck when he was a freshman at Valdosta High School. You could tell even then that he had confidence. That was something we had to temper a little bit when he got to Georgia. Buck had an immediate impact on our team as a true freshman. Sometimes, when a young player sees action so early, he feels that every time he touches the ball, it is a big play. He hasn't learned that the other team might occasionally have some success. A quarterback has to learn not to turn a bad play for his team into a great play for the other team. But once Buck learned that, he became one of our greatest quarterbacks.

As a freshman he rallied us from a 20–7 deficit against Georgia Tech to a 29–28 victory. He threw a touchdown pass on fourth down and made a two-point conversion to give us that win.

Then, of course, he led us to the national championship in 1980 and took us to another SEC championship as a senior in 1981. He is the only Georgia quarterback ever to lead the Bulldogs to two consecutive SEC championships.

Buck was a guy who I always believed would be a great Bulldog. I'm glad it worked out that way.

Kevin Butler, Place Kicker, 1981–1984

The best testimonial I can give Kevin Butler is that he is the only place kicker in the College Football Hall of Fame. We've had a lot of great kickers at Georgia because we believe so strongly in that part of the game. None were better or could deliver in the clutch more often than Kevin Butler.

He possessed incredible confidence. Every time we would cross the 50-yard line he would start walking in front of me, just to remind me that he was available. A time or two I had to push him out of the way so I could focus on trying to score a touchdown.

There were so many big kicks. He made a field goal in the rain to beat BYU (17-14 in 1982). He made a 60-yard field goal to beat Clemson (26-23 in 1984). He hit that ball, and it just kept going and going. I know Danny Ford, the Clemson coach, could not believe it.

He ended his college career on an almost incredible note. We were playing Florida State in the Citrus Bowl, and the score was tied in the final seconds. The clock was broken, we did a lousy job of managing our time, and our play selection wasn't very good. I sent him out there to kick a 70-yard field goal on the last play of the game. It was just a foot short. It was the most remarkable miss I ever saw.

Mike Cavan, Quarterback, 1968-1970

In 1968 we had a senior-laden team but we did not have a proven quarterback after Paul Gilbert got hurt. But Mike Cavan, a sophomore, stepped in and led that team to the SEC championship.

Mike was no ordinary sophomore. He was the son of a coach, and because of that he had a very confident air about him. The seniors liked Mike and they believed in him. Mike was the easy choice for the SEC sophomore of the year in 1968. But things did not go well for Mike in his final two years at Georgia. To start, we lost a lot of great players from the 1968 team. Second, things might have come too easy for him as a sophomore. He didn't play as well in 1969 and 1970, and our team showed it. To be fair, Mike simply didn't have the supporting cast he had in 1968.

I think Mike was a little bitter about the way his football career ended, but eventually I brought him back as an assistant coach. He was a very good one. I knew him and I knew his daddy, who was a legendary high school football coach. I knew he had a great knowledge of the game and could help us. He was the most loyal and enthusiastic coach we ever had. He was always full of personality and a great recruiter—just ask Herschel.

Mike stayed with us a long time and then went on to become a head coach at Valdosta State, East Tennessee State, and SMU. Now he is back working in Georgia's development office. Mike Cavan is a great Bulldog through and through.

George Collins, Guard, 1975–1977

A very natural football player who used every ounce of his talent. He wasn't very big but, boy, could he block. We started him at tight end, and he just sort of ate his way into a guard position. It was a good thing for us because George went on to become an All-American. He is still a high school coach.

Cowboy and Moonpie, Guard and Tackle, 1974–1976

We never had a better blocking combination than Joel "Cowboy" Parrish (guard) and Mike "Moonpie" Wilson (tackle). Cowboy was just like George Collins, a real natural as a football player. I remember going to see Moonpie in high school. He was just a big old guy with a lot of potential, but once he got to Georgia, he really didn't want to stay. It seemed like freshman coach Doc Ayers had to go back to Gainesville and get him every two weeks. It's a good thing he stayed. He went on to have a very long pro career in the NFL. The 1976 offensive line might have been the best we've ever had at Georgia; Cowboy and Moonpie were two big reasons why.

Knox Culpepper, Linebacker, 1981–1984

Knox was a wonderful, wonderful individual who came from a great family. He was always very serious-minded and always wanted to do the right thing. He was also a great player.

Knox was, by far, the most conscientious player we had on the team. One time we were over in Mississippi eating the team meal the Saturday before the game. We checked around the room and no Knox. After 15 minutes *still* no Knox. We figured something must be really wrong!

We sent somebody to look for him and, as it turned out, his roommate had inadvertently locked him in the bathroom, and he couldn't get out. When he got to the meal his face was white and he couldn't speak. He didn't have to tell me. I understood.

We've had a number of father and son combinations play at Georgia. Knox and his dad, Knox Sr. (1954-1956), are a terrific example—they were both captains of their respective teams as seniors.

Freddie Gilbert, Defensive End, 1980–1983

I remember going to Freddie's home in Griffin when we were recruiting him. We were sitting around and his mother was serving tea. Freddie reached over and poured tea for everyone without ever having to get up from the couch. He had the longest arms I had ever seen!

And what a great athlete! He could really, really run with incredible speed for a man his size. I was glad that he was playing for us. He is a quality young man who always returns for reunions and get-togethers.

Ray Goff, Quarterback, 1974–1976

When Ray came to Georgia from Moultrie, he had a reputation for being a great high school passer who couldn't run very much. As it turned out, the opposite was true. Actually, he was a good high school passer, but I probably took him down a notch or two with my coaching. Once we installed the veer offense, Ray proved to be a great option quarterback.

In 1976 we used two quarterbacks, Ray and Matt Robinson, to win a championship. Matt established himself as the starter early in his career but then got hurt. Once Ray got the job, he just never gave it up—he was that good.

Ray had a lot of great games for us. He had an incredible day against Florida in 1976 when we rallied from 27-13 down to win 41-27. The following week against Auburn he never threw a pass because he couldn't raise his right arm high enough. It didn't matter because we just ran the ball every play and won 28-0.

Ray returned as an assistant coach and then became our head coach when I retired after the 1988 season. It was a very tough decision when I let him go as head coach in 1995. As a result, we don't talk as much as I wish we did. But Ray has become a tremendously successful businessman.

Bill Goldberg, Defensive Tackle, 1986–1989

He could be one of the meanest guys on the field and one of the sweetest guys off the field. He was a great player for us but then went on to earn international fame as a professional wrestler and a Hollywood actor. He sent my grandson Matthew, who has cerebral palsy, a photo of them arm-wrestling together. On the photo Bill wrote, "Matthew—you are the man!!"

I remember talking to Bill, one of our few Jewish players, about the religious services that were part of our Saturday morning routine. Those services were Christian-oriented for the most part, and I wanted Bill to know that he didn't have to be at the devotional if he didn't feel comfortable. He told me, "Coach, I want to be with the team. I understand what you're saying. You don't know how much I appreciate that."

He was a relentless player. When he left Georgia he held the school record for most career tackles by a defensive lineman (348). That meant he was really chasing the ball.

A lot of people don't know this, but we had three players who went on to become professional wrestlers: Goldberg, Dan Spivey (1972–1974), and Jim Wilson (1963–1964).

Steve Greer, Nose Guard, 1967–1969

He was an All-American nose guard at 190 pounds. He had more quickness, drive, and determination in that 190 pounds than in any player I have ever seen. What made Steve so effective was that he was incredibly quick and competitive. We knew we couldn't let him stay in one position when the ball was snapped or a larger player would just move him out of the way. But he was so quick that it was very hard to block him.

Here's a funny story about Steve and Kent Lawrence, our great running back. When those guys were at Georgia, we had a rule that none of our players could drive or ride motorcycles—period. We had to put that rule in because of Jake Scott, who once rode a motorcycle over the top of the Coliseum! So about 2:00 on a Sunday afternoon I went to the office, planning to meet the team at about 4:00. As I pulled into

17

the Coliseum parking lot, Steve Greer and Kent Lawrence were both sitting on a cranked up motorcycle.

Well, as soon as they saw me, they turned the accelerator wide open, and the motorcycle went flying up into the air while they hit the ground. Their first reaction was to run. They ran from the Coliseum across the street into the alumni house parking area and then over the top of the hill. They just disappeared. The funny thing was that Greer, the defensive lineman, was outrunning Lawrence, who was a world-class sprinter when he came to Georgia!

I just stood there for about a minute. After all, where could they run? Pretty soon they came back all skinned up and bleeding all over the place. I told them to come with me to the training room to get them patched up. I put merthiolate on their open wounds, and I knew it was burning the fire out of them, but they never said a word, though I could see they were gritting their teeth. After several applications I said, "See you at 4:00."

I never mentioned the motorcycle again.

Rodney Hampton, Running Back, 1987–1989

We didn't get a lot of players out of Texas. But at the time the old Southwest Conference was beginning to break up, and Texas became good, fertile recruiting territory. Ray Sherman, a great coach and recruiter, got Rodney to come to Georgia.

Ray told me that Rodney was a good one. I heard the same thing from other people. It didn't take long to find out just how right they were. Rodney could stop and start as well as anybody we've ever had. He had all different kinds of moves. He could give a defender a limp leg better than anybody I have ever seen! Rodney was one of the most natural running backs we've ever had at Georgia, and I was proud to have him on my final team in 1988.

Glynn Harrison, Running Back, 1973–1975

Dan Magill nicknamed him "Glidin'" Glynn Harrison. That was because Glynn could make a cut without slowing down better than anybody. He had a lot of great runs for us. I remember one year he had a great run against Florida—one of the greatest I've ever seen because he cut back and forth and seemed to run through their entire team. Unfortunately, Glynn's great run was called back because of a penalty.

We struggled for a couple of years when Glynn was here, but he was a big part of us getting it turned around and going to the Cotton Bowl in 1975. He was such a nice young man he could have been called "Gentle Glidin' Glynn."

Craig Hertwig, Offensive Tackle, 1972–1974

I remember going down to Lanier High in Macon to see a running back we wanted to recruit playing a game. While I was there I saw this incredibly tall offensive lineman. I turned to somebody and said, "Who is that guy?" That guy turned out to be Craig Hertwig, who was so tall that we called him "Sky." Craig didn't know a whole lot about football when he got here, but he made himself into a great player. As a senior in 1974 he was the team captain on offense and an All-American.

We had to redshirt him as a freshman, and he became the team's biggest fan. He went to all the games on the road and would be in the middle of the student body. It was hard to miss him, and he's the same way today. He is still at all the games and he still loves Georgia.

Terry Hoage, Rover, 1980–1983

It was 1980 and we were in the process of signing the best recruiting class we've ever had at Georgia, but we had a couple of scholarships left. I told our coaches to go out and find a couple of players with good potential. I wanted some good students who would hang around and be overachievers for us.

We got a call from a college professor in Texas who had talked to Steve Greer. He told us about his young man who was an excellent student and loved to play football. He had gotten hurt halfway through his senior year so nobody really knew about him. The kid sounded like just the kind of guy we were looking for, so Steve and later Bill Lewis, our secondary coach at the time, went out and liked what they saw.

But I certainly had no idea what we had in Terry Hoage. As it turned out, that year (1980) we got the most sought-after recruit in the country in Herschel Walker. At the same time you could say that Terry Hoage was the least sought-after recruit in Division I-A. Both became consensus All-Americans and both are now in the College Football Hall of Fame.

Terry proved to be the ultimate overachiever. As a freshman he kept blocking field goals and extra points in practice, so we took him with us to the Sugar Bowl in 1980, and he blocked a field goal against Notre Dame.

He was so relentless in practice that I had to threaten him not to go full speed anymore because he was getting hurt all the time. I've said it many times and I still stand behind it: Terry Hoage was not the most talented player, but all things considered he was the best pure defensive player I have ever coached or seen.

He played in the NFL for 13 years, winning a Super Bowl with the Washington Redskins in 1992. Today he owns a vineyard in California. He is a special, special person and was a great player for us.

Andy Johnson, Quarterback, 1971–1973

Andy was one of the best athletes I have ever seen. He was a great football player, but he was also an outstanding basketball and baseball player. I remember watching him play one time in high school. He turned to make a lateral pitch but the back had gone the wrong way. The ball sailed loose and he outran the entire defense to recover it near the sideline. And the defense was already going full speed! It was an impossible play, but he made it.

Andy played at Athens High, and I remember one of their games against Valdosta. Everyone thought the first half was over, and the players were heading to the locker room. But the officials brought everybody back out on the field and said that there was one second left on the clock. Andy took the ball and ran 70 yards for a touchdown.

There is no question that Andy was the best running quarterback we've ever had. But a lot of our fans remember him for passing us down the field to beat Georgia Tech 28-24 on Thanksgiving night of 1971. Andy made a bunch of big passes on that drive, including the most critical on fourth down to Mike Greene, the least likely receiver to throw to in the clutch. But Greene made the catch. And, of course, the drive ended with Jimmy Poulos going over the top for a touchdown.

Randy Johnson, Offensive Guard, 1973–1975

I said that George Collins was a natural blocker, and so was Randy Johnson. Those two were probably the most natural offensive linemen we ever had at Georgia. Randy was a raw talent with no real background when he got to Georgia. He was somewhat shy and wasn't really sure that playing college football was what he wanted to do. He just wasn't sure if he wanted to leave home.

But on the practice field we could see his great natural ability. He had the leverage. He had the feet. He knew instinctively how to make contact and drive the other player. So he stayed with us and became an All-American in 1975. Today no player is more appreciative of the opportunity that was given to him at Georgia. He's been a teacher and a coach for a long time and when he sees me he is so thoughtful. Randy is a special guy.

John Kasay, 1965–1966, and John David Kasay, 1987–1990

John Kasay was one of a large group of Pennsylvania guys who were here when I first came to Georgia in 1963. John was not an overly gifted player but a real bulldog who would just keep on keeping on. He always kept trying and kept working, and ended up being selected to the All-Bowl team when we played SMU in the Cotton Bowl in 1966. He had grown that much. Then he stuck around to serve as the off-season coach, the weight training coach, and the offensive line coach, among other jobs. He is still with Georgia today, working in the athletic department.

John was also my connection to most of the players. If I wanted to know something about a player 10 years after he left, I would ask John to tell me some inside stories. A lot of the players today still call John and stay in touch. The late Royce Smith, our great All-American guard in 1971, named his daughter (Kaysie) after him. In fact, a number of our players, including Mac McWhorter (Georgia captain in 1972 and now the offensive line coach at Texas), have named children after John.

21

One day I looked up to find John's son, or "Brief Kasay," as Erk Russell called him. He started hanging around the team when he was only five or six years old. Of course he grew up around our great kickers like Kevin Butler and Rex Robinson and became a talented kicker himself. He kicked for me for two years (1987–1988). In fact, he made it a little easier for me to retire when he kicked a field goal with no time left to beat Arkansas (20–17) in the 1987 Liberty Bowl. I was determined not to retire until we beat Arkansas after losing to them twice. Of course, John has gone on to have a great career in the NFL.

I'm lucky to have coached several father-son combinations. The Kasays are very special people.

Horace King, Running Back, 1972–1974

Horace King was one of our trailblazers. He was among the first group of five African-American players that we signed for the fall of 1971, and one of three that year from Athens High. Horace was very careful and very suspicious, but not in a negative way. His attitude was, "I only have time to go to school and play football. I don't want anything to interfere with that." He was very focused, and he ended up being a heck of a running back for us. I remember we discussed the possibility of moving him to fullback because he was so strong, but Horace didn't want any part of that.

We'll always be grateful to Horace. He played for nine seasons with the Detroit Lions. He still lives there today but always comes home to Athens at every opportunity.

Bill Krug, Rover, 1974–1977

He was one of the few players we recruited from the Maryland area. He came recommended by Joe Tereshinski Sr., a great former player whose sons (Joe Jr. and Wally) and grandson (Joe III) have all played at Georgia. We thought Bill was a pretty good player when we signed him, but we never thought he would develop into one of the best big playmakers that we've ever had at Georgia. Bill played the rover position, which is a combination of safety and linebacker, and it suited him perfectly. We gave him great freedom to make plays, and he did—game after game. Bill will always be remembered for recovering a big fumble late against Georgia Tech in 1976. That gave us the chance to kick a field goal in the final seconds and win 13–10.

John Lastinger, Quarterback, 1981–1983

John was one of the few quarterbacks I have ever known who would have rather played another position, but he had too much inner strength not to be a quarterback. He was maligned at times during his career at Georgia but left here with a 21–2–1 record and an SEC championship. Not bad for a guy who once said, "I just don't think I should be the quarterback."

John had a bad knee injury at one point in his career, and it looked like he might not ever recover to play again. But he went home and found somebody to help him, and when John returned, he was stronger than ever and ready to go.

With John running the show, we went undefeated and won an SEC championship in 1982 and played for the national championship. We almost won another championship in 1983 and played No. 2 Texas, who would have been national champions if they had won, in the Cotton Bowl.

John will always be remembered at Georgia because, in his final game, he ran for a touchdown to beat Texas 10-9, shouting "Glory, Glory, to old Georgia!" He had had some tough moments in his career, but he ended it in pretty grand style.

Tommy Lawhorne, Linebacker, 1965–1967

Of all the overachievers we've had at Georgia, Dr. Tommy Lawhorne might be the greatest. I remember that we decided to redshirt him as a sophomore because he was very small. But he went home during the off-season and put on a bunch of weight and muscle. He also spent that time studying our defense, and when he came back to school, he knew everything about it. Then the guy in front of him got hurt. All of a sudden he went from not being in the program to starting the first game in 1965, a major upset (18–17) of Alabama, the defending national champions!

Tommy had a brilliant mind. Back then football was based on trends and formations, even more so than today. When it came to looking at formations and knowing what a team liked to run in certain situations, nobody was better than Tommy Lawhorne. Tommy was smart, to be sure, but like most successful people he was also willing to put in a lot of hard work. That's why he became a great football player for us. That is also why he was the valedictorian of the 1968 senior class at Georgia. He finished second for the Rhodes Scholarship and then went to medical school at Johns Hopkins. He now lives in Columbus, where he has his own practice. He has served his alma mater for many years on the UGA Foundation and the athletic board.

One of the most gratifying things in coaching is to watch your players succeed in life after football. People like Tommy Lawhorne are why you coach.

Kent Lawrence, Running Back/Wide Receiver, 1966–1968

During our early years at Georgia we had a lot of recruiting success in South Carolina. Kent Lawrence is a perfect example. As a senior in high school Kent was one of the fastest kids in the country. He had already run a 9.3 in the 100-yard dash. I wish we could get an 18-year-old Kent Lawrence and match him in a race with a young Herschel Walker—it would really be something to see.

We didn't know exactly what we were going to do with Kent, but we did know that we wanted him at Georgia very badly. Thanks to Frank Inman, we had a bunch of good players from South Carolina in that great 1965 signing class, and Kent was one of them.

He started as a running back on the 1966 championship team, but by 1968 we had enough depth at running back to move him to wide receiver. With Kent, the speedster, on one side and Charlie Whittemore, the possession receiver, on the other, we were hard to stop.

Kent was a great player for us, especially on the 1966 and 1968 championship teams. He went on to become a judge here in Clarke County, Georgia. Today he remains a great representative for our program. He is as solid as they come.

John Little, Rover, 1983–1986

John Little was another high school quarterback who we converted to defense. By the time he left Georgia he was a great football player. John had some big shoes to fill at the rover position, which was a very important one in our defensive scheme. Terry Hoage had been a two-time All-American at rover and had basically set the standard for all future players at the position. John was certainly up to the task. He did not become a big-play rover like Hoage or Bill Krug, but he was very reliable and I felt very comfortable having him back there.

Tommy Lyons, Center, 1968–1970

Like Tommy Lawhorne, Lyons was a classic overachiever. We played Tommy in a lot of positions when he first got to Georgia. He was not big, but he was extremely quick, confident, and competitive. He became a great center because he had confidence that he was going to control whoever was in front of him. It didn't matter who the opponent was; Tommy's mentality was that over the course of the game, he was going to whip the guy.

After he went to the Denver Broncos, they would try to replace him every year. They would always say, "We need to find a bigger guy to play the position." But Tommy had intelligence, quickness, and a bulldoggedness about him. He played a lot of years in the NFL despite the fact that he was undersized.

Tommy was truly a Renaissance man. He was a concert pianist who directed the Denver symphony orchestra, all while playing football and going to medical school. Today he is one of the top ob-gyn doctors in the country and has been a pioneer in laser surgery.

Willie McClendon, Running Back, 1976–1978

We had Willie at linebacker for a while and he was really good. In fact, when I wanted to move him to tailback, we had quite a fight on the staff about it. He was that good. In 1978 we went back to the I-formation running game, and Willie was the ideal guy for tailback. He broke Frank Sinkwich's record for rushing yards in a season. [Editor's note: Willie

McClendon ran 287 times for 1,312 yards during the 1978 season. Sinkwich held the previous record with 1,103 yards in 1941.] But he didn't hold it long because Herschel broke it in 1980 with 1,616 yards.

Willie McClendon was as good a captain as we have ever had at Georgia. In fact, he was voted captain by the largest number of votes to that point. He was our spokesperson when it came time to say the prayer after the game. I got to where I called on him to give the prayer all the time. He had a great ability to deliver a prayer with some true meaning to it. And now, I know he is especially proud of his son, Brian, who is an excellent wide receiver for the Dawgs.

George Patton, Defensive Tackle, 1964–1966

George was signed by the previous staff, and, when I look back on it, we were lucky to get him. He was from Alabama and all of his brothers had gone to Alabama and Ole Miss. He was a high school quarterback but not highly recruited.

When the staff and I got to Georgia we started timing all of the players to see what we really had. George had a pretty decent time. Lanky by today's standards, George was a big guy who just wanted to play. He had big hands, long arms, and was pretty strong, so we put him over at defensive tackle to see what he could do. Turned out that George was a natural for the position. I would say he made as many big plays on defense as anybody we've ever had. He returned an interception for a touchdown in our big (18-17) upset of Alabama in 1965.

He was voted captain of the team as a senior in 1966, and was a really fun guy to coach.

George will always be remembered for his last game, when he got to play quarterback against SMU in the Cotton Bowl. When he signed in 1963, the coaches on the previous staff promised that he would get to play quarterback at some time in his career. So in his final college game, we delivered on that promise. We let George wind up and throw it as far as he could. I was told later that some of the SMU players didn't appreciate what we were doing. They thought we were making fun of them, and I felt bad about that. But when I saw George throw, I knew we had made the right decision moving him to defense.

I will always remember George because he was in with that bunch of players who were here with the previous staff and who helped us win that first championship. They bought in to what we were trying to teach them, and for that I will always be grateful.

Billy Payne, Defensive End, 1966–1968

I used to call him the "sixty-minute man" because Billy could play just about any position and help the football team. He started at tight end. He played split end. He became an All-Conference defensive end. I wanted him on the field on just about every play.

He was a great scholar-athlete at Georgia, vice president of the student body, and went on to law school. Of course Billy has become famous not for being a football player at Georgia, but because of his extraordinary accomplishments as a citizen, such as bringing the Olympics to Atlanta in 1996. We all knew that Billy would go on to do great things after football. I'm proud to say that we are still close friends. I especially feel like a proud dad when I am around him.

Jimmy Payne, Defensive Tackle, 1979–1982

We had two great defensive end–defensive tackle combinations at Georgia. In 1966 we had Bill Stanfill and George Patton. We didn't see anything quite that good again until the early eighties when we had Jimmy Payne and Freddie Gilbert.

Jimmy was a great athlete who could have played a lot of positions for us. He was extremely quick.

Whenever I think of Jimmy Payne I think of his daddy, who worked for us. James serviced my athletic director's box for 25 years. One day I was in the coaching tower, and James came up the ladder to see me. He said, "Coach, can I borrow $20? I've got a little boy who plays football and I want to buy him some cleats." That little boy turned out to be Jimmy. Two years later James gave me the $20 back. Jimmy came to Georgia and was All-SEC three times and an All-American in 1982. I would say that $20 paid a pretty good dividend.

Matt Robinson, Quarterback, 1974–1976

Matt was as good a passing quarterback as we ever had, and he proved it by playing for a long time in the NFL. He had a quick release of the ball that Bill Pace, our offensive coordinator back then, just loved. He was also a great competitor and knew how to lead a team.

At the time we were beginning to install the veer offense, which placed a premium on the quarterback's ability to run the ball. We had a great running quarterback in Ray Goff. Both guys brought good qualities to the table, so the challenge was to find a way to use them both. Matt was in the running to be the starter going into the 1975 season, but he got hurt. Once Ray moved in, he played so well that it was impossible to move him out. I had several sessions with Matt over those years trying to keep his spirits up. The fact is, we could not have won the 1976 SEC championship without him. He ran for one touchdown and threw for another in the Alabama game (a 21–0 win by Georgia) which jump-started the championship season.

Rex Robinson, Kicker, 1977–1980

He was the kicker on our national championship team of 1980, which gives him a special distinction among all of the great kickers that we had at Georgia. He was "that kid out of Marietta," as Munson described him after Robinson made the kick at the buzzer to beat Kentucky 17–16 in 1978 in a great comeback. He went on to have a great college kicking career and ended up being the guy who got us on the board first in the national championship game in the Sugar Bowl against Notre Dame. There were so many big kicks. In the nationally televised game against South Carolina and George Rogers in 1980, he kicked field goals of 57 and 51 yards. We needed them both for the 13–10 win. Rex is a special young man and made a great contribution to Georgia.

Buzy Rosenberg, Defensive Back, 1970–1972

To look at Buzy you would think he was too small to be a great player. But all you had to do was watch him jump. There is a great picture of him jumping over me. We called him the Super Frog. He had a great day against Oregon State in 1971. [Editor's note: Rosenberg returned five punts for 202 yards and two touchdowns in a 56-25 win over Oregon State in 1971.] But really Buzy was a joy to coach because he was always full of life and enthusiasm. I remember, too, back in the eighties or early nineties we had an alumni game and Buzy showed up in incredible shape. None of us could believe it. He and Bob Taylor ran circles around the other "has-beens."

Troy Sadowski, Tight End, 1985–1988

I wasn't so sure about Troy when he got to Georgia. He had a lot of hype surrounding him out of high school, and I was always wary of that. But Troy showed that he was willing to work to become a great player, and by the time he left us, he was an All-American. He was a member of our last senior class and, to me, that will always be a very special group of guys. Troy went on to have a very good career in the pros.

Jeff Sanchez, Safety, 1982–1984

We didn't sign very many junior college players during my time at Georgia. Our philosophy was that he had to be an exceptional player with the ability to come in and fit right into the system. If the junior college player could not make an immediate contribution, I did not see the logic in signing him.

Jeff Sanchez was exactly that kind of player. He was playing quarterback at a California junior college when Bill Lewis, our defensive coordinator, saw him. Jeff came in and won a spot at safety. He and Terry Hoage turned out to be an incredible combination. [Editor's note: In 1982 Jeff Sanchez was second in the nation in interceptions with nine. His teammate, Terry Hoage, led the nation in interceptions with 12.] By the time Jeff left, he had been All-SEC twice and an All-American once. That's what I call making a contribution.

Jake Scott, Safety, 1967–1968

He was a free spirit, but I've never had a player who loved football more than Jake Scott. He never utilized his talents in the classroom. He did just enough to stay eligible, but Jake was really smart. He could always get it done when he had to. But when it came to football, I never had a player who studied film harder than Jake. He absolutely loved the game, was really gifted, and, when it came time to play the game, he didn't hold anything back. We got everything Jake had. Most people who become great players work at it, and Jake worked at it.

Yes, we had some problems, but those problems were never about football. He was never late coming to practice or meetings. The problems were with other things (like cutting class or missing curfew) because Jake, for all of his talent, walked to the beat of his own drummer. He still does.

In 1968, the second or third time we had a problem with Jake, I had to sit him down. I was about fed up with him, but I thought that before I kicked him off the team I would let the seniors decide. I talked to the team about it and then left the room. I think Billy Payne was the spokesperson for the group. He basically said, "We don't like what Jake did, but we want to win the championship and we need Jake to win it." So I agreed to let it go one more time. Fortunately, nothing else happened, and we won the championship.

After the 1968 season Jake took a trip to Canada, which a football club up there paid for. Taking the trip made him ineligible, but to be perfectly honest about it, I think he was ready to go. He was a little older than the rest of the guys, so he was ready to leave.

I remember when he was named Most Valuable Player in the conference. I had a highlight film put together, which was easy—in every single game he made at least one big play. What an extraordinary talent!

Lindsay Scott, Wide Receiver, 1978–1981

Lindsay was a very talented high school player and we had to endure quite a recruiting battle before we got him to come to Georgia. Buck Belue was coming in as quarterback in that same class, and I believe that helped.

Lindsay showed early in his career that he was a very special player. As a freshman he ran the second-half kickoff back for a touchdown in a game at LSU. But then I thought we had lost him when he went home and got into a horrible car wreck. There were some real doubts whether he would play again. Then he had some personal problems that forced us to take him off scholarship for a while. I am proud of the way he has addressed his problems.

In the end Lindsay had a great career for us and will always be remembered for scoring the winning touchdown against Florida in 1980. Some say it was the biggest play in Georgia history because, without it, we wouldn't have won the national championship. It's hard to argue against that. In fact, I believe it.

Royce Smith, Offensive Guard, 1969–1971

When we signed Royce Smith, he was basically a 197-pound track guy. We knew he could run. What we didn't know was that Royce loved to be in the weight room and was determined to build himself into a football player. That's exactly what he did. By the time Royce left Georgia he was a 250-pound guard (that was big in 1971) and an All-American.

Back then we knew weights were important to strength development, but I was always cautious about overuse. I was always worried that too much lifting would hurt flexibility and speed, which was more important than size at the time. I always believed in using the weights modestly. Because of this belief I had to threaten Royce with disciplinary action several times if he didn't stop spending so much time in the weight room. Of course, he never did. He had his own key made to the weight room so he could work out when none of the coaches were looking. I knew, but I never said anything. Royce knew what he was doing.

Through hard work and sheer will, Royce Smith made himself into an All-American football player and was drafted by the NFL in the first round by the New Orleans Saints. He taught high school in south Georgia and became a remarkable bicycle rider in superb condition. He was a great man and we lost him way too soon. [Editor's note: In 2004 Royce Smith died suddenly at the age of 54.]

Bill Stanfill, Defensive End, 1966–1968

What can you say about the greatest defensive tackle/end to ever play for us? Bill Stanfill was one of the most gifted high school athletes I ever saw. Besides what he could do on the football field, he was the MVP of his high school basketball team, and in track he set a state record in the discus.

I remember that Bill Yeoman, the old Houston coach, said that Stanfill was the only defensive player he ever saw who could single-handedly take away all three options in the triple option offense. He was that good; no wonder he won the Outland Trophy, which goes to the nation's best lineman, in 1968. Bill could do it all, and with him in the lineup we won a couple of SEC championships (1966 and 1968).

No one was surprised when Bill went on to have a great career in the NFL with the Dolphins, where he won a couple of Super Bowls. In 1998 Bill was inducted into the College Football Hall of Fame. He has also had a successful business career in Albany and is a model south Georgia Bulldog.

Richard Tardits, Defensive End, 1985–1988

When I first heard that we were going to get a walk-on from France I thought, "Good. It's always good to have some diversity around here." Turned out that Richard had some natural ability, but he knew absolutely nothing about football. We had to get somebody to show him how to put the uniform on!

We put him at tight end first. Then he fired off and tackled the man in front of him, so we immediately moved him to defense. We could tell that he had a great explosiveness, but we didn't know what would happen *after* he exploded. It took him a long time to distinguish between a pass and run, but he was extremely committed. He had a great ability to get off at the snap, and that made him a tremendous pass rusher. [Editor's note: Tardits was Georgia's all-time leader in quarterback sacks with 29 until the 2004 season, when All-American David Pollack passed him for the record.]

He was a joy to coach in a lot of ways. He was another Renaissance man. He enjoyed and wanted to do so many things. I would venture to say that he is the only player we've had who ran with the bulls at Pamplona. He took advantage of the great opportunities he had at

Georgia and has given back to the university ever since he left. I truly believe that Richard Tardits is one of the great success stories in college athletics, and he is always sharing the good news about the Bulldogs with his hometown of Biarritz, France, where he resides with his family.

Herschel Walker, Running Back, 1980–1982

In many ways there seem to be no words left for such an incredible individual, but I will say this: I've always believed that talented people can be overachievers too—those are your superstars—and there is no better example than Herschel Walker.

For all of his great gifts, and he was an immense talent, nobody worked harder and nobody was mentally tougher or had more self-discipline than Herschel. He had a complete package that I have never seen before or since in one man. He had great speed—world-class speed. He was tremendously strong. And he had the mental toughness that all champions have. When you combine those skills with intangibles like determination and self-discipline, then you have a once-in-a-lifetime player. That's what Herschel Walker was.

Today he remains a self-disciplined man. He is in his forties now, but he looks like he could still play. As a coach, you hope to have one player in a lifetime like Herschel. All of us at Georgia are very fortunate that he came our way. To top it all, he has stayed close to Georgia and is still in many ways the same very nice young man who came out of Wrightsville a quarter century ago.

Charlie Whittemore, Wide Receiver, 1968–1970

They call them "possession receivers" now. They are guys who run great routes and have great hands. They catch everything that is thrown their way. That was Charlie Whittemore. He led us in receiving for three straight years (1968–1970). Charlie came back and joined our coaching staff in 1978. I kept him on when he got out of coaching, and he has worked his way up as assistant athletic director for facilities.

Jim Wilson, Offensive Tackle, 1962–1964

Jim was one of the guys we inherited from the previous staff, and when we got to Georgia, he was an individual who was strictly about himself. Many of the guys were that way, and that was one of the things we had to change.

Back then we weren't a team. We had Southerners sitting only with Southerners. The guys from the North, "Yankees," would sit only among themselves. We had the south Georgia crowd in a group separated from the Atlanta crowd. But as time went on and we started implementing our program, guys like Jim Wilson started to understand team unity and how important it was if we were going to succeed.

About the third or fourth game, Lynn Hughes made a bad play at a crucial time and we lost. In the locker room, Lynn was beside himself and more than once he said, "I lost the game." At that moment Big Jim Wilson put his arm around Lynn and said, "No, *we* lost the game."

That's when I knew we had arrived as a team.

He was a super offensive lineman, but we would also use Jim on defense when teams got inside the 20-yard line. He and his buddy, Ray Rissmiller, were a big part of that first team in 1964. Jim was a great athlete and proved it by going into professional wrestling when he was done with pro football. He wrote a book on that sport exposing some of its evils.

Scott Woerner, Safety, 1978–1980

Scott was a great All-American and was perhaps only exceeded by Jake Scott among the great safeties who played for us at Georgia. He came out of high school as a quarterback, and we actually used him some at running back. He and Andy Johnson were very similar as athletes and players. But eventually we wanted to move him because we thought he had a chance to be great as a defensive back. He didn't care because he just wanted to play and do whatever it took for us to win.

Herschel got a lot of the recognition on that national championship team in 1980, but there were a couple of games in that undefeated season that we just would not have won without Scott Woerner.

In the 20-16 victory over Clemson he returned an interception 98 yards and ran back a punt 67 yards for a touchdown. Then he had two big interceptions in the Sugar Bowl victory over Notre Dame, although he ran one of them out of the end zone when he shouldn't (but he did get it past the 20, so it was OK). He was one of the great playmakers we've ever had at Georgia. Like Jake Scott, when Scott Woerner was on the field, he almost always made something happen.

Tim Worley, Running Back, 1985-1988

We didn't recruit a lot of players from North Carolina, but we knew that Tim was something special. I think Tim really wanted to go to Oklahoma, but his mother didn't want him to be that far from home. It ended up between us and Clemson. I think we got an assist from Jim Donnan, who was an Oklahoma assistant at the time. When Jim found out that Tim wasn't coming to Oklahoma, he recommended Georgia.

We're sure glad Tim picked Georgia because he turned out to be a great back for us. He led the SEC in rushing in 1988 (1,216 yards) and made a lot of big plays for us. He played on our very last team at Georgia and was drafted in the first round by the Pittsburgh Steelers in 1989. Today he is back in his home town of Lumberton, North Carolina, where he is preaching the good news about the Lord.

Ben Zambiasi, Linebacker, 1974-1977

When I would talk to the team in the locker room right before the game, the person I kept going back to with my eyes was Ben Zambiasi, the great linebacker from Macon. That was because he was always on the edge of his seat, and I could see his eyes get wider and wider the more I talked. The more I talked, the more he got fired up, and the more he got fired up, the more I got fired up.

We had a great tradition with Ben: he would always throw up before the game, and when he did, everybody in the locker room shouted. Then we knew we were ready, and I'd say, "OK, men, let's go!"

One time it took him a while to get going. I suppose he was having an off day. Ben had not thrown up, and our guys would not take the field until he did. He finally did it, but I thought we were going to get penalized for coming onto the field so late.

We used the saying "Intelligent Fanaticism." We wanted our guys to play like fanatics but it had to be with intelligence. They couldn't be running all over the place; they did it within the framework of the defense. That was Ben Zambiasi. If the opponent stayed between the white lines, Ben would get him. He went on to become an MVP in the Canadian League and was recently inducted into the CFL Hall of Fame. Pound for pound he was probably the best linebacker we ever had.

There are so many more great guys I could name here, but time and space just won't allow it. Here are just a few more men I'd like to mention:

- Mixon Robinson and Chuck Heard, who both became orthopedic surgeons

- Happy Dicks, Tom Nash, and Lee Daniels, who were great players for us but also went on to become great alumni. They later served on the UGA athletic board

- Leroy Dukes, the oldest and most loyal player I ever had, who became a lifelong friend

- Little Bobby Etter, a wonderful kicker and person; his run to the end zone after a botched field-goal attempt helped us beat Florida in 1964

- Edgar Chandler, a magnificent tackle who helped us beat Michigan in 1965

- Mack Guest, who went on to become president of the Letterman's Club

- Frank Ros, who came to this country as a child from Spain speaking no English and went on to become captain of our 1980 national championship team

- Jimmy Poulos, the "Greek Streak," who went over the top to beat Georgia Tech in 1971

- Kirby Moore, a successful attorney who was a quarterback on our first SEC championship team in 1966

- Gene Washington and Richard Appleby, who combined on the great end-around pass to beat Florida in 1975; the phrase "Appleby to Washington" will live forever in Georgia history

- Alphonso Ellis, who was a fullback on my last team at Georgia (1988) and went on to became a police officer in Dallas

There are many more names and so many more great stories I could tell of the men who wore the Red and Black for us. I wish I could thank each one of you personally for what you did for me and my family.

3

The Assistants:
Brother Billy, Hootie, and Erk

Perhaps the most important thing a head coach does is put together a staff. I don't care how good the head coach is and how hard he works, if he doesn't have a strong staff around him, he will not be successful over the long haul.

When I became head coach at Georgia in 1963, I had a pretty good idea what kind of people I wanted for my first staff. I wanted coaches who I knew would be loyal and trustworthy. But combined with that, I wanted some coaches who had strong Georgia backgrounds and who would be beneficial for what we needed to do at Georgia.

The coaches I knew well were my brother, Billy, and Erk Russell. I knew Hootie Ingram from a distance because he was an Alabama man. Then there were the others with strong Georgia backgrounds—Sterling DuPree, John Donaldson, and Doc Ayers—who also came on board.

That was my staffing philosophy at the start. My goal in the future was to eventually get all my own people—people who had played for me and who had played in my system. I always wanted to have two-thirds of the staff be people from my system and the other third be from the outside. I never wanted to be totally inbred because I always needed new people with new ideas. At the same time, I thought it was important to have a foundation of loyalty and proven success. We pretty much were able to stay with that formula for most of my time as head coach.

I've often been asked what I was looking for in an assistant coach. First of all, he had to be a pretty good person—very trustworthy. I believed that if I just got the right person, who was committed and loyal and willing to work, it didn't matter if he was a superstar coach. If he just had those base qualities, the rest would come.

The beauty of that first staff was that we all knew we had to start from scratch. Everybody was very enthusiastic because basically we were all starting over. We all came from different backgrounds using different types of terminology and there we were, trying to build our own playbook.

Not long after we got started at Georgia we moved out of old Stegeman Hall into the new Coliseum. We had been in Stegeman for four months and the office space was pretty Spartan. I had an office that only I could fit into. Then there was one office where all 12 of the assistants could fit in—but only if they faced the wall!

When we went to the Coliseum it was like we had gone to heaven. We had an offensive coaching room for four coaches, a defensive coaching room for four coaches, and a freshman coaching room for three coaches. I had an office that was twice the size of the one I had in Stegeman.

Of course you have to remember that coach Joel Eaves, our athletic director, was very frugal. We held our staff meetings at a long table surrounded by folding tin chairs. We would sit in those hard chairs for as long as 10 hours a day when we were first getting organized and putting our playbook together. My coaches didn't care. Most of us had come up the hard way. It was an exciting time for us because we were building a new program!

After our first game with Alabama (a 31–3 loss) I decided to make some major changes on the coaching staff. I've always believed that it's important to play a good team early in the schedule so that you don't have any illusions about your football team. A good team will show you what your problems are.

Well, I thought we had some problems on our coaching staff, and I decided to shake things up. When we went into that first game, I just didn't feel confident that I had the right people in the right spots—both players and coaches. Looking back, I should have made the changes before the game, but I didn't. The Alabama game just confirmed some things that I already thought were true.

For example, I thought that Erk Russell would be better coaching the down linemen on defense, while Jim Pyburn would be better coaching the ends. I made that switch and then I switched some players. After those changes the team got better and better as the season went on. And by the end of the year, I thought we were one of the most improved teams in the country.

I had a lot of assistant coaches during my 25 years, and I'm proud to say that I never fired one of them. I might have moved them around or had them reassigned elsewhere in the organization, but I didn't send one out on his own. I guess I was just from the old school that believed that loyalty is a two-way street. It must flow up and down. If I expected loyalty from my staff, I had to first be loyal to them. And the fact is, they were loyal to me and they were loyal to Georgia. I was often criticized for not getting rid of certain coaches, but in those days, with the low salaries, it was a good approach. Today, with the high salaries paid to coaches, loyalty takes a back seat to consistent performance.

Here are fond memories of the assistant coaches who were so important to my career as the head coach at Georgia.

Howard "Doc" Ayers, 1964–1980

Doc was the perfect example of what a freshman coach ought to be, someone special who could help those guys make the tough transition from high school to college. Doc was a master at it. Kids would get homesick and just leave college and go home. Doc was great at going to get them and then sitting down with their parents to talk it out. When freshmen were ineligible to play, they really had to be handled with tender, loving care. Doc Ayers was the ideal individual for that task. I wish we could go back to those days.

Mike Castronis, 1969–1986

"Coach Mike" was one of the most lovable individuals who ever worked at Georgia. He played at Georgia and did just about every job you can name. He taught physical education classes, he was director of intramural sports, he coached the cheerleading team, and for almost 40 years he was a fixture at the Athens YMCA. He was a freshman football coach and later became a varsity assistant coach.

Mike was committed and loyal and you always knew where he stood. Because of his dedication to and love for Georgia, coach Mike was inducted into our Circle of Honor in 2003. Since 1992 Georgia has presented the Mike Castronis Award to a varsity football player who, like coach Mike, "never, never, never gave up the fight."

We also have a football scholarship endowment in Mike's name. He was a very special individual and the Georgia people miss him every single day. [Editor's note: Mike Castronis, who was a three-time All-SEC football player at Georgia in the forties, died of cancer in 1987.]

Mike Cavan, 1977–1985

Mike had been through our system before becoming an important part of our program. He was a great player for us, and he had the perfect background because his father was a coach as well. After he quit playing, he tried private business for a while but decided that he really missed football. I brought him back because I was convinced he would be an outstanding coach, and he was. Mike stayed with us a long time and then went on to become a head coach at Valdosta State, East Tennessee State, and SMU.

Dicky Clark, 1981–1995

Dicky was a great player for us but proved early on that he had the right qualities to be a coach. He was a graduate assistant in our program and got an offer from Vanderbilt to be a full-time assistant. Right after he accepted, I had a position open on my staff and wanted to hire him. I knew Dicky wanted to coach at Georgia, but he said no and kept his commitment to Vanderbilt. I thought that was a very good trait. But when the next opening came up, I went and got him back.

Ken Cooper, 1963–1970

Ken was a Georgia man, and I just had a hunch about him. He was a holdover from the previous staff, and some people told me not to keep him. But I liked Ken and thought he would be a very good coach for us. So I hired him as the assistant freshman coach. I was right about him—he went on to become the head coach at Ole Miss and even beat us a couple of times.

Dick Copas, 1964–1991

Dick served our football program for 28 years in a lot of different capacities. I knew him at Auburn, where he graduated in 1960 with a degree in physical education. He joined me at Georgia when I became head coach in 1964 and was our head trainer for two years. He then served as our academic counseling coordinator, helped run McWhorter Hall (the athletic dormitory), and somehow found time to win seven SEC championships as our men's golf coach from 1970 to 1996.

During our games Dick was always on our sideline serving as what we called the "Get Back" coach. When the players who were not in the game kept moving onto the playing field, Dick was in charge of telling them to get back so that we didn't get in trouble with the officials.

I can't think of a more respected person in the athletic community than Dick. He did a multiplicity of jobs for us and did them all well.

Bill Dooley, 1964–1966

I had to scrutinize him twice as much as I did any other coach because he was my brother. But the fact is, I was looking for the best offensive line coach I could find and he was clearly the best out there. If you talk to some of the players on our early teams they will tell you that. Billy was a very good football coach, and he proved it by very quickly becoming a head coach. He was with me for only three years, and in that stretch we beat North Carolina two years in a row (47-35 in 1965 and 28-3 in 1966). The athletic director up there was impressed and hired Billy as his head coach. We would later face each other in the 1971

Gator Bowl. He was a successful head coach for 26 years at North Carolina (11 years), Virginia Tech (9), and Wake Forest (6).

John Donaldson, 1964–1968, 1971–1972

Anybody who knew John would always call him "Hubba Hubba" because that's what he always said during practice to get his guys going. He was a good south Georgia boy and a devoted Bulldog. He was also a tough, old fundamentals running backs coach. He had some great drills to make our backs better. And if you talk to the guys who played for him, they will tell you that they loved the guy.

Sterling DuPree, 1950–1960, 1964–1976

When I first got the job at Georgia, I made it one of my early goals to bring Sterling DuPree back to Athens. He was an Auburn graduate, but I knew him from scouting when he was first working for Georgia. Sterling was known as a great recruiter. Then he left, went to Florida, and recruited in south Georgia for the Gators. We couldn't have that. Through Sterling I got to know John Donaldson, and when I hired them both, we started recruiting well in south Georgia again.

Alex Gibbs, 1982–1983

He is one of the best coaches I've ever had even though he was with me only a short period of time. He was as demanding on the field as any coach I've ever seen, but when practice was over, he could stay out on the practice field with the players and put his arm around them, talk to them, joke with them. They couldn't stay mad at him, and they appreciated him. He was great at being as demanding as he could possibly be but then afterward just love them. A coach needs to be able to do that, and he did it better than anyone I've ever known. Alex is one of the best offensive line coaches in the history of the game and has proven that over and over in the pros, especially with the Denver Broncos. He joined the Atlanta Falcons in 2004 and made an immediate difference.

Ray Goff, 1981–1988

Another one of our men—a true Georgia boy. He was a great player for us and then had a chance to go to South Carolina and work with Jim Carlen for a year. We brought him back in 1981, and he became one of our very best recruiters. Ray had a lot of friends and was very good at talking to people. He was as good as anybody I've known at making contacts. Ray took over as head coach at Georgia when I retired after the 1988 season.

Steve Greer, 1979–2001

He was an All-American nose guard for us and then was with us for one year as a graduate assistant. Then he went to Auburn for several years and got some good experience. When we brought him back in 1979 he was a very good fit for our staff. Just as he was as a player, Steve was a very intense defensive line coach. He was also one of the best recruiters we had on our staff. He was very loyal and I always appreciated that.

George Haffner, 1980–1990

George was a good fundamental football coach who knew what to do in the framework we provided. He and I both wanted to have a sound offense that didn't make a lot of mistakes. George knew the passing game pretty well. He was not a Spurrier-type genius in the passing game but a solid guy. For what we wanted to do at Georgia, I thought George was the perfect fit.

Bob Harrison, 1988–1991

Bob was a very good coach who came in to replace Ray Sherman in 1988, my last year as coach. Bob was an outstanding recruiter and stayed on when Ray Goff became head coach.

Bill Hartman, 1974–1994

Bill was an All-American at Georgia in 1937 and had been on Georgia's coaching staff a couple of times before leaving to enter the insurance business, where he was very successful. As chairman of the

Georgia Student Educational Fund, he was always close to the program. So in 1974 I offered him the job of volunteer coach working with the kickers, which he accepted. Such arrangements were allowed by the NCAA at that time. I felt that kickers are often ignored, but to me it is such a very important part of the game. Coaching the kickers was always a secondary duty for one of the other assistants, and as a result they often got ignored. Plus, I wanted someone who could defend the kickers because they would always get beat up by the staff. Bill had a good relationship with the kickers, and their performance showed it. For this job, Bill was the ideal person with the right background. He was really terrific.

Pat Hodgson, 1972–1977
Pat was a great tight/split end (they did both in those days) for our early teams, and he was really the start of former players becoming coaches for us. Pat is a Georgia boy through and through, and he's an emotional guy about it. His father played at Georgia. His grandfather played at Georgia. And any time you mention Georgia and all it meant to him, he will tear up on you a little. He's a wonderful coach and a very good man.

Joe Hollis, 1985–1990
He had worked under Alex Gibbs, and it really showed. Joe had a broader knowledge of offense than most offensive line coaches I've known. He was very concerned with the overall picture, and that impressed me. He left Georgia and went to Ohio State, where he was very successful for many years as their offensive coordinator.

Hornsby Howell, 1983–1991
Hornsby was my first black coach, and he was an absolutely perfect fit for our staff. He was an Athens native and would come by to watch practice when he was in town. My brother knew him and had a lot of confidence in him. I had complete confidence that he would be the right person for the job. Hornsby was a very good people person and

was always likeable. The players called him "the judge." They couldn't put anything over on him.

Cecil "Hootie" Ingram, 1964–1965

I knew of Hootie because we were contemporaries. When I was playing and coaching at Auburn, Hootie was doing the same at Alabama. Everybody I knew in the profession thought highly of Hootie. He would go on to become the head coach at Clemson (1970–1972) and would later be the athletic director at Florida State and Alabama.

Frank Inman, 1964–1978

When I took over as head coach, there were two coaches from the old staff whom I decided to keep. Everybody I talked to said that Frank Inman would be a great asset if I retained him, and they were certainly right about that.

Frank was from North Augusta, South Carolina, where he had been a high school coach. He had really good connections up in South Carolina and did a great job of recruiting for us there. He took a lot of pride in his recruiting and really made South Carolina his territory. The results speak for themselves when you look at players like Kent Lawrence, Steve Greer, and Dennis Hughes, who hail from that state. Frank was also a great overall coach and played a big role in getting our program established.

John Kasay, 1970–1995

We never had a more loyal player and coach than John Kasay. He was here as a player when we arrived in 1963, and he just never left. He has been an assistant coach, a strength coach, and has held many more jobs. He loves Georgia and still works for our athletic association. He worked the players hard in the weight room, but they loved him. He had some humorous sayings the players will never forget. He was and still is my inside guy with the players.

His son, John, was a great kicker for us. Every organization needs people like John Kasay to be successful.

Bill Lewis, 1980–1988

Bill was well thought of when we brought him to Georgia in 1980. He had worked for Frank Broyles at Arkansas. He had struggled as a head coach at Wyoming, so we had to look into that before we could make a decision. We found that he was a very good football coach, and he would be a good fit at Georgia. We brought him in as a secondary coach under Erk, and he grew from there. After Erk left for Georgia Southern in 1981, I promoted Bill to defensive coordinator. It was not an easy decision because Dale Strahm, our linebackers coach, had done good things as well. It was a tough decision but the right one. If I had any fault with Bill it was that he was too much of a perfectionist. He couldn't leave anything to chance—unlike Erk, who did leave some flexibility in his game plan. But if that's the only fault you can find, then that's pretty good. Bill Lewis was an outstanding football coach.

Wayne McDuffie, 1977–1981

He studied the game. He knew the game and he knew offensive line play. McDuffie was very dedicated and worked extremely hard—in fact, he would coach his players so hard that on Thursdays during the season we would send him recruiting instead of letting him come to practice.

Wayne's intense personality and desire for perfection stayed with him on and off the field. Whenever he had a strong feeling about something, he found it very difficult to let it go. There is no question that this personality trait affected his ability to get a head coaching job. He was often frustrated by not getting a head job because he saw others who didn't know nearly the football that he knew get jobs. But sometimes the fact that Wayne was so focused and so demanding made him appear as though he did not have a wide view of things—not someone who could be the head man. It was a real disadvantage to him. It's just tragic the way it ended for him. [Editor's note: McDuffie returned to Georgia in 1991 as assistant head coach and offensive coordinator under Ray Goff. After the 1995 season Goff, McDuffie, and the rest of the Georgia staff were fired. McDuffie, who suffered from depression, committed suicide on February 16, 1996.]

Sam Mitchell, 1975–1978
I coached Sam at Auburn, so I was very familiar with him when he arrived in 1975. We brought him in to help us put in the 4-4 defense that had been so successful at Auburn and Notre Dame. He was here for our 1976 championship. He's still in Athens in the security business and has been very successful. He is a good friend.

Sam Mrvos, 1968–1977
He was from the old school. When I got here he was the B-team coach and the weight coach. He was part of the diverse personalities we had in our staff. John Kasay trained under him, and at times that was pretty entertaining. One was a Serb and one was a Croat. Needless to say they had their disagreements. They were two great characters and individuals.

Bill Pace, 1974–1979
I knew Bill from Arkansas and had always liked him. He had been the head coach at Vanderbilt (1967–1972) but was at Georgia Tech when I hired him. We knew he had a good offensive mind, and, for us, he really came along at the right time with the right group of players. Bill was a solid football coach who helped us a lot while he was here. He left us to go up to Tennessee to work for Johnny Majors.

Fred Pancoast, 1970–1971
I knew Fred in the Marine Corps; we were at Parris Island together. I first saw him coach at Florida and was impressed. In 1970 I really wanted to get somebody with new ideas to come in here and really coordinate the offense. It took a year to get his feet on the ground, but then he did a terrific job. We were really good in 1971 with Andy Johnson at quarterback and Jimmy Poulos at tailback. We were so successful that the next year Memphis stole Fred away to be head coach.

Jim Pyburn, 1964–1979

Jim and I were teammates at Auburn. He was always a great competitor and later became a successful high school football coach. He was part of our original staff in 1964 and stayed for 16 seasons, but there were some problems at the end.

His son, Jeff, was a great high school athlete and came to Georgia as a quarterback. It was tough to ignore that Jim was on the defense as a coach and his son was on offense. Then there was the situation with Buck Belue, who came in as a freshman and challenged Jeff for the starting quarterback job. This was tough on the family, no doubt about it. Jeff was a great competitor, but it just so happened that Buck came in and did some things that we were not doing particularly well until he got in the game. The whole thing was tough on Jeff's family, and when you get the whole family involved, there are bound to be repercussions. I think it was the reason that Jim left us as a coach. The whole episode with Jim was very tough but it's part of making decisions as a head football coach.

I'm happy to say that all is well now. I've seen Jeff several times, and he's a successful attorney. I was proud to help Jim get into the Alabama sports Hall of Fame, where he deserves to be.

Erk Russell, 1964–1980

I coached with Erk at Auburn, so I had known him for quite a while when I got the job at Georgia in 1963. He had been a successful high school coach in Atlanta and was at Vanderbilt as an assistant recruiting in Atlanta when I was hired at Georgia. So he just picked up the phone and called. The first words out of his mouth were, "Hey, Vince! How about a job?" That's how Erk Russell became our defensive coordinator. And for the next 17 years he was just great.

Erk is a hard man to dislike. In fact, I don't think I have ever heard anybody say anything bad about Erk Russell. He had a maturity that was a complement to me, the 31-year-old head coach. I always thought it was important to have a diverse staff. Erk made sure that we had a great collection of characters. Erk had his own style, too. He was one of the best motivators I have ever seen and had a funny story for every situation.

In the pregame he would literally butt heads with his players until his forehead was bleeding. The players loved it but his wife, Jean, didn't, so he stopped doing it. But one time our defense was playing lousy and we had a meeting. I told Erk that the players loved the head-butting thing, so he did it in the next game. Jean got mad at me but it helped the team, and we started winning again.

I can say that in 25 years as a head coach, there was only one Erk. There is no one else like him.

Rusty Russell, 1979–1980
Rusty was a good player for us and learned a lot about being a coach from his daddy. He was with us for a couple of years and then went to Georgia Southern when Erk became the head coach there in 1981.

Ray Sherman, 1986–1987
I really can't say enough good things about Ray Sherman. I just wish we could have kept him longer. He was a good football coach, a good recruiter, and a very good person. He was well respected throughout the profession. He was a really great fit here. He is definitely head coach material.

Dale Strahm, 1981–1988
Dale was a very organized coach who was very ambitious. He spent some time at the Naval Academy, which was a help. His linebackers played very well for us, and he was a valuable member of our staff. When I retired as coach, he began campaigning for my job, and he had some support. But ultimately I felt that Ray Goff, a Georgia man, deserved a chance. It was difficult because I liked George Haffner and Strahm; both had their strengths.

Jimmy Vickers, 1971–1976
Jimmy was a good offensive line coach who had trained with my brother at North Carolina. I knew that he had the same ideas that I

had. He was also a Georgia guy. We had some of our very best offensive lines during the time he was with us.

Charlie Whittemore, 1978–1990

Charlie was another one of our players who came back to Georgia to work for us. He was with Fred Pancoast in Memphis, and I hired him from there. He was a fine coach and loves Georgia. He is still with Georgia in charge of facilities and has done a splendid job.

Barry Wilson, 1971–1973

Barry played on our first team at Georgia (1964) and ended up being the captain. He coached with us and then at Ole Miss. He later became an assistant coach with Steve Spurrier at Duke. Then he took over as head coach at Duke when Spurrier went to Florida. Today he is living in Chattanooga and remains a loyal Dawg and good friend.

Chip Wisdom, 1975–1980

Intense. Intelligent. He grew up in the sixties and played for us from 1969 to 1971. During those years there were a lot of social changes going on, and Chip was certainly a product of his time—a real independent thinker. But when it came to football he was a company man—that is to say, a Bulldog first.

He was a great linebacker for us and then became an enthusiastic assistant coach and recruiter for our program. Chip bounced around and ended up at Alabama with Bill Curry. Curry fired him, but I never asked why. Since then he's been very successful in the publishing business in Tuscaloosa.

4

The Characters:
Bear, Shug, Woody, and
Assorted Others

You can't spend 41 years as a coach and administrator in college athletics without meeting some colorful and interesting characters along the way. Some were friends. Some were just acquaintances. All of them were memorable. Here are just a few of my favorites:

Bobby Bowden

Bobby and I coached against each other only once (1984 Citrus Bowl), but I have known him for a very long time.

I got to know him quite well when he was at Samford University in the fifties and early sixties. I was at Auburn at the time, and I went by to say hello with fellow Auburn coach Claude Saia. I met with him on many other occasions, mostly on coaching trips that were sponsored by Nike. We made these trips each year after recruiting was over. We were able to take our wives, so Barbara and I got to know Bobby and Ann really well. It's hard not to like Bobby Bowden.

I will never forget the one game we played against each other. It was a 17–17 tie—a good tie for him but a bad tie for us. We had played so well during the game and led 17-9 late in the game. We had been preaching all week that blocking punts was their specialty. And doggone it if they don't block a punt and run it in for a touchdown. I think it was the first punt we had had blocked in about 15 years! Then they ran a reverse for the two-point conversion to tie the game.

We still had time to win, but then the clock broke and time was kept on the field. We did a very poor job of clock management. We should have gotten our kicker, Kevin Butler, a little closer. We sent him out there to kick a 70-yard field goal on the last play of the game, and he was just a foot short!

James Brown

In 1975 Erk Russell approached me about calling our defense the "Junkyard Dawgs" because we were a small but scrappy bunch of guys who would really get after the other guys. I thought it was a great idea and agreed. Happy Howard, who worked on our radio broadcasts, wrote a song called "Dooley's Junkyard Dawgs" and got James Brown to record it. It was quite a rock'em, sock'em song. The students really loved it. Because of that there were several occasions when I was around James Brown. I was even on his television show when it was taped over at the TBS studios in Atlanta.

James Brown was a very interesting character. It was clear that he always enjoyed being where the action was. On the other hand he could be very sensitive and would always say, "God bless you." Then there were all these personal issues that seemed to get in his way from time to time.

We had no idea how popular he was internationally before we started working with him. But I can tell you one thing. He loved the Bulldogs. He went to the Cotton Bowl with us in 1975 and spoke to the team on several different occasions. What a character!

Paul W. "Bear" Bryant

Needless to say, coach Bryant was a colorful individual with his own unique style. A lot of people in Alabama loved him. A lot of people who didn't wear Crimson hated him. But I believe that everyone respected him. He was one of the greatest motivators I have ever seen, and he had the ability to change with the times. That's why he was so successful over such a long period of time.

I was lucky as a young coach to work under Shug Jordan at Auburn. And when he would send me to scout, I would always want to scout Alabama because of coach Bryant, and Georgia Tech because of Bobby Dodd. Jordan, Bryant, and Dodd were three very different people who handled coaching in three very different ways. But I learned a lot from all of them.

Coach Bryant was really larger than life. He could come into a room and say things that nobody else could say—and get away with it. His personality was that strong. But at the same time, if coach Bryant said something he knew was out of line, he would come back later and apologize for it. He was a very big man in that regard. And when his teams lost, he always took responsibility and never backed away from it. That is what made him such a great leader.

Coach Bryant also had a playful side to him. One year a bunch of us were sitting together with our wives at the SEC spring meetings. Coach Bryant was on the phone talking to his stockbroker, which was something the rest of us couldn't really relate to at that time. Barbara just had to ask coach Bryant what he was doing. Bryant put his arm around her and said, "Young lady, don't you forget that I'm the man who made your husband famous." He was referring to our 18–17 win over Alabama in 1965, which was the first big win that got us national recognition. Alabama was the defending national champion that year and, as it turned out, we were the only team to beat the Crimson Tide during the entire 1965 season! But coach Bryant handled the loss with class. I remember him coming into our dressing room and congratulating our entire team. It was those kinds of things that made him special.

One time we played over there and Joel Eaves, our athletic director, became ill and had to be admitted to the hospital in Tuscaloosa. On Sunday night, when he would normally be getting ready for his next game, coach Bryant was in the hospital visiting Joel Eaves. He did so many things like that that people never knew about.

Another year we were in a conference meeting in Birmingham, and we were in the process of looking for a new commissioner. The coaches were meeting downstairs and the presidents, who would ultimately make the decision, were meeting upstairs. Coach Bryant came in late to our meeting. Let's just say he was in very good spirits. It was Sunday

afternoon after they beat Auburn the day before, and perhaps the celebration from the previous night had not worn off.

He bellowed, "Why are *we* here when the presidents are up there?
I move that we send somebody up there to let the presidents know who
we like as commissioner!" But nobody seconded coach Bryant's
motion. We knew better. He got up and walked out of the room saying, "You're all a bunch of yellow-bellied son of a guns!" Needless to
say, I cleaned that up a bit. Only coach Bryant could do things like that
and get away with it. He was just great. I still miss him.

Nick Chilivis

For 41 years Nick Chilivis has been a loyal confidant and friend during
both the good and bad times. He is a highly respected individual whom
I first met when I came to Athens. He served for many years as the
attorney for the Athletic Association. He later moved to Atlanta as state
revenue commissioner under then governor George Busbee, and then
established his own highly successful law firm. Nick and his wife, Patti,
and their children have been close family friends.

Interestingly his wife, Patti Tumlin Chilivis, was a cheerleader on
my first Georgia team in 1964 and accompanied that team to the Sun
Bowl. She is fondly remembered for an incident that took place at the
team Christmas party in El Paso that year. Erk Russell, who was playing Santa Claus and calling names out while handing out presents to
team members, reached in his sack, pulled out a present, paused as he
looked at the name, and said: *"Who the hell is Patti Tumlin?"* Of course,
that broke up the party, and the story is still told today.

Bobby Dodd

I always respected coach Dodd for being an honest, straightforward person who always did what he thought was right. Naturally my fellow
Bulldog supporters did not share my opinion, especially after the eight-
year drought inflicted on us by Georgia Tech prior to my arrival.
[Editor's note: From 1949 to 1956 Georgia Tech won eight straight
games against Georgia.]

I remember the terrible situation in 1961 when Georgia Tech's Chick Graning was severely injured when he was hit in the face with an elbow by Alabama's Darwin Holt. It was a terrible episode, and it brought a lot of criticism to both sides of the field. Not long after that, one of Georgia Tech's defensive ends kicked one of our Auburn players in the face. Coach Dodd didn't hesitate to suspend that player for the rest of the season.

He was very good with the media. He didn't put any false spin on what he had to say, and if something was Georgia Tech's fault, he would say it. He never made excuses.

I remember that before professional sports came to the state, we would have the annual Kiwanis Club meeting in Atlanta, and coach Dodd and I would speak on the Tuesday before preseason practices started. The meeting was a pretty big deal back then and would always be front-page news. Coach Dodd would always steal the show and say something more newsworthy than I would. But afterward he would always tell me that he knew that I had to drive to Atlanta for the meeting (while all he had to do was drive from Georgia Tech, just over on North Avenue) and that he really appreciated me being there. He was always very considerate of others.

In 1966, when we won our first SEC championship, we met Georgia Tech in the last game of the regular season. Georgia Tech was undefeated and headed to the Orange Bowl. We had a very strong team and were in a position to beat them pretty badly. But from watching Dodd, Bryant, and Jordan, I knew that once the game was in hand, you didn't run up the score and embarrass a fellow coach. Besides, the tables might be turned one day soon. Tech got a late touchdown and made it a very respectable score (23-14).

The next day we saw each other as we were getting ready to tape our respective television shows. "You were very kind to me yesterday," coach Dodd said. "I want you to know that I appreciate it." Coach Dodd retired after that season so we only met on the field three times. I feel very fortunate that we were able to win all three games. He was a great coach and an even greater man.

Claude Felton

I had a chance to get to know Claude when he was first at Georgia (1975–1976) as an assistant to Dan Magill. Claude went to Georgia Southern in 1977 as the public relations director for the entire university.

When I became athletic director in 1979, Claude was one of the first people I wanted to bring back. I still kid him that I recruited him just as hard as I did Herschel Walker. I even got President Fred Davison to call him. He wasn't sure that he was going to get complete control of the sports information department because of Dan Magill's longtime influence. So I had to sell him. He agreed, and the University of Georgia has been much stronger for it. He is still in place today and is generally regarded as the best in the nation at what he does.

I have never seen anyone better at knowing how the public is going to react to a set of circumstances. He has a great feel for public relations. During the rest of the time I was head coach and for all of my time as athletic director, I would always ask for Claude's help before I did anything that would get a public response. I always wanted to make sure I had all the bases covered. He knew exactly the right way to get a point across without irritating people, even if it was a tough decision.

Claude is very efficient in what he does and he always does it in a quiet, understated manner. He is also very, very loyal. Most sports writers consider Claude to be the very best in the business. The proof is in the pudding: on June 30, 2004, Claude was honored in Canada with the Arch Ward Award. It is a lifetime achievement award in the field of sports information. That day was also my last as Georgia's athletic director, and I was in Canada to see Claude receive that award. I cannot think of a more fitting way to spend my last day as athletic director.

In an early draft of a letter to UGA president Michael Adams, I recommended that Claude be promoted to the number two position in the athletic department when Damon Evans replaced me. I told Dr. Adams that I thought the team of Evans and Felton would make "a great one-two punch" to lead Georgia. I took that paragraph out of the final version of the letter because, given my conflict with Adams, I was concerned that my recommendation would hurt more than it would help. Claude did not get that opportunity, but I still believe he deserved it.

Woody Hayes

I never met the Ohio State legend on the field, but one year he agreed to speak at my coaching clinic on one condition. I was thinking that he would want a lot of money. Instead, he said he wanted to have dinner with my entire family.

So Woody came to our house and we had a delightful evening. We talked about history, leadership, warfare, and all kinds of things. To this day, my children, who are now grown with children of their own, still talk about the night Woody Hayes came to the Dooley house.

But I also remember a very different kind of meeting with coach Hayes. In 1973 I became the chairman of the ethics committee of the American Football Coaches Association. I took over from John Pont, the head football coach at Indiana. The year before I took over, coach Hayes was asked to appear before the ethics committee due to a transgression. Back then somebody would just go down to the lobby of the hotel where the coaches convention was taking place and simply fetch the person and, without any warning or prior notice, that coach had to appear before the committee. Woody refused, and I didn't blame him.

When I took over I spent a year rewriting the rules so that a coach would receive plenty of advance notice before he was asked to appear before the committee. I was still the ethics chair in 1977 when coach Hayes punched a TV photographer during the big game with Michigan. He had to go before the ethics committee again. He was playing Alabama in the Sugar Bowl, and it fell upon me to tell him.

Coach Hayes had a suite set up in New Orleans and granted me an audience. I simply told him it was important for him to appear before the committee and that it would set a terrible example if he didn't. So coach Hayes made the appearance and immediately began making excuses for his behavior. But then he conceded that he shouldn't do such things—it was sort of a General Patton–type apology.

Lou Holtz told me that coach Hayes would get so mad during staff meetings that he once picked up a Kodak projector and threw it out a fourth-story window. Woody got a bill for about $300. After that they chained the projectors down.

Unfortunately, it did not end well for coach Hayes after he hit a player from Clemson (Charlie Bauman) at the Gator Bowl. I remember that Bo Schembechler and I went to see him after he had been forced to resign. It was a great and rewarding visit, but coach Hayes never acknowledged that he hit the player and, of course, refused to watch the film.

Lou Holtz

I only went head to head with Lou Holtz a couple of times (1972, 1973) when he was the head coach at North Carolina State, and I just remember that they had the Buckey twins (Don and Dave). One played quarterback and one played wide receiver; they both played us really tough. In one game I went for it on fourth down because I knew we couldn't stop them. We had to keep the ball for the last six and a half minutes of the game to win (28-22 in 1972). Our families were together in Tokyo for the Japan Bowl, and Barbara and I were with his lovely wife Beth on many occasions, especially trips sponsored by Nike.

Of course Lou went on to become head coach at Notre Dame, where he won a national championship, and then took over the program at South Carolina, where he recently retired. Lou was always a very demanding coach, but his teams were always very well coached. He is really good at all aspects of the game and a great, great motivator.

Frank Howard

I can't remember a more colorful coach than Clemson's Frank Howard, the man they called "the Baron of Barlow Bend." He got that name from his hometown in Alabama. You always had to be on your toes around coach Howard because you never knew what he was going to say or do next.

Right after I got to Georgia, I remember coach Howard coming to our first spring game. His reaction? "Ain't nothing out there that scares

Dooley (left) in 1949 with McGill High School teammates Bobby Duke (center) and Bubsy Partridge.

Vince Dooley, that "bright young coach," took over at Georgia on December 4, 1963.

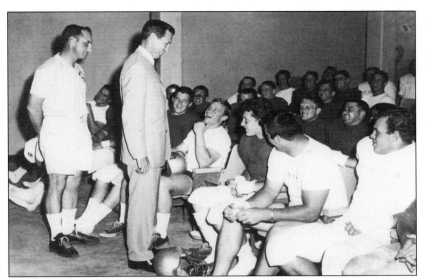

Coach Dooley introduces Georgia governor Carl Sanders to Dooley's 1964 team, his first.

Coach Dooley receives congratulations from Georgia Tech legend Bobby Dodd after another Georgia victory. Dooley was 3–0 against Dodd.

Coach Dooley is congratulated by Alabama's Bear Bryant after the Bulldogs upset the Crimson Tide 18–17 in Athens in 1965. Alabama was the defending national champion. PHOTO COURTESY OF BILLY DOWNS/THE ATLANTA JOURNAL-CONSTITUTION.

Coach Dooley is congratulated by his former coach and mentor, Auburn's Shug Jordan, after Georgia upset the Tigers 31–17 in 1970.

Coach Dooley with legendary Oklahoma coach Bud Wilkinson. Wilkinson, who became a TV analyst after his retirement, encouraged Dooley to pursue the job offered by Oklahoma in 1965.

Coach Dooley with his younger brother Bill. Bill Dooley was on Vince's original staff at Georgia and later became a head coach at North Carolina, Virginia Tech, and Wake Forest.

Coach Dooley with four of the first five African-American players at UGA, who signed in 1971. From left: Chuck Kimmebreu, Clarence Pope, Larry West, and Horace King. PHOTO COURTESY OF DAN EVANS/UNIVERSITY OF GEORGIA.

Coach Dooley with Charles, Prince of Wales, who visited Sanford Stadium in 1977.

me!" he said. I still like to tell the story of the first time our teams met in 1964. As an assistant coach, I always wondered what the head coaches said to each other when they met out on the field before the game.

So there I was, a rookie head coach right before our game with Clemson. Out on the field is the legendary Frank Howard. I knew I was supposed to walk out there and say *something* to him, but I just couldn't figure out what it should be. So I walked out to coach Howard and extended my hand. He never gave me a chance to speak. "Hey Vince," he said with that booming voice. "You been to Atlanta lately? They got some great nightclubs over there!" So this is what coaches talk about before the game?

Howard had something to say about everyone and everything. He knew my brother, Billy, who was on my staff. He would always call me "Big Brother" and call Billy "Little Brother." He would always call our league, the SEC, the "knucklehead league" because he thought the ACC's academic standards were higher. But he didn't spare his brothers in the ACC, either. One time he came back from North Carolina and said, "They've got a bunch of communists up there!" I remember he used to call Marvin Bass, the coach at rival South Carolina, "Largemouth Bass." But I will say this: his teams were always tough and he knew how to motivate them.

Squab Jones

Harry "Squab" Jones was listed as one of our trainers, but he was truly a jack-of-all-trades. He made what we called "Squab juice," which our players drank during their breaks in practice.

He would give a five-minute whistle warning to the players that a meeting was soon starting. Then he would give a final warning right before the meeting was about to start. He would come into the locker room and say, "Last call. Coaches and all." Then we would all go to our meetings.

He would often take it upon himself to be the security at practice. He was the guardian of the gate, so to speak. Sometimes he would take that job a little too seriously. One time people were just jogging around the track near our practice field, and he jumped out of the bushes and scared them! He even did it to some faculty members. I had a little public relations problem to deal with on that.

He would also help some of the players sell their tickets (back when it was legal to do that). I came to find out that he would take the "Squab commission" on those sales. He might have even scalped a ticket or two, and that was *not* legal. One time we came back from Florida and he was not with us. We had to go back to Jacksonville to get him out of jail for scalping tickets.

Squab was always good about giving me Dutch uncle advice, particularly when we began to integrate the team in the early seventies. I would bounce ideas off of him about what we should do and what we shouldn't. When we stopped playing the song "Dixie" at games, he thought that I should be supportive of the decision, and I was. A lot of the fans resented that decision, but he felt it was very, very important to understand why our minority athletes wouldn't want it to be played. I really appreciated that good advice.

He was a good and loyal friend. When I went to his funeral, I looked into the casket and he had on his SEC championship rings—all six of them—and his national championship ring.

Ralph "Shug" Jordan

I was already at Auburn when coach Jordan took over the program in 1951. But I learned my base set of coaching skills and philosophies from him, and that's something that you never forget.

I learned some of the most important things from coach Jordan. Certainly patience was a great character trait of his and, as an impetuous young coach, I needed to learn it. Some of the other coaches on our staff would get nervous when I would speak up and express my opinions in the staff meetings, but coach Jordan appreciated it and understood that it was part of learning. Just being around him, watching him in various situations, was a great learning experience.

Coach Jordan gave me my first chance to practice running an organization when he put me in charge of the freshman team. It was a really big step toward becoming a head coach, and I'll never forget it.

Back in those days, coaching a freshman team that played a five-game schedule was great experience for an aspiring head coach. Since I coached the quarterbacks on the varsity along with the B-team, a lot of people thought I had taken a demotion. But in my mind I needed the overall experience of coaching all phases of the game, which I got as head freshman coach.

A lot has been made of the fact that I had to beat coach Jordan for our first championship at Georgia in 1966. The truth is, I never really thought about him being my coach until the game was over, and I had to walk across the field and shake his hand. It was a little like beating your father. But as I have said many times, "better he than me" when it comes to losing a game.

Coach Jordan was everything people said he was. He was a fiery competitor but, at the same time, the most noble of gentlemen. I was very fortunate to play for him and then learn how to be a coach from him.

Don Leebern

Don Leebern, who played at Georgia under coach Wallace Butts, and I have been friends for more than 40 years. The basis for that friendship was the relationship that Barbara and I had with Don and his wife, Betsy.

The four of us did a lot of things together. Every year, we all went to New York for the College Football Hall of Fame dinner. After I became athletic director in 1979, Don and Betsy would sit with Barbara in the athletic director's box while I coached. Many times they would stay at our home on the Friday night before a home football game.

Of course our friendship changed when Don began his relationship with Suzanne Yoculan, our gymnastics coach. Given the sensitive nature of the situation—that Suzanne reported to me and that Don's wife, Betsy, was close to Barbara—it was only natural that our friendship would never be quite the same.

When you know somebody for as long as I've known Don, you don't always agree with everything they do and every decision they make. But I will say this: Don Leebern was a tremendous source of support for the vast majority of my time at Georgia. Unfortunately circumstances change and people change. I understand that and I accept it.

Dan Magill

I always tell the story about how valuable Dan Magill has been to the University of Georgia. When I came to Georgia in 1963 Dan had three jobs: sports information director, secretary of the Bulldog Club, and men's tennis coach. Today we have 38 full-time employees doing what Dan Magill used to do by himself.

He is, without question, Mr. Bulldog—more so than anybody I have ever known. He set the standard in sports information work and became the most successful college tennis coach of all time. He built a college tennis complex and Hall of Fame that is second to none.

He was also a good sounding board. He would come in and talk, and, because he was a coach and had seen a lot of football, he would tell me what he thought. I respected his opinion. He had a great sense of humor and our sessions would always include two or three really good laughs.

Dan and I did have some tough moments when I began to make changes after I became athletic director in 1979. He was used to doing everything, and I wanted to split up some of his duties. I wanted to bring Claude Felton back to Georgia and put him completely in charge of the sports information department. Claude knew it would be tough for Dan to let go, and so did I. Dan and I sat down and talked about it. We made the move, and I promoted Dan to assistant athletic director.

Dan and I also had a problem with the gender equity issue. Through his own hard work and resourcefulness, he had built an incredible complex for his men's tennis program. But the rules of gender equity dictated that the women's team must have equal access to all of our facilities for that sport. Now understand, Dan did everything he could to help the women build their program. I hired Jeff Wallace as the women's coach on his recommendation, and since then Georgia's women's tennis program has been among the best in the nation.

Dan's position was that it had taken decades to build these facilities for the men's program and, from his perspective, the women were not entitled to just walk in and have everything the same after his years of hard work. It was just hard for him to understand and, in many ways, it was for me, too. He wanted to help them build their program (and did so in many ways) but philosophically, as he would often say, he felt that "the girls need to pull themselves up by their own bootstraps." He did everything to help them build a facility, but he wanted the men and the women to be "separate but equal," which did not fly with Title IX and equal access.

Ultimately, there had to be equal access to that facility. Our president, Chuck Knapp, made that very clear. Dan had to accept that, and it was really tough on him. And it finally put strains on some relationships within the department. When it came to pass, he felt like Liz Murphey, our women's athletic director, and Jeff Wallace were undercutting him.

Throughout those years I asked Dan to compromise on this issue just a little more each year—which he did, allowing the women to practice and play matches when the men were not using the main courts. But finally it got to the point where access had to be completely equal, and I was responsible for telling Dan. It hit him hard, and that is probably what moved him to retire.

When Dan retired I went over to his house to see him. He was hurt. And no doubt some of his family was hurt too. But out of respect for him, I felt I owed him the courtesy of going to his house and talking about it. He told me it would take him a while to accept everything, and I understood.

I'm sorry that it ended that way for Dan because he has been a great and loyal friend. I can't think of one person who has meant more to the university than Dan Magill. I think time has soothed some of the hurt.

Since retiring Dan has played tennis competitively in various age brackets (80 to 85 now) and, most importantly, runs the Collegiate Tennis Hall of Fame, which he was able to bring to Athens through the generosity of Marianne and Kenny Rogers. He is still a great friend and the greatest Bulldog of them all.

Johnny Majors

I remember going to see Johnny Majors play in the Sugar Bowl for Tennessee against Baylor after the 1956 season. Johnny was a great football player on an undefeated team, but that day Baylor upset them (13-7) and ruined their perfect season. Johnny did not play well that day, and I will never forget what his mother said after the game: "Some days I have been known to burn the biscuits, too."

Johnny then coached at Mississippi State with my brother, so I knew him there. Then he went on to Pittsburgh, where he rebuilt that program, and we ended up playing him three times (1973, 1975, 1976) in a four-year period. His 1976 team, which we played in the Sugar Bowl, ranks as one of the two best teams we ever played (Nebraska in the 1969 Sun Bowl was the other).

Then finally he went to Tennessee, his alma mater, in order to rebuild their program. We had a chance to play against him there several times, including the unforgettable game in 1980 (a 16-15 victory) that began our run to the national championship.

Johnny was tough on his assistant coaches, that much I knew. But he was an outstanding football coach and a great competitor.

Larry Munson

My first two years at Georgia, our radio play-by-play voice was Ed Thilenius, a highly respected man with a lot of experience. But after the 1965 season, Ed had a chance to do some other things in professional sports, and suddenly we were looking for a new radio voice.

I really wasn't involved in the search. That fell to Joel Eaves, our athletic director, and Dan Magill. They discovered Larry Munson. Little did I know at the time what a find he was.

There was not a lot of excitement when we hired Larry Munson. Dan felt he was good, and he was OK as far as I was concerned. But he certainly wasn't the legendary Larry Munson that we know now.

Larry was doing Vanderbilt games and living in Nashville when we hired him, and in the early days, he would simply commute to Athens on game day or meet us on the road. I didn't like that idea because I thought he should have been in Georgia promoting our team. If he was really going to be a part of our team, then I wanted him around to promote us. Eventually he moved to Atlanta because he had some other opportunities there, and I was very happy.

There is a lot of debate about when Munson really became a "Georgia man" and a "homer" and was finally embraced by our fans. I do know that it didn't happen overnight. Sometimes love takes a while. I know I started hearing more about him during the week after we upset Florida in 1975. That's when his call of the winning touchdown told us that Gene Washington was "thinking of Montreal and the Olympics" and "ran out of his shoes" when he caught the end-around pass from Richard Appleby.

I think that call, the 1976 championship team, and the 1978 "WonderDawg" team that won so many close games turned Larry into the legend he is today. Who can forget Rex Robinson's field goal in 1978 against Kentucky in the closing seconds and Munson just yelling, "Yeah, yeah, yeah, yeah!" He never said it was good! All those close games brought out the best in Munson, and once the fans knew he really cared, they embraced him and he became a folk hero.

Munson is quite a character away from the radio booth, too. I would go fishing with him and he would talk to the worm! He'd tell the worm to "hunker down" and find a fish. He is also the biggest pessimist I have ever met. It finally got to the point where I couldn't be around him on game day because of all the negative thoughts he would put into my head. I would be feeling pretty good about things right before a game, and he would come up smoking that big cigar and say something like, "You realize, of course, that we don't have enough speed in our secondary to cover their receivers."

But, of course, nobody loves the Bulldogs the way Larry does. It's hard to believe that the 2005 season will be his 40th with Georgia. It's hard to imagine Georgia football without him.

Joe Paterno

I first got to know coach Paterno when we coached in the college All-Star game together back in 1968. Back then the game was played in Atlanta, and it gave us a good chance to get to know him and his wife, Sue.

Joe is a professional, a gentleman, and a very, very strong competitor. We had a great relationship. We never met on the field, however, until the end of the 1982 season in the Sugar Bowl—with the national championship on the line. Penn State won the game (27–23) and finally gave Joe his first national championship after coming close so many times.

I have to say that I am surprised he is still coaching at his age (77), but he has taken good care of himself, and I'm sure he still feels up to it. I certainly hate to see him going through these tough times because it hasn't been just one year of losses, it's been several years. I really got a kick out of watching him chase that official to the locker room at the end of a game a few years ago. Those old bird legs of his were moving pretty good. I sure hope I can move like that when I'm 77.

Barbara and I have spent some great times with Joe and Sue. Nobody has done more for college football than Joe, and I hope he will leave the game in the glorious way he deserves.

Billy Payne

When Billy played for us (1966–1968) we knew he would be a great success after football. He was vice president of the student body. He went to Georgia law school and actually coached for me while he was there.

I have to say that what Billy did in bringing the 1996 Olympics to Atlanta has to go down as one of the most amazing accomplishments in the history of the state, if not the nation. I just don't think the average person realizes what an incredible challenge it was. Just think of all the things he had to overcome to make it happen: Atlanta was not particularly well known as a big-time city; the Olympics had just been in the United States (Los Angeles, 1984) and they rarely bring it back to the same country that soon; it was the Centennial Olympics and Athens, Greece—where it all started—was heavily favored to be the host in 1996; no city in the history of the Olympics won it the first time they bid.

Sharing the dream with me was one thing, but sharing it with the sponsors was another. They told him he was crazy. The only way he got things started was to have several of his close friends put up $10,000 each. From there he upset Minneapolis for the right to represent the United States in the bidding process.

Through his leadership and a great staff he assembled, he was able to pull it off. Then, what is even more amazing, nobody who has ever spearheaded bringing an Olympics to a particular city has remained to spearhead putting it on. Usually, somebody like that gets involved in politics. Most people are incapable of doing both, but Billy was able to do it.

His dream for Atlanta came from the Barcelona Olympics in 1992. I was fortunate enough to be there when he formed it. He wanted to leave something—a legacy—to the city and the state. He invited me to be his guest in Barcelona. Barcelona has many fountains that attract people to come downtown. Later in his office in Atlanta he showed me the plans for Centennial Park and pointed the area out to me. He told me about his dream of the park and the fountains. It was his vision that the park would become the center of economic development in the area.

And that's exactly what happened. Today we have Centennial Olympic Park in downtown Atlanta, and it has transformed and renewed what used to be a pretty depressed area of the city. That is the legacy that Billy has left for the city of Atlanta and the state. He is one incredible individual and I am proud to call him one of my former players. More importantly, I am proud to call him my friend.

Prince Charles

We didn't have a great year in 1977. In fact it was our only losing season (5-6) in 25 years. But there was a lot of excitement around the campus when it was announced that Charles, Prince of Wales, would be visiting Georgia and attending our game with Kentucky.

69

Before the game, I took my captain to the center of the field, and the Kentucky coach, Fran Curci, brought his captain, Art Still. Art was a huge man and a great football player. I can still see Prince Charles, a small man, looking up at Still and wondering how a human being could be that big! I also remember Fran, who had put together quite a football team, walking over to the Prince and pulling out a stick of gum. He pulled the foil back and said, "Gum, Prince?"

Prince Charles was aghast at such a common American gesture, and in royal fashion snobbishly said, "No, no thanks." I almost broke up but managed to keep my composure. I have to say that was the last funny thing that happened that day. Kentucky beat us 33-0 and went on to win the SEC championship. I heard many people say that was the best Wildcat team "that money could buy." They got hit with major sanctions two years later.

Pepper Rodgers

I knew Pepper was a little bit different the first time I met him. We were in the lobby of a hotel during the national coaching convention when he turned to me and said, "I'm going to go page myself!"

When he came back to Georgia Tech, his alma mater, he couldn't resist bringing part of California with him (he was the coach at UCLA). He had a motorcycle, wore his hair in a perm, and carried a pocketbook. We didn't see that a lot in the South, but I always told people that if you're winning, nobody cares what you wear. I found that out in 1974 when he brought Tech to Athens and beat us 34-14 on the most miserable weather day I can ever remember. I knew that if we hadn't come back the next year and beat them bad in Atlanta (42-26), somebody might have suggested that I start carrying a pocketbook!

They called his tenure the "Pepper Generation" because his carefree style seemed to appeal to a lot of young people. He even let cameras in the locker room and was really good with the press.

But underneath all of that was a very good football coach. We had a lot of tough, hard-fought games. Our 1978 game in Athens (a 29-28 win) was one of the best games ever in the series. I liked competing against Pepper Rodgers, especially since he made me look like a passing genius! His wishbone offense threw a lot fewer passes than our offense.

Bo Schembechler

I got to know Bo really well when we spent a couple of weeks together on a lecture tour across Europe, which was sponsored by the Air Force. We went to beer gardens throughout Europe. We "Punted on the Backs" of the River Cam, which has nothing to do with football. A punt is a flat-bottom boat and the Backs is a long stretch of the Cambridge River in England. During that time we shared a lot of our football experiences and a lot of our personal lives. He was a former lieutenant in the army, and I had been a Marine captain. We just had a lot of things in common.

Bo was a good, sound football coach and a tough son of a gun. Of course, to compete against Woody Hayes every year, he *had* to be tough. He and I never coached against each other, but I would always give him a little reminder that we won at Michigan in 1965. He would always quickly respond, "But I wasn't there." He and I have remained friends all these years and have served on some important committees together.

Frank W. "Sonny" Seiler

By the time I got to Georgia in 1963, Sonny Seiler was already our man in Savannah. Sonny was a valuable and trusted friend because nobody promoted Georgia in Savannah like Sonny did. He kept me informed of everything that was going on down there that could affect Georgia.

And of course, he is the owner of UGA, our internationally famous mascot. It was 1966, our third year, that we had the first "changing of the Dawg," as UGA I retired and was replaced by UGA II. I was there for that most solemn occasion and have been on hand for the changing of all six UGAs. Charles Seiler, Sonny's son, was only five years old when UGA I retired. He and Sonny's daughter, Swann, have been helping Sonny with UGA as the years have gone by, but of course the real keeper of the Dawgs is Sonny's wonderful wife, Cecelia.

The best thing I can say about Sonny is that he has been a 40-year friend. He's one of the people who make Georgia such a special place.

Loran Smith

I'll never forget my first meeting with Loran Smith. As you might imagine, the day I was introduced as head football coach at Georgia in 1963 was a very long one. When it was over and I finally got back to my hotel room at about 10:00 P.M., I started going through my stack of messages. Then came a knock on the door. It was Loran Smith. He was a stringer for the Athens paper and wanted to interview me some more.

That story typifies Loran and what has made him so successful. He has a great ability to get to know people and get stories from them—no matter who they are. He doesn't hesitate to knock on the door at 10:00 at night if that is what it takes to get the job done or to travel to the backwoods (or anywhere) on a moment's notice to interview the likes of Satchel Paige or Ted Williams.

The thing I really like about Loran is that he has very good initiative. He is a good writer and will try anything. And any shortcomings he might have, which are few, are overcome by this persistence. Best of all, nobody knows the Georgia people better than Loran. That's because his role model is Dan Magill. He absolutely loves Dan because Dan is always for Georgia first, which is a great example for Loran. Whatever is best for Georgia, that is what Dan wants to do, and Loran tries to pattern himself after Dan.

Because of his persistence, he has traveled all over the world, especially to golf tournaments, to interview people. In that respect he has led the good life. Bill Simpson, a very humorous Athens marketing and public relations guru, often said, "I don't want to make the money Loran makes. I just want to lead the life Loran leads."

Barbara and I have shared many great times with Loran and his wife, Myrna, and their children, Camille and Kent. We have been friends for 41 years. Loran is, and will always be, a very important part of the Georgia tradition.

This chapter could go on for a long, long time. There are so many more people, including members of my own extended family, whom I should talk about. There are people like Dick Bestwick, one of the best people and college administrators I have ever known; Lee Hayley, who was an invaluable friend and associate over the years; and John Shafer, my right-hand man who did such incredible work for Georgia. There are so many more I want to mention but the constraints of time and space will not allow it. Needless to say, when you have done what I have done for so long, you make a lot of friends who help and influence you.

5

Glory, Glory Days: Champions and Those Who Walked with Champions

When you're a coach, every team is special and every team is a challenge. In the spring you begin with a pretty much blank piece of paper, and it's up to you and your coaches to take the players you have and write the story for that particular season. And, like a good story, there are always some twists and turns that you don't expect. How you and your players react to those unexpected things—both good and bad—usually determines what kind of story is going to be written about your season.

In my 25 years as head coach, we won six SEC championships and had a number of other teams that were good enough to walk with champions. I'm proud to say that more often than not, we were in the hunt for the championship.

We had a lot of high moments, like the early eighties when we had a 43-4-1 stretch, and some low moments as well—after a 6-6 season in 1974, I was probably as down as I've ever been. But I'm proud to say that every time the program went down, we rededicated ourselves to bringing it back up and getting back in the race for the championship.

Each of our six championship teams has a special story.

1966: Super Sophomores Put Georgia Back on Top
I've said many times that the 1965 recruiting class was the second best group that we ever had (the 1980 class with Herschel Walker was the

best). In 1966 those great players—like Bill Stanfill and Billy Payne—were all sophomores, so we really didn't know what to expect.

We certainly didn't start off the season like champions. We opened up at Mississippi State in a real dogfight. The game was tied (17–17) late, Mississippi State was deep in our territory and looking like they were going to win the game. They threw a pass into the end zone and it appeared to hit their guy in the chest for the touchdown. But just as the ball got there, Terry Sellers hit the receiver in the back and the ball popped right into the arms of Happy Dicks, a sophomore who had turned and raced for the ball after it was thrown, and he caught it for the touchback. We took the ball and drove it about 70 yards to kick a field goal to win, 20–17, in the last minute of play. That's how close we were to being champions or not being champions.

That team had some great growth potential. Even when we went down to Miami and got beat (7–6) by the heat and a great Hurricane defense, we could tell that it was going to be a good team at some point. It was just great that from that game on, we were a really good team and proved it every week. We got stronger with each game and solidly beat everybody down the line.

We had an incredible defense that allowed us to dominate a Florida team (27–10) that had a Heisman Trophy quarterback in Steve Spurrier. We fell behind 13–0 at Auburn at halftime, but then drove the length of the field three times to win, 21–13, and capture our first SEC championship since 1959. Obviously winning our first championship at Auburn against my old coach, Shug Jordan, was special.

And then we played a Georgia Tech team that was undefeated and headed to the Orange Bowl. We beat them soundly, although if you look at the final score (23–14), you wouldn't have guessed. That was an era when you just didn't run up the score on another team when you had them beat. We were up 23–7 and felt like they could not move the ball on us, so we took that opportunity to put in some seniors who had not gotten a chance to play. Tech got a late touchdown on us to make the game a little more respectable.

We went out to the Cotton Bowl to play SMU, and that game will always be remembered because at the end, when we had the game in hand, we let George Patton, our All-American defensive tackle, play quarterback. (See pp. 26–27 for the full story.) But we won the game and finished 10-1.

The 1966 team was a solid group of seniors who had been through some tough times before we got to Georgia, combined with some talented young players who were ready to win. The quarterback on our first SEC championship team was Kirby Moore, who is now an attorney in Macon. As a player, Kirby's feet were so quick that I called him "my little sandpiper." The first championship is always special, and that group of guys will always be special to me.

1968: A Championship Team Fit to Be Tied

I believe our 1968 championship team was as talented as any group we've ever had. The players from the great recruiting class of 1965 were now seniors. Our offense averaged almost 200 yards rushing and 200 yards passing, and for a team to post 400 yards of total offense per game was unheard of back then. Our defense led the nation in scoring. Only one time all season did our team give up more than 17 points, and that was in a win, 21–20, over South Carolina.

We became a strong offensive team when Mike Cavan emerged as our starting quarterback. Not a lot of people played sophomores at quarterback back then, but the older guys on the team liked Mike and could relate to him. Mike was the son of a coach and showed great leadership qualities.

This team was really good and we knew it. We had a chance to be great but some things didn't go our way—like the first game at Tennessee.

Some ties feel like a win; some ties feel like a loss. The 17–17 tie at Tennessee definitely felt like a loss because we outplayed them. They were down 17-9 and scored on the last play of regulation on what should have been an incomplete pass. Tennessee threw the ball into the end zone and the ball bounced on the turf and back into the receiver's hands. The officials ruled it a touchdown, Tennessee went for two with no time left on the clock, and they made it. It was a lousy way to let a game slip away. Because the touchdown pass was completed down the middle in his zone, Jake Scott really felt bad. The loss no doubt made Jake and the team more resolute the rest of the year.

That was the first game ever played on Tennessee's new artificial turf. Joel Eaves, our athletic director, called it "the Brillo pad" and he wasn't far off. Coach Eaves really hated that thing. He didn't want us to be the guinea pigs who broke in that surface and said so. He was very upset about it, but we really didn't have a choice.

I made a big coaching mistake leading up to that game. The more we talked about that darn turf, the more I thought we were not focusing on the game. The guys were coming to practice wearing all these things on their arms and elbows. They looked like gladiators (or armadillos) coming out of the locker room. So I put my foot down and told our players they couldn't wear anything for this game that they didn't normally wear. We were going to focus on the game—not the turf.

What a mistake! We went up there and guys got skinned up everywhere. As a result, we had an outbreak of boils. I think about 19 players got infected by scrapes from that turf. It might have brought us closer together as a team, but it was a hard lesson to learn about that stuff.

We had a tough win at South Carolina (21-20). That was the third game and we were still uncertain about who to start at quarterback. We threw a couple of interceptions before the fans even got settled in their seats, and at halftime we were down 20-7. We decided to go with Cavan full time and he brought us back to win. From that point on we knew Mike would be our guy, and from that point on I knew we would be a very good team.

Then we had another tie, but that one felt like a win. Houston came to Athens with their incredible offense and a great group of athletes led by Elmo Wright. They were averaging 410 yards a game, an incredible number back then. Erk Russell, our defensive coordinator, told his unit during practice, "Nobody is ever going to have 400 yards against us."

Erk was right. Houston had 532.

Most of that yardage was between the 20s. They scored only one touchdown and led 10-7 late in the game. Cavan then drove us down the field, and Jim McCullough kicked a field goal at the end of the game to give us a 10-10 tie.

What I remember most about that game is Billy Kinard, our assistant coach. He used to complain all the time about kickers, especially McCullough, whom he detested, and one of my standing rules was that if anybody complained about something, they were put in charge of it. So Billy was put in charge of the kickers. When McCullough made that field goal I thought Billy was going to hurt Jim by hugging him so hard. It was hilarious.

That team rolled on to beat Florida and Auburn and win another SEC championship. I didn't know it at the time, but most of the players wanted to go to the Orange Bowl and the Orange Bowl was ready to invite us. But there was something the players didn't know.

The Sugar Bowl Decision

The bowl process was very different back then. Not a lot of people know this, but Bear Bryant of Alabama basically controlled the whole system and pretty much dictated who would go to what bowl. Deals could be made at any time, and sometimes you had to grab the best bowl deal that you could, when you could.

It was the week of the Auburn game and the Orange Bowl was prepared to take us if we won the game and the championship. The Sugar Bowl came to us and said they would take us regardless of what happened in the Auburn game. After discussing the situation with then-athletic director Joel Eaves, we decided to take the unconditional Sugar Bowl offer. In hindsight, we probably shouldn't have made the deal, but we did.

After we went down and beat Auburn I remember coach Eaves coming to me and saying, "Now, what is your feeling?" Despite the dilemma, I told coach Eaves, "My feeling is we told them [the Sugar Bowl] we would do it. We made a commitment and should not back out, regardless of the circumstance." He wholeheartedly agreed.

On the one hand I take my hat off to myself because a commitment is a commitment. But on the other hand I still second-guess myself because I shouldn't have made that commitment. I should have waited until I discussed it with the team so that I would at least have had a feel for what they wanted to do. That would have been better, but it was just not done that way. We had made a commitment to go to the Sugar Bowl and that's what we did.

Back then coaches didn't really consult the players very much, and that, perhaps more than anything else, accounted for the fact that we didn't play like we wanted to play in New Orleans (losing to Arkansas 16–2). I tried to tell the team some of the great things about playing in New Orleans but it really didn't work. I told them I couldn't back out and break my word to the Sugar Bowl. Now I just hope that as the players got older, they understood. They might not ever agree, but I hope they understand.

That was a good lesson for a young coach to learn.

1976: Shaved Heads and Stout Hearts

You never know what will make a team jell, make them feel they are a unit instead of a bunch of individuals. In 1976 all it took was a sharp razor, a little shaving cream, and a lot of courage.

After the 1975 team went to the Cotton Bowl, we thought we looked good for 1976. We had a great offensive line coming back and a really solid group of seniors led by quarterbacks Ray Goff and Matt Robinson. I really didn't think there would be any surprises with this team.

I was wrong.

I came into the meeting room the first day of the preseason to discover that practically all the guys had shaved their heads as a show of solidarity. They were laughing and cutting up and were pretty proud of themselves. I figured I had to say something, so basically I told them that if they won the SEC championship and beat Georgia Tech that I would shave my head too. Of course, I didn't think a whole lot about it after that because, frankly, I didn't think we were quite good enough to win the championship.

Well, I was wrong again. We did win the championship. We did beat Tech, and I had to keep my promise. But more on that later.

It didn't take long for that team to show it had the stuff of champions. Our first SEC game was at home against Alabama. Anybody who was there will tell you that it was a day they will never forget. I remember a crowd on the tracks outside of Sanford Stadium at 2:00 P.M. on Friday. By 7:00 that night the tracks were packed!

You have to remember that Alabama was the dominant program in all of college football in the seventies. But on that day we dominated them, 21-0, with Matt Robinson directing two of three touchdown drives. I was at home when most of the celebration was going on, but I know that they had to close off Milledge Avenue because there were so many people parading in the street.

I don't know if we were still celebrating or what, but we slipped up the next week at Ole Miss (in a 21-17 loss). It was the second straight year we had been to Oxford and lost. The 1975 loss cost us a share of the championship. We couldn't let that happen again.

We didn't. A few weeks later we were in trouble in Jacksonville against Florida. We were trailing 27-13 at halftime, but in the locker room things were pretty calm. We thought we could move the ball, and if we got a break or two, we'd be right back in the game. We got that break in the third quarter after we cut their lead to 27-20. Doug Dickey, the Florida coach, decided to go for it on fourth and inches at his own 29-yard line. I'm sure he felt they had to do something because we had the momentum and were starting to take control of the game.

I didn't second-guess coach Dickey for going for it, but I did second-guess the play he called. If he had given the ball to his fullback, there was no way we could have stopped it. But Florida decided to run the option wide. He went for all the marbles and the big gain. Using the option play at that point could have been a big gain or a big loss. Johnny Henderson made a great play and we stopped them. That just poured more fuel on the fire, and we went on to dominate the rest of the game and win 41-27.

The next week we beat Auburn (28-0) without throwing a pass. We didn't throw a pass because we *couldn't* throw a pass. Ray Goff was hurt and couldn't lift his arm high enough to throw, but the win was good enough to give us our third SEC championship.

After winning the championship Ray was feeling his oats. He came out to the press and said that Georgia Tech was no longer our biggest rival. Instead teams like Auburn and Florida were, especially since we were dominating Tech and they were not in the SEC. I'm sure he was speaking his feelings and probably the feelings of a lot of Georgia fans, but even now it's something you just don't say. I did have a little talk with Ray about his remarks. That's when I started to think we might be in trouble against Georgia Tech.

We got up 10-0 in the third quarter, and it looked like it might be easy. But Tech hung in there and eventually tied it up at 10-10. And then it got serious. Really serious. Our ballclub came alive and started acting like champions. We drove the length of the field and got inside their 30. But then Ray fumbled the ball and Tech recovered. Well, everybody thought that was it. It was going to be a tie and that would *definitely* feel like a loss.

Ray came off the field so mad that he threw his head gear into the hedge. Then the next play somebody hit the Tech ball carrier hard and Bill Krug recovered the ball for us. Ray couldn't find his head gear, so I started yelling, "Where is Goff?" Ray found his helmet (or somebody else's, I found out later), and we just hammered the ball as best we could and put Allan Leavitt into position to kick a field goal. I remember it was so foggy that you couldn't really see the upper deck of the stadium. It seemed like it took forever for the official to give the signal, but Allan's field goal was good, and we won 13-10.

We had won the SEC championship. We had beaten Tech. And now the time had come for me to keep my commitment to shave my head. I wanted to find a way to do it without a lot of fanfare, so I looked in the phone book for a barber I figured might not know me. I found a man named John Salvadori. I figured he might be an Italian immigrant and would know nothing about football or about me.

As it turned out, John Salvadori was an old blocking back from West Blocton High School in Birmingham, Alabama. His family came to Birmingham from Italy to work in the steel mills. Today he and his wife Mary are still some of our best friends, and he still cuts my hair. Salvadori shaved my head and fitted me with a wig to wear to the team banquet.

People looked at me funny, thinking something was strange, but I never let on and, when it was my turn to speak, I tried to keep it serious. After all, we were set to play Pittsburgh in the Sugar Bowl on New Year's Day. If we won, we would have a chance to win the national championship. And so I began my speech:

> Our football team can walk with any champion that we've ever had. But our football team has an opportunity on January 1 to walk *ahead* of any champion that we've ever had here at the University of Georgia.
>
> From the time that we started the season, it was evident to all of us that this team would be very special . . . would be special to the extent that we've never had a team with more character and more heart and with more unity of purpose than this football team.
>
> Shortly after we finished our two-a-day practice sessions, when they had perhaps more time than they needed on their hands, about 15 of our players elected to show their unity by shaving their heads. They were soon joined by some 10 others for a total of 25. Soon joined by members of our coaching staff who pledged themselves each and every game to shave their heads.

At that point the noise among the players was starting to build. They knew what was coming. I put my hand on the wig. A commitment is a commitment.

> So I want to pay my tribute and say *hail to the champions!*

I ripped off the wig and the crowd went nuts. It took the players forever to settle down. Too bad we didn't play the game that night.

I went around and lectured all year with the wig, and when I would pull it off, the high school coaches I lectured to around the country would also go nuts. Barbara used to turn over and wake up in the middle of the night and scream because she thought there was some strange person in the bed. Erk Russell, of course, said I set bald heads back 30 years.

1980: Undefeated, Untied, and Unforgettable

A lot of our great seasons came right after very difficult seasons, and that was certainly the case in 1980. In 1979 I should have been voted ACC Coach of the Year because I certainly helped a lot of other schools in that conference. We lost to Wake Forest (22-21) in our opener. Then we went to Clemson and lost (12-7). Then later on Virginia just thumped us (31-0). We also lost to a former ACC member, South Carolina (27-20).

But with all that, we still had a chance to share the championship because we were 5-0 in the SEC when we played Auburn. We lost (33-13) and Alabama won the championship, but at least we beat Tech (16-3) to go 6-5.

We knew the guys we had coming back in 1980 were pretty good, but we had to have a tailback, a position we never filled in 1979. We had to wait until Easter Sunday of 1980 before we finally signed Herschel Walker to fill that spot. People ask me all the time if I knew what we had when we signed Herschel. I did know what I had, but I honestly didn't know he would be that good that soon. There was so much attention and pressure being put on him, I wanted to temper that a little bit. So I made some statements publicly that he was kind of a stiff back, kind of a fullback type. That was true compared to some of the more flexible backs who had played for us. But I was also trying to take a little pressure off him and off us and remove some of the excitement around him.

I was going to give Herschel a chance to be good, but I also had an obligation to let the players who had been around start in the first game against Tennessee. Donnie McMickens was a fifth-year senior, then there was Carnie Norris, and then finally Herschel. I played each one of them two series. If Herschel was going to win the job, he would have to win it on the field. And that's exactly what he did.

When he went in there was a surge of electricity. I often said of Herschel's performance that night that he might not have known where he was going, but he was going there in a hurry. The fans could see it and the team could see it. Based on that, we started him in the second half against Tennessee, and the rest is history.

Everybody has a memory of what happened at Tennessee. We were behind 9-0 at halftime and not doing a lot on offense. In the locker room, Mike Cavan and George Haffner and the rest of the offensive coaches were in a huddle. By that time I had already made up my mind that Herschel was going to start in the second half, but the coaches thought they needed to come tell me that Herschel needed to start. Nobody wanted to tell me—they finally made Mike come. Mike claims I agreed and said, "Well, it [our offense] couldn't be any worse." I might have said that.

We came back to win at Tennessee (16-15) because Herschel scored two touchdowns. But I don't think we really knew how great he was going to be until the next week against Texas A&M. When Herschel broke his first long run (for 76 yards and a touchdown) against Texas A&M, I think a lot of people sat up and took notice. That run, and the long run later in the season against South Carolina (76 yards for a touchdown) are two that I will never forget.

The South Carolina game took a lot out of our team, and the following week we had to go down to Jacksonville to play Florida. We had the lead most of the game, but at the end they jumped back ahead of us (21-20).

People ask me what I was thinking on the famous play from Buck Belue to Lindsay Scott. [Editor's note: Belue hit Lindsay Scott for a 93-yard touchdown pass with 1:03 left to give Georgia a miracle 26-21 victory over Florida.] All I was thinking was that we needed to get a first down and get out of the hole. And when Lindsay caught the ball I just thought, "Great, we got it! Now we have a chance." Then when Lindsay hit the ground and started running I thought, "Good, he's got a little more than a first down." Then I realized there was no one between him and the goal line, and I started running down the sideline with him. I outran him for the first 10 yards, and then he outran me to the end zone.

Of course it was a crazy, wild celebration. I got irritated because I knew we were going to get an excessive celebration penalty—we had players coming off the bench and fans joining the celebration in the end zone—and we still had to kick off to Florida with a minute left.

Bobby Gaston, who is now the SEC supervisor of officials, was working the game and came over to tell me about the penalty. According to Bobby, this is the way the conversation went:

Bobby: "That's a celebration penalty, Coach."

Me: "How much is that?"

Bobby: "It's 15 yards, Coach."

Me: "That seems a little harsh."

Bobby still remembers my remark and kids me about it.

But we beat Florida, and then wrapped up the SEC championship by winning at Auburn (38-20). We also beat Georgia Tech to finish 11-0. We were ranked No. 1 when the invitation came to play Notre Dame in the Sugar Bowl for the national championship.

Dawgs Strut Their Stuff in New Orleans

We knew how good Notre Dame was when we agreed to play them in the Sugar Bowl. Defensively they were truly great—no player had rushed for more than 100 yards on them all season. Their defense was so good that their offense didn't really have to do much for them to win, but we knew we were going to have our hands full.

There are so many memories I have from that game, but today I am still in total awe of what Herschel Walker did that day at the Superdome. To me, Herschel had three things that I've never seen one other back have in one package:

Speed: He was a world class sprinter.

Strength: Physically, he was incredibly strong.

Mental toughness and self-discipline: The tougher the game was, the better he liked it and the better he played. He was a classic example of training and self-sacrifice.

And the Notre Dame game was as tough as it gets. On the second play Herschel came out holding his shoulder.

I used to call our trainer, Warren Morris, "Dr. Death" because he always had to deliver the bad news, and he appeared to enjoy it. After Herschel went out Warren came up to me and said, "He's finished. He's out for the game and can't play any more. His shoulder is dislocated." Warren kept going on and on and finally, in a stern voice, I told him I got the message!

I was thinking, "Well, that's it. We have got to find a way to win without him and I have got to provide leadership to portray that attitude."

But when we got the ball back, Herschel took the field and Warren came back to me and said, "His shoulder is back in place. He's going back in." Herschel went on to rush for 152 yards, and we won the game and the national championship. I'm just glad we didn't have to find a way to win without him.

I'll always remember the sea of red that flooded the Superdome floor when the game was over. One of the really great thrills in coaching is to be in the locker room after a great win. The players picked me up and passed me around the room. It was really fun. I don't remember a lot about what went on that night after the game, but I knew I had to get up early the next morning and keep a commitment I had made with Loran Smith. Barbara said she woke up in the middle of the night, and I was in bed with my clothes still on, my sideline pass still attached to my sweater, and a smile on my face.

I get asked a lot if my coaching career would have been complete had we never won a national championship at Georgia. I say it would have been a satisfying career, but I just don't think a coaching career can be complete without an undisputed national championship. You need at least one year when you win them all and your team is recognized unanimously as the best in the nation. It took 17 years to do it, but we finally had one.

1981: Finding a Way to Stay Hungry

One of the biggest challenges after winning any kind of championship is to make the team stay hungry—to be willing to put forth the same effort as the year before. Besides, we had lost some good seniors, and for the first time in 17 years, Erk Russell would not be with us to lead the defense. He had accepted the challenge of resurrecting the football program at Georgia Southern.

In 1981 our coaching staff first challenged the team and then we challenged each other. If we were not going to win it all, it was not going to be because we eased up or slacked off or we got satisfied. It was going to be for some other reason.

During our incredible run in the early eighties (43-4-1) I kept reminding our teams, "Whoever we play, they are going to be at their best. And that's your fault. That's not my fault. It's your fault because of what you have done and what you have accomplished. You will have to pay that price, and you'll be challenged every time out there."

By 1981, and throughout the run, we had a lot of games that went down to the wire. But we got into a wonderful pattern of believing we were going to win. Every week it was different, and that was true for four years. Our guys were determined to find a way to win, and each week it was a different person in a different phase of the game who stepped forward to make the difference.

The 1981 team could do everything. We had senior quarterback Buck Belue. We had the best running back in the country—Herschel Walker. We had added place-kicker Kevin Butler, who would eventually be named to the College Football Hall of Fame. The defense was stout and talented. The team was capable of winning it all again.

But we ran into a buzz saw in our third game against Clemson. We laid it on the ground nine times. Nine turnovers! We still had a chance but ended up losing the game 13–3. The fact that we were still in the game after all those turnovers tells you what a good team it was. What we didn't know at the time was that it was Clemson's year to win them all and to win the national championship.

After that we rolled along pretty well until we got to Jacksonville to play Florida. Just like the year before, we found ourselves behind, 21–20, in the fourth quarter. But this time there was plenty of time left, and we were able to drive 95 yards with Herschel and Buck doing a lot of the work. We won the game by the same score, 26–21. That drive, and the 99-yard drive we had two years later against Florida, were two of the most impressive I've ever seen.

For the first time we were able to clinch a championship at home when we beat Auburn (24–13). Herschel had his usual great game (165 yards), and Buck threw a couple of touchdown passes. After the game Buck gave me the game ball, but the way I looked at it, he was the leader of the team and was a big reason why we won the championship. So I gave it right back to him.

We went into the Sugar Bowl against Pittsburgh ranked No. 2. Clemson was No. 1 and was playing Nebraska in the Orange Bowl. If we could win and Clemson stumbled, we could win it again.

Unfortunately, neither happened. Clemson took care of Nebraska and won the championship. It was just their year. And we got beat with a great play by Hall of Fame quarterback Dan Marino.

The game bounced back and forth, but we had the lead late. Pittsburgh had the ball around our 30-yard line, and it was fourth-and-five with 24 seconds left on the clock.

All game long we could never get any pressure on Marino. So we decided to blitz, hoping to make Marino hurry his throw. Our safety played man coverage on their tight end, John Brown. Brown ran the post into the end zone, and Marino threw the ball right into his chest. Cornerback Ronnie Harris hit him hard just as he caught the ball, but it was a perfect strike for the touchdown and they won, 24–20. Marino went on to make a lot more big plays in the NFL.

1982: Georgia Gets First SEC Three-Peat

During the preseason it was hard to look at this team and think that we would go through the regular season undefeated. We had lost Buck as our quarterback and our new quarterback, John Lastinger, didn't particularly care about being a quarterback. John would rather have been a wide receiver and let somebody else be the quarterback. But John was also a great leader—if you gave him the responsibility, he would take it and make the most of it.

I really liked John. He had a lot of great stuff about him. Sometimes he would frustrate you with some of his passes, which would go into the ground or sail into the stands, and sometimes I thought, "What in the heck is this guy doing?" But he was a tremendous leader and a great competitor and that's what I liked.

We had a tremendous opportunity to open the season with Clemson, the defending national champions, on Labor Day night. It was a meeting of the last two national champions, and all of Athens was really excited. The fans could afford to be excited, but I was nervous and worried because we were going to play most of the game without Herschel Walker, who had an injured thumb. Herschel gave us some tough yardage under extreme adversity with his injury. But that game showed that this team really had the right stuff. We turned a blocked punt into a touchdown, and Kevin Butler kicked two field goals. We won 13-7, but little did we know that it was just the beginning of an 11-0 regular season.

We almost paid a big price for playing that Monday night game. Due to a scheduling problem, we had to turn right around and play BYU the following Saturday at home. I did my best to try to change the game. Both Georgia and BYU had open dates the following Saturday, so we could have moved the game to September 18. But my good "friend" Lavell Edwards, the BYU coach, knew he had me in a weak position. I offered to add another $100,000 to BYU's payout if he would move the game to a week later. I thought he would understand that it was not fair for my team to have only a few days of rest while his team had 10 days to prepare. I guess we weren't such good buddies after all, at least when it came to competing. I would have done the same thing, no doubt.

I was worried about the BYU game, and I really got worried when we came out to practice on the Tuesday after the Clemson game. Everybody was basically asleep. The fact that we were able to beat BYU (17-14) was one of the most outstanding accomplishments any of my teams ever had. To beat Clemson, the defending national champions, on Monday night and come back five days later to beat BYU was something special. It was even more special given the fact that Steve Young, another future Hall of Famer, was BYU's quarterback.

That BYU game shows you how much scheduling has changed. Back then we could bring in great intersectional teams and they would come to our place for one game (for a very good guarantee), but we wouldn't have to return the game. We brought in California, UCLA, BYU, Oregon, Oregon State, Baylor, Texas A&M, Virginia, North Carolina State, and Pittsburgh, to name a few. And we never had to go to their place. Now teams of that quality want a "home and home" arrangement—they want you to play a game at their home as well. Fortunately, the new 12-game schedule will allow Georgia to play more quality nonconference opponents at home.

Behind Herschel's running and a great defense, that team sailed along. We took care of Florida much easier than I would have imagined (44-0), and then we headed to Auburn, where we had a chance to clinch our sixth championship.

So much happened in that game. I'll never forget Herschel running down the sideline (47 yards) to give us the lead at halftime (13-7). I'll never forget the man Auburn called "Little Train." Lionel James took off on a long run (87 yards) to put them on top 14-13 in the fourth quarter. We put together a heck of a drive (80 yards) to retake the lead 19-14. Then they came right back down the field with Bo Jackson and got into position to score and win the game. Jeff Sanchez had to knock down a pass on fourth down for us to win the game. [Editor's note: Auburn drove to the Georgia 21-yard line in the closing moments of the game before the Bulldogs stopped the drive.] It was an incredible game and the perfect way to wrap up our third straight championship, with "sugar falling out of the sky," as Munson kept repeating on the radio when the game was over.

After beating Georgia Tech 38-18 to go 11-0, we had a chance to go back to the Sugar Bowl ranked No. 1, knowing that a win would give us another national championship. It was the third year in a row that we had arrived at New Year's Day in the mix for the national title. It was a great feeling.

Penn State was ranked No. 2, and they were on a mission. For all the great things that Joe Paterno had done at Penn State, he had never won a national championship. Penn State had lost a game to Alabama 42–21 early in the season and had fought their way back up the rankings. We knew it would be a difficult game.

They had a great start and really jumped on us early (20–3). But then we fought back and came within three points (20–17) in the third quarter. I thought we were getting ready to take control of the game. Our defense was playing really well, but Todd Blackledge threw a long touchdown pass (47 yards) over Tony Flack, and their receiver (Gregg Garrity) made a sensational catch in the end zone to make the score 27–17. We scored again late but missed a two-point conversion when Herschel turned up too soon and the Penn State defense made a great play on him. We were hoping to get the ball back one more time, but Penn State was able to run out the clock.

It was a great, great football game but we just didn't make the plays we needed to. It was a tough loss to take. They always say the highs are never as high as the lows are low. That day I believed it. It was a real low. Little did we know that we were getting ready to experience another low. On national signing day we found out that Herschel had signed with the New Jersey Generals of the USFL. His career at Georgia was over and we would have to enter the 1983 season without an established tailback.

While we won six SEC championships at Georgia, we had a number of other teams over the years who were good enough to walk with those champions. They were teams that had the grit and tenacity of championship teams, but through bad luck, injuries, or circumstances they were never able to wear a championship ring. Even so, they were very special teams.

1965: Flea Flicker Beats 'Bama

I've often said that if freshmen had been eligible, the 1965 team could have been one of our very best. We had a pretty talented team in our second year at Georgia, but we didn't have any depth. The 1965 freshman class was the second best one (to 1980) that we ever signed. That was the class that included Bill Stanfill, Jake Scott, Billy Payne, Kent Lawrence, and many other quality players. Those guys went on to win two SEC championships. We could have played at least eight of them as backups and would have been really good.

The year started out great. We beat Alabama 18–17, the defending national champions, on the famous flea flicker pass from Kirby Moore to Pat Hodgson to Bob Taylor. Kirby then completed a pass to Hodgson for the two-point conversion and the win. It was a great victory for our program in only its second year and was a sign to everybody that we were headed in the right direction.

Two weeks later we went to Michigan and won a game (15–7) that I thought was just as big. We were a small team compared to Michigan, but we had a ragged bunch of tough old guys who had been through the wars before we arrived in 1964. They were like the army of Northern Virginia. They didn't impress anybody just by looking at them, but they would fight every minute of the game. Guys like Bob Taylor, Joe Burson, Doug McFalls, and Preston Ridlehuber weren't going to back down from anybody.

When we went into Michigan Stadium, I remember Preston saying, "This stadium isn't that big, we've played in the Gator Bowl." Michigan Stadium, even back then, held more than 100,000 screaming fans.

I'm glad the players weren't intimidated, because I sure was.

We were a quick, dogged team that was really relentless. We were in good shape and we just wore Michigan down. The reception we got back in Athens is something that all of us will remember for the rest of our lives. Cars were lined up from the city of Athens all the way to the airport. Some fans just parked on the side of the road and walked to the airport. There must have been ten thousand people there. People would always go to the airport to see us off and they would be there no matter what time we got back.

Some students got on our team bus and rode back to Athens with us. It was one of the greatest celebrations we ever had. I really missed celebrations like that when we had to stop flying out of Athens and started flying out of Atlanta.

We were undefeated and ranked pretty high (No. 5) after our first four games, but then we started losing players. We lost Bob Taylor, who broke his leg at Florida State and never played again. We lost Doug McFalls. We lost Joe Burson. We lost four or five first-stringers, which really affected us, but we hung in there until the end. We had to play Ridlehuber, one of our starting quarterbacks, at tailback against Kentucky (a 28–10 loss) because we were so banged up.

We struggled at North Carolina (winning 47–35) where we needed to recover an onside kick for the win. Little Billy Cloer earned his scholarship in that game. He was on the onside kicking team, and I think it was the only team he was on. Billy went under the pile and got the football, and we scored after that.

We got McFalls back for the Florida game, but he had his jaw wired shut and we lost 14–10. We almost beat Auburn (losing 21–19). We had the ball and a chance to win but Ronnie Jenkins fumbled on the 1-yard line. By the time the Georgia Tech game rolled around we had just about everybody back but Taylor and we were a pretty good football team again. We beat a good Georgia Tech team pretty handily (17–7). That Tech team went on to beat Texas Tech in the Gator Bowl.

In today's environment, given what that team had accomplished, we could have definitely gone to a bowl game. We beat an Alabama team that had won the Associated Press national championship the year before and would go on to win it again in 1965. We beat a Michigan team that had been in the Rose Bowl the year before. They were a tough group of guys who deserved better than 6–4, but they set the stage for our first championship in 1966.

1971: Sullivan, Beasley Deny Perfection

We were always fortunate to have our big years at the right time. After winning the championship in 1968, we broke even for a couple of years (5-5-1 in 1969, 5-5 in 1970). We were really below average, to tell the truth.

In 1971 we had a really terrific group of seniors. Mixon Robinson was on that team, and so was Chuck Heard. Robinson and Heard were both defensive ends and both later became orthopedic surgeons. And that was the year I made a commitment to myself to try to be a little closer to the players and get to know them better. Overall it was a veteran team but the skill positions would be filled by some very talented sophomores like quarterback Andy Johnson and running back Jimmy Poulos. We went through the season undefeated, and it all came down to one game with Auburn. And what a game it was.

The buildup to that game was incredible. We were undefeated. They were undefeated. Both of us were ranked in the Top 10. Looking back on it now, there was actually too much excitement, too much going on at the campus. We would have been better off going on the road to get away from the excitement. It is one of the reasons that the road team seems to have the advantage in the Georgia-Auburn series.

We went out to practice on Tuesday, which is usually a tough practice, but the players were just crazy. If I had been a more experienced coach, I would have stopped practice right then, gotten mad, and sent everybody in. We were that ready—too ready, too early. Then we had a pep rally at the dorm and thousands of people showed up. It was just too much.

Auburn got off to a good start (taking a 14-0 lead), and then we made a good comeback. We scored and should have tied the game, but we missed the extra point and Auburn led 21-20. At that point I really thought we were gaining momentum and were going to take control of the game.

Then came that one play.

All I remember now is that Auburn's Pat Sullivan threw it out to Terry Beasley. Don Golden and Jerome Jackson converged on

Beasley to make the tackle. They knocked each other off the tackle and suddenly Beasley was in the open. He went the distance (70 yards) for a touchdown. It was a deflating moment after such a great comeback. They went on to beat us 35–20 and knock us out of the championship.

Sullivan went on to win the Heisman Trophy after that performance, and he deserved it. I said at the time that he was a super player having a super day. I still believe that's a game we should have won but didn't.

We had to recover from that disappointment in time to play at Georgia Tech on Thanksgiving night. We had to play the game without our best linebacker, Chip Wisdom, who had pulled his hamstring against Auburn and could not play. We knew Tech was certainly not going to feel sorry for us.

They really jumped on top of us early (14–0), and it took us a while to wake up. We finally fought back and took the lead in the fourth quarter (21–17), but Tech would not quit and they jumped back ahead of us 24–21. We got the ball back in our own territory (the 35-yard line) with not a lot of time left (1:29). Then it all came down to one dramatic drive.

I will always remember that we had a fourth-and-10 with less than a minute left, and for some reason we decided to throw it to the worst hands on the team. But that was our best option, and Andy Johnson found a wide-open Mike Greene, who caught it for 18 yards to give us a first down at the Georgia Tech 25-yard line. Then Lynn Hunnicutt made a couple of catches out of bounds, and Andy hit Jimmy Shirer at the 1-yard line. There were only a few seconds left (14) when Poulos went over the top for the touchdown. It was a great finish.

That set up the Gator Bowl game against my brother, Billy, the head coach at North Carolina. We won the game but when it was over, I hoped I would never have to face my brother again. Number one, his team was really good. Number two, he and I had put in the same offense back in the summer, and during the season we would talk every week and compare notes. By the time we played, we both knew exactly what the other team could do, and I wasn't surprised when it was a defensive struggle. We finally put together a long drive (80 yards) in the third quarter and Poulos ran 25 yards for a touchdown. We won the game 7-3.

When I went out to shake my brother's hand and saw the expression on his face, I had a lot more empathy than I normally have for a losing coach. I really felt for him. But as I have said so many times, I would rather it be him than me. Not everybody in my family felt the same way. When I got back to the hotel I found out that my sister, Rosezella, was in the bathroom crying. Turns out that she and Barbara had had a little misunderstanding. My sisters, Margaret and Rosezella, were pulling for Billy in the game because he was the baby and always the underdog. I understood that, but Barbara really *didn't* understand. Barbara thought, at the very least, Rosezella should have been neutral.

So I never wanted to play my brother in a game again, and we didn't.

1975: Junkyard Dawgs Pick Cotton

If you coach for 25 years, you're going to have high points and low points. But if there was a lowest point for me as a coach, it was at the end of the 1974 season. We were 6-6 and we weren't a very good or a very disciplined team that season. I was more disgusted with myself than anything else. I got really mad at myself and decided if I couldn't make us play the way we're supposed to play, I was going to get out of coaching. That's how disgusted I was after losing to a good Miami of Ohio team. Thanks to the Junkyard Dawgs and some great offensive linemen, the next two years were great, and I got to keep doing what I loved.

The 1975 team is the perfect example of a team that didn't win the championship but deserved to walk with champions. They did the same thing that all of our championship teams did: they closed out the season by beating Florida, Auburn, and Georgia Tech.

And it all started with a nickname.

In the off-season, Erk was down in Albany visiting Jimmy Matthews, a great friend of our program. Jimmy mentioned that "Junkyard Dawgs" might be a good name for our defense. Erk came back and told me about his conversation with Jimmy and I just said,

"Let's do it." It was a good rallying cry. We did have a bunch of small but tough, quick guys on defense. Jim Griffith and Ben Zambiasi, our linebackers, weren't very big at all but they would fight on every play.

We had to open against Pittsburgh at home, and they were really good and beat us 19-9. That was Tony Dorsett's junior year, and the following season the same team would win the national championship. We played Mississippi State the next week, and I will always remember that as the game where Dicky Clark made amends. The year before Dicky was our starting quarterback against Mississippi State but didn't play well and lost his job. He became a defensive end, and against Mississippi State a year later, he picked off a pass and ran it back 71 yards for a touchdown. That day he found a permanent home on defense.

We really played only one bad game, losing at Ole Miss, but we almost got embarrassed against Richmond because of a mistake that I made. I did something before the Richmond game that I had never done before and haven't done since. We had the big game with Florida coming up the following week, and one of my assistants, Sam Mitchell, talked me into working on Florida on Monday and Tuesday and then spending the last two days on Richmond. I should have known better.

As it turned out, we trailed most of the game and had to drive the ball 60 or 70 yards on the last possession of the game to win (28-24). We survived and I vowed I would never do that again, though Sam has the satisfaction today that, despite it all, his plan worked.

All season we had been having success with an end-around play with our big, lanky tight end, Richard Appleby. But the week of the Florida game Bill Pace, our offensive coordinator, told me he wanted to use the option where Appleby would throw the ball instead of run. I told him to put it in the game plan. I sure didn't know how big that play would become.

Florida was really good but time after time our Junkyard defense kept finding ways to keep them out of the end zone. We were still behind 7-3 when we got the ball at our own 20 late in the game.

Everyone knows what happened next. We called the end-around pass and Richard stopped and threw the ball long and high. Gene

Washington was out there to catch it and turn it into a touchdown to give us the lead (10–7). Everyone was excited but I was still worried. I was afraid that we had scored too early. There was too much time (3:12) left on the clock.

I was almost right. On Florida's first play from scrimmage they threw a 46-yard pass down to our 35-yard line. But on the next play, their quarterback fumbled and David Schwak recovered for us at the 40-yard line. We couldn't move the ball and had to give it right back to Florida after just three plays. They moved all the way down to our 21-yard line and tried for a field goal that would have tied the game. Fortunately, we blocked it and held on for a great victory. After the game Richard Appleby made his famous statement, "I just rose to the occasion." Yes, he did. That year, all of our guys did.

"Dad, Don't Worry"

In 1975 we were very anxious to play Georgia Tech because they had beaten us so badly (34–14) the year before. We got up 42–0 early in the third quarter and started to let our second-string guys play. The final score was 42–26. That's when Dan Magill nicknamed me "St. Vincent the Merciful."

But what I remember most about that night was a story involving my youngest son, Derek. The game was on Thanksgiving, so I wasn't at home to take part in the family activities. Barbara knew she could take advantage of that. Derek was always pleading to be on the sideline, but I wouldn't let him on until he reached a certain age. Barbara knew I would be in a weak moment, so she got him to ask me. I said if we're really up a lot and beating Tech, then he could come on the sideline. I never thought we'd beat Tech that badly.

I found out that earlier in the day Derek had prayed that Georgia would beat Tech badly enough so that he could come down on the field. When the score hit 42–0, she brought him down, leaned him over the bench, and Squab Jones grabbed him. I said he could come on the field, but he still had to stay away from me. About that time Tech scored and made it 42–7. Then they scored again. I looked down to find Derek pulling on my leg. Then Tech scored again and it was

42-26. I shooed him away. Finally, I said, "Derek, what do you want?" Derek said, "Dad, don't worry. Jesus is just having a little fun."

The "Shoestring" Backfires

That wonderful season ended on a bad note when we lost to Arkansas in the Cotton Bowl. We had been a team that had run a bunch of trick plays all season, and I have always believed that if you live by the sword, you die by the sword.

Earlier in the year we ran a "shoestring" play against Vanderbilt where the quarterback would bend down next to the ball and pretend to be tying his shoe. In that game, Ray Goff then just shoveled the ball back to Gene Washington who ran behind some blockers for a touchdown. It worked that time, but I still didn't like it. The coaches wanted to run a variation of the play against Arkansas. Instead of running it, there would be a counter, and we would throw the ball. Because it had been successful earlier in the season, I felt I couldn't say no. That decision really backfired.

We were ahead 10-3 when we called the play. We fumbled it and they recovered. Arkansas scored a touchdown right before the half to tie the game 10-10. That just poured fuel on the fire, and Arkansas went on to win pretty big (31-10).

So we got strung by the shoestring. I tell the story that not long after that I was in the Little Rock, Arkansas, airport and kneeled down to tie my shoe. Four people jumped on me.

1978: From Underdogs to Wonder Dawgs

In 1977, our only losing season in 25 years (5-6), we broke a Georgia record for fumbling the ball. I think we broke it by 18 fumbles. We went through five quarterbacks that season because of injuries, and ended up using a transfer from the Naval Academy named Steve Rogers. I remember Steve being so tough he could clear out a bar all by himself! He has matured now and visits often.

So in 1978 we put away the veer option attack and went back to the I-formation. We put Willie McClendon at tailback, and he was so good that he broke Frankie Sinkwich's rushing record for a single season.

That team had a knack for winning close games. In fact, we won four games that year by a total of six points. We just kept finding new ways to win. We beat Baylor by two (16–14). We went to LSU and Lindsay Scott ran the second half kickoff back for a touchdown to help win another close one (24–17). I remember in that game that our goal was to make sure that Willie outrushed their super back, Charles Alexander, who they called "Alexander the Great." Willie did outrush him.

At Kentucky we were in trouble, trailing 16–14 with about four minutes left. But again, our guys found a way to win. I remember Amp Arnold making a huge play on a hitch pass, which he turned into a big gain. And then Willie let us control the ball and the clock to set up a field goal by Rex Robinson with only seconds left to give us a 17–16 win. Later I found out that Munson just screamed, "Yeah, yeah, yeah, yeah," when Rex kicked the winning field goal.

We went to Auburn undefeated in the conference and had a chance to win the championship. We scored late to come within a point, 22–21. I didn't go for two because I thought we had the momentum and there were three or four minutes [Editor's note: 4:35 to be exact] left in the game. I thought we could stop them, and we had an All-American kicker in Rex Robinson.

I really miscalculated. Auburn had great running backs, like Joe Cribbs and William Andrews, and they just kept making plays on third down. We never got the ball back and the clock ran out. Looking back on it, I should have gone for two and given us a chance to win the championship. Instead, Alabama finished undefeated and won the SEC title.

But there was still the state championship to play for, and I've always said that the Georgia–Georgia Tech game of 1978, from a purely spectator standpoint, was one of the greatest games ever played in Sanford Stadium. That game had everything that anybody could hope for: an onside kick, a punt return for a touchdown, a kickoff return for a touchdown, a fourth-down play that turned into a touchdown, and a two-point play that won the game, but had to be run twice.

What people forget is that we fell behind 20-0 in the game, and Tech looked like they were going to run us out of the stadium. We fought back and finally took the lead (21-20) on Scott Woerner's punt return (78 yards) for a touchdown. Then Drew Hill of Tech ran the kickoff back over 100 yards for a touchdown. They made the two-point conversion and led 28-21. I remember that Eddie Lee Ivery, their great tailback, ended up hurt and was not available in the fourth quarter. That was a big blow for them.

When we were behind 20-7 we called on Buck Belue, our freshman quarterback, because we needed a change of pace. He was back in there late when it looked like we were facing our final possession, down 28-21. I can't tell you exactly where we were on the field, but we were facing fourth down. We had to go for it, and when Buck rolled to his right, he just stopped, double pumped, and found Amp Arnold behind the Tech secondary for the touchdown to make it 28-27.

After not going for two against Auburn, we *had* to go for two in order to win the game. The first play we ran was a pass over the middle to Mark Hodge, our tight end. He was tackled before he could catch the ball and flags went everywhere, giving us another chance. Then Buck executed an option to Amp again for the two-point conversion to give us the lead (29-28). Our tailback actually busted the play and went the wrong way, which probably helped.

But even after we scored, quarterback Mike Kelley brought Tech back down the field into our territory. We decided to put a young freshman, David Archer, into the game as an extra defensive back. It might have been the only time he played in a game. David stepped in front of a pass, intercepted the ball, and saved the game for us. David then transferred to West Georgia and quarterbacked them to a national championship.

1983: Moving on Without Herschel

Obviously, we expected to have Herschel Walker as a senior when the 1983 season began. But Herschel signed a professional contract with the New Jersey Generals of the USFL and had to give up his last year of eligibility.

I really thought that we could still be good without Herschel. I thought we would be in contention for the championship, but whether or not we could get over the hump and *win* the championship without Herschel was another question. I knew this team could be good because Herschel had always had a great supporting cast. The players of the great freshman class that Herschel came in with, the best that we ever had, were now seniors. They were used to winning: they expected to win.

Fans think one player makes the team, but on this team, time after time, a different guy would step up and make a play. The team had great chemistry, and it certainly had the intangible qualities of a championship team. As it turned out, we came up just a little short. Would we have won the championship if we had had Herschel? No question our chances would have been better, but we'll never know.

We opened at home against a good UCLA team coached by Terry Donahue. Rick Neuheisel was the quarterback. How we got that game is an interesting story. It was originally scheduled as a home game by our former athletic director, Joel Eaves. When it was scheduled, UCLA wanted us to come out there first in 1983 because they thought Herschel would still be with us and he would be a tremendous draw at the Rose Bowl. We said no. There was no way we were going to play an extra road game in Herschel's senior year.

UCLA said that because their crowds were smaller, they couldn't pay us what we promised to pay them in Athens. So we agreed there would be just one game between us—and that the game would be played in Sanford Stadium. What a great game it was! We didn't put it away (19-8) until Charlie Dean intercepted a pass to stop a last-minute UCLA drive and ran it back for a touchdown at about 12:15 in the morning.

There are so many memories from that season. I remember that John Lastinger was struggling at quarterback but would eventually find himself and have a perfect ending to his career. We went to Vanderbilt and held on (20-13) thanks to Terry Hoage, who stopped a sure touchdown pass with the tip of his finger. There was a tough game with Florida in Jacksonville (trailing 9–3) when D. J. Jones intercepted a ball on the 1-yard line. I thought, "Oh my god! We've got the ball on the 1-yard line!" But we drove it 99 yards for a touchdown to win the game 10–9. Clarence Kay had a big play on a screen pass, but the rest of it we just punched out the yards. And to think: we did it without Herschel!

Had Herschel stayed, our showdown with Auburn would have been his last home game. It was a huge game anyway because the championship was on the line, and we almost pulled it out. We scored with only a couple of minutes left to get within 13–7. Then we recovered the onside kick! I really thought we were going to do it one more time, but Auburn stopped us and won the game.

This group of guys finished the regular season off in style by beating Georgia Tech in Atlanta 27–24. I remember that Tony Flack had to intercept one late for us to hold on, but that was in keeping with the character of that team.

I gave the team a couple of options when it came time to choose the bowl game. We could go to the Fiesta Bowl in Arizona and have a lot of fun. Or we could go to the Cotton Bowl and play No. 2 Texas. Our guys wanted to play the best team we could. If we couldn't win the national championship, we just might have some say in who did.

Texas had one of the best defenses I have ever seen, and man, did we struggle! We ran a reverse that got us a field goal, but we just couldn't get very many first downs against them. We were very good defensively, and our kicking game was good with Kevin Butler, so we decided to hang in there and keep it close in the hopes that something good would happen at the end.

Late in the game, trailing 9–3, we faced a fourth down in our own territory. I knew our guys wanted to go for it, but I thought if we could stop them again and get another shot we could still win. If we had tried for the first down and not made it, then the game was over.

As the guys came off the field I was telling them, "We're going to get it back." Of course, I didn't think we would get it back quite so fast.

We punted the ball and their return man let the ball slip through his hands, and we recovered down there deep. [Editor's note: Georgia recovered the ball on the Texas 23-yard line with 4:32 left in the game.] We got to third down and the call came from George Haffner, our offensive coordinator, and Alex Gibbs, our offensive line coach. They wanted to run the option. At first I did a double take because we needed a pretty good bit (four yards) to get the first down, but they convinced me that it was the right call and would be better than throwing the ball.

All I remember about John Lastinger's run is that when he got to the goal line he dove at the pylon and got in for the touchdown. I learned later that John said, "Glory, Glory to Old Georgia," when he looked back to see the official give the hands-up signal for the touchdown. Kevin Butler kicked the extra point and once again our guys had found a way to win (10-9).

After the game I told Fred Akers, the Texas coach, that it was the only way we could win. As it turned out, that loss was the beginning of the end for Fred at Texas. Had they won, Texas would have won the national championship. [Editor's note: After losing to Georgia in the Cotton Bowl on January 1, 1984, Akers' next three teams at Texas were a combined 20-14-1. He was fired after the 1986 season.]

That game capped a remarkable (43-4-1) four-year run for us. It was a tribute to that senior class that we could win 10 games and finish with such a great win at the Cotton Bowl. In 1983 we didn't have a proven tailback because, as long as Herschel was there, we couldn't recruit one. But that team found a way to win games.

6

The Last Waltz:
25 Years Seemed Like
a Good Number

It was the summer of 1988, and I was about to enter my 25th season as the head coach at Georgia. It seemed like a good time to take stock of where I was in my life and my career. In 1985 I had been in a similar situation and had given some serious thought to stepping down as coach and running for the Senate. I felt some restlessness and thought that if I was going to do something else with my life I needed to get on with it. But at that time I felt there was still some unfinished business that I needed to get done in athletics and as a coach. So I stayed. By the time I got to my 25th year at Georgia, I started to get those restless feelings again.

As I thought more about it, 25 years seemed to be a good number. Coach Shug Jordan stayed at Auburn for 25 years. Bear Bryant stayed 25 years at Alabama. I was still relatively young (at 55) to do something else if I wanted to. I never wanted to coach deep into my sixties like coach Bryant. I felt like I could do other things and be fulfilled.

Somebody once said you need to win 200 games before you leave, and going into that season, I knew that goal was attainable. [Editor's note: Dooley had 192 career victories headed into the 1988 season.] But more important than that, I wanted to leave when things were good in the program and it was stable. I also hoped to win another SEC championship.

Obviously, all of this was on my mind during the 1988 season, but I don't believe I thought seriously of retiring until we beat Georgia Tech (24-3) in the last regular-season game, which was victory number 200. I just couldn't think about it during the season because there was always another game coming up. At times the idea would pop into my head, but I would never allow myself to give it much thought. I would just dismiss it and continue to focus on the next game. But after we beat Georgia Tech, Barbara and I had some time to talk while we made our annual trip to New York for the Hall of Fame dinner. When we got back to Georgia, we went to Our Lady of the Holy Spirit Monastery in Conyers and visited with my old friend and counselor the abbot, Father Gus. We talked on many occasions and found commonality in, among other things, personnel problems we both had—he as head of the monastery and me as the head of the football program and athletic department.

Barbara didn't want me to give up coaching at that point, and I understood how she felt. She enjoyed her role as the First Lady of Georgia football. She asked me, "Why would you work so hard for so long and get to the point where you are finally making decent money, and *then* decide to leave?"

I told her that the obvious answer must be that it was not all about money. I knew it was time to go. I had done everything that I ever wanted to do as a coach and I needed a new challenge and a new opportunity. I thought I had found that in a whole new world—the world of politics. There was an opportunity to run for governor of Georgia, and I was strongly considering it.

Barbara understood that it had to be my decision, and when I was at the monastery I got the feeling that the time had come for me to do something different with my life. We had won 200 games, we had won six SEC championships, and we had an undefeated national championship season in 1980, which is something I believe every coach should experience to make a career complete. I would have liked to have won one more SEC title, but I felt we were leaving the program in pretty good shape, much better shape than we found it, to say the least.

So I felt ready to step aside. I felt like I had another good option in the area of public service. I informed our president, Dr. Charles Knapp, of my decision, and it didn't take long for the word to leak out.

I remember the press conference on December 14, 1988, to announce my retirement. It was quite a turnout. I remember Barbara crying through most of it, and that was understandable. It was an emotional time because we were saying good-bye to a place that had been our life for 25 years. When I stood up there that day in December, my intention was to leave the university and run for governor. The subject did come up in the press conference. I avoided a commitment but did respond when questioned about my philosophy, saying, "My political philosophy is very much akin to my offensive philosophy in football—conservative." As it turned out, running for governor was not meant to be. I just never felt right. My head wanted to do it, but not my gut or my heart, and I finally listened. I discussed it with President Knapp. He called off the search for an athletic director. I returned to Georgia and stayed 16 more years. But on that day I thought my time at Georgia would be over after the Gator Bowl.

My bottom line, when it came to coaching, was this: I never wanted to coach until I dropped dead. I never wanted to be like Bear Bryant. Fortunately, I got into it early (at age 31) and got out of it relatively early after my 25 years. After I stepped down as coach and decided to remain as athletic director, I knew I had many more years to go in what would be a very challenging profession. I never wanted to stick around just to coach. I wanted to show that I could do something else and do it well. But I will say this: after that press conference, I was very happy that I still had one more game left as Georgia's coach.

A Recommendation for Erk

I was not on the search committee for the new football coach, but I did make a recommendation to President Knapp. I recommended that Erk Russell, who had been with us for 17 years before going to Georgia Southern, be named the head coach. I suggested that he come in and be given a contract for five or six years or whatever he wanted to coach. I felt Erk would be a sort of bridge to begin the process of bringing in someone young who could stay at Georgia for a long period of time. But first Erk could keep the continuity going with what we had been doing, which was, I am proud to say, very good.

Erk had been a big part of our program for a long time. He was someone with the maturity who could come in and continue with a good program. I really thought that with his enthusiasm and leadership, Erk could quickly lead us to another championship. I called and told him what I had done and that he had my support, and he thanked me.

A search committee was appointed and Bob Bishop, an Athens banker and longtime friend, was named chairman. I told Bob that I had talked to Erk and to Dr. Knapp, and that I felt like Erk was the one. But I don't think the people at Georgia did a good job of recruiting Erk. Maybe it was because he was not the guy they really wanted. I really don't know. I just don't think they recruited him hard enough. Maybe they took it for granted that he would come, but I think a guy like Erk, just like most people of his stature, needs to be recruited and feel like he is wanted.

The committee talked to Erk, and I think they implied strongly that he had the job. He really believed the job was his, and I think that was with good reason. But because the recruiting job wasn't good enough, he decided that he was happy where he was. So he basically turned the job down, at least in his mind. Erk made the announcement in Montgomery, Alabama, where he was coaching in the Blue-Gray game.

In Dr. Knapp's mind, Erk was never offered the job because he alone had the power to offer it. So Dr. Knapp publicly said that Erk, despite his announcement, was never really offered the job. I am very fond of Dr. Knapp and have a great deal of respect for him, but I think he made a very serious public relations mistake with that announcement. It would have been just as easy for him to say that Erk would have been great, we would have loved to have had him at Georgia, but we respect his decision and wish him the best. He could have let it go at that.

If he had done that, the Georgia people would have been fine, but that was not the case. The Georgia people were not fine with it because

Erk Russell was one of the most beloved people ever associated with our program. And while Dr. Knapp was right, he didn't officially offer the job to Erk, from a PR standpoint he would have been much better off to handle it another way. I certainly can't speak for him, but if Dr. Knapp had it to do all over again, he probably would have done things differently. I do know this much: it took Erk a good while to get over that.

The Dick Sheridan Decision

With Erk out of the picture, the process turned in the direction of Dick Sheridan, the highly respected coach at North Carolina State. Given the way things happened with Erk, I began to think that Dick was the guy that Dr. Knapp really wanted. Perhaps he didn't see the need for any kind of transition.

Dick had a good background in coaching and was well thought of by people in our profession. I certainly thought he would be a very good fit at Georgia. I talked to Dick on the phone, and he told me he was in a dilemma. He was really interested in Georgia but he felt a very strong obligation to go with his North Carolina State team to their bowl game. [Editor's note: North Carolina State had accepted an invitation to play Iowa in the Peach Bowl on December 31, 1988.]

Dick really saw Georgia as a great opportunity but he could not come at that moment. It would have had to be after the bowl game. I thought if there had been some patience with Dick Sheridan, Georgia would have ended up with him. But I remember that Dr. Knapp took off, had breakfast with him, and basically said, "You've got to come now. The job is yours but you've got to take it now." I certainly understand Dr. Knapp's thinking.

I don't think Dick was ready to do it. I think the pressure from Georgia, combined with the pressure he was feeling back from North Carolina State, forced him to stay. It was the only way the pressure could be taken off him. It certainly didn't help that media reports in Atlanta claimed that Dick had already taken the job.

Right before Christmas Dick announced that he would stay at North Carolina State. It was too bad because in my conversation with him, I really felt like he wanted to come to Georgia. So we left to go down to Jacksonville for the Gator Bowl still looking for a head coach.

Ray Goff: The Grassroots Candidate

With Erk and Dick Sheridan no longer candidates, the focus turned to members of the current staff. George Haffner and Dale Strahm were the most experienced coaches of that group. I knew that Dale Strahm was campaigning behind the scenes for the job, but I really didn't know the full extent to which he was campaigning until later. Dale had strengths and George had strengths, but at that particular time I think George was the best candidate.

A grassroots campaign had begun among the Georgia people for Ray Goff, one of the youngest coaches on our staff and a former quarterback for us. The Georgia people knew Ray as a player, and they hadn't had a "Georgia man" as head coach. Despite 25 years at Georgia, to some people I was still an "Auburn man," I guess. I understood where they were coming from, though.

After practice one day at the Gator Bowl, Bill Hartman, our kicking coach, came by. We walked around and talked about the coaching situation. Bill, of course, is one of the university's greatest assets—academically and athletically—and had been a great confidant of mine. He reminded me that we hadn't had a Georgia man as head coach. He had had so many phone calls that he felt like Ray, a young guy, should be given an opportunity. He was 33 years old. When I became head coach at Georgia I was 31. The more I thought about what Bill was saying, the more I agreed with him. At that moment I believed the best way to go was to give Ray a chance, as I was given a chance.

One thing was very obvious: Chuck Knapp was anxious to make a decision. He had gone through the Erk Russell situation and had gone through the Dick Sheridan situation. Needless to say, Dr. Knapp was tired of going through these situations. I told him that I did not think it was appropriate to name a head coach before the Gator Bowl, because that would be distracting to the team. It would work just as well after the Gator Bowl because the first big weekend of recruiting was still over a week away. As long as the coach was named shortly after the bowl game there was plenty of time.

I told Bill Hartman that I agreed with his assessment and that we should communicate that to the members of the athletic board. Ray knew the program and gave us the best chance for consistency. He was very personable and a very good recruiter. The Georgia people liked him and it would obviously be a very popular choice. I went into the Gator Bowl with Michigan State knowing pretty much that the decision had been made, but then I had to let that go. There was still one more game to coach.

Victory 201: The Final Ride

The biggest challenge of playing Michigan State in the Gator Bowl, besides stopping Andre Rison, was trying to get the focus off the fact that it was my last game. I didn't think it was fair to the team because there were a bunch of seniors who were in their last game too. I wanted the players to be the focus; I didn't want it to be me.

But the truth is once the game starts, all of that stuff goes away because you are so focused on trying to win. We did win the game (34–27), thanks to Wayne Johnson, who had a terrific night throwing the ball (227 yards, three touchdowns). I kept thinking we were going to put the game away but Andre Rison (252 yards receiving, three touchdowns) made sure it stayed close, so the fans didn't go home too early.

I'm so glad that we won. It was a good feeling that in the last game everybody was happy. It would have been sad for the team and the Georgia people if we had lost. All I remember now is that I had to get up early the next morning to be at the press conference where Ray was introduced as our head coach. Since all the media was still in Jacksonville, it only made sense to make the announcement then so that Ray could get started.

Then, for the first time I can remember, I didn't have to go recruiting. My mind was on all the speaking engagements I had committed to as I contemplated running for governor. I had coached my last game, but I really didn't have any time to reflect on exactly what it all meant and how I really felt about it. There was too much to do.

I can say this: while I would have loved to have won another SEC championship or two, I did everything I wanted to do as a head football coach. When I walked away, there were no regrets. Not many people get to leave coaching on their own terms. I felt very fortunate to be one of them.

7

Temptations:
Why I Never Left Georgia

When we got to Georgia in December of 1963, I remember one of the first things I told Barbara: "Don't get comfortable, and keep a suitcase nearby." Because even then, being a football coach was a very unstable profession. There were a few coaches noted for their longevity but not very many. That was the nature of the business, so I wanted Barbara to understand that any year we could be picking up and leaving. It might be our decision, but more than likely it would be somebody else's decision.

It's hard to believe that we had that discussion over 41 years ago and that, after all that time, we're still in Athens at the same address where we started. Given where the professions of coaching and athletic administration are now, it's hard to believe that anybody will stay at one school for 41 years again. In that sense I know we are very fortunate.

In all that time I can truthfully say there were only four times I gave serious consideration to leaving Georgia—two opportunities were in athletics and two in the political arena. There were other times after we had had some success when people called and wanted to know if there was any interest on my part, but I would politely but firmly say no. I didn't say anything about it at the time, but there were calls from several schools. The University of Miami in particular tried to recruit me. I actually had a conversation with Father Edmund Joyce at Notre Dame. I remember walking along the practice fields with young Rankin Smith Jr. of the Atlanta Falcons—they were really struggling and wanted to know if I was interested in being their coach. But in all the cases like that, I never let it go beyond the original conversation because I didn't want my name in the papers. Plus I really had no interest in leaving Georgia.

Like I said, there were four times where the opportunity was interesting enough or I thought the timing might be right to consider something else. I never said yes, but the opportunities were tempting.

1965: Oklahoma Looks "OK"

We had just finished our second year at Georgia with a good team hit hard by injuries. We felt really good about 1966 and the recruiting class that would be sophomores in the fall. Then Oklahoma called because they were looking for a new head coach. I really wasn't all that excited because I had been at Georgia for only two years, and we were just getting the program going in the right direction.

I really didn't think anything more about Oklahoma until I got a call from Bud Wilkinson, the Sooners' legendary coach. You have to understand how much I respected coach Wilkinson. When I was a young coach, he was very much a role model of mine. I had read a lot of things he had written and really emulated him.

Coach Wilkinson told me, "You ought to at least make a trip to the university and visit." Because of him I did go out there, and they made me a very nice offer. What made the job attractive, besides the nice financial offer, was that the timing was good. Coach Wilkinson had retired in 1963 after his Hall of Fame career and his top assistant, Gomer Jones, had taken over. But the Sooners struggled under Jones for a couple of years. In 1965 they had their first down year in a long time (3–7) and lost to Oklahoma State. So the timing was right, just like it had been for me at Georgia, for someone new to come in and rebuild the program.

When I got back to Georgia there was an overwhelming response asking me to stay. I have to say that I really didn't expect it to that degree. I remember the late and beloved Elmo Ellis, the well-known radio personality on WSB, who wrote and played a song that went to the tune, "Hang down your head, Tom Dooley." But the words to the song were something like, "Please stay at Georgia, Vince Dooley." It seemed like they kept playing that song over and over again. The incredible outpouring of support was very heartwarming, to say the least.

We had just gotten the program started at Georgia, and with the strong reaction from the Georgia people, combined with a boost in pay from the administration, they convinced me to stay. My salary almost doubled, but you have to remember that my base salary when I came to Georgia was $12,500 a year with a small housing allowance. They asked me to stay and then they showed they wanted me to stay.

I can remember an editorial cartoon by Clifford "Baldy" Baldowski, who was the cartoonist for the *Atlanta Journal-Constitution* at that time. It was a big old bulldog licking me on the face because he was so happy I was staying. I was happy, too, and the next season (1966) we won our first SEC championship. You could say that everything worked out the way it was supposed to.

1980: Auburn Says "Come Home"

I can honestly say that after the Oklahoma offer in 1965, I never seriously considered a job at another school—until Auburn called in 1980 to offer me a position as both coach and athletic director. Any other calls I would just dismiss. I was happy at Georgia. We were having a great season. We were undefeated and getting ready to play Notre Dame for the national championship in the Sugar Bowl. Things couldn't have been better.

But when Auburn called, I had to listen. It was where Barbara and I went to school. It was where we met and fell in love. We had so many friends back there and, of course, they wanted us to come home. Fob James, the governor of Alabama and my teammate and roommate in college, was recruiting me. When people you care about call, you have to listen to what they have to say.

I think Barbara was interested because of all the ties we had there. And there is something to be said about taking on a new challenge and feeling reinvigorated. I went to Auburn to talk to the selection committee, and I let them know that I was interested. There were people on the committee who I knew, and some who I had coached when I was at Auburn.

117

They were all encouraging. Lee Hayley was there and willing to pass the torch to me as athletic director. Lee is a great Auburn man and would later work for me at Georgia. Bobby Lowder, the well-known Auburn booster, was also there. It was pretty clear that if we were going to move forward, Lowder would be in charge of putting together the financial package.

In that regard, I think it was the first time Auburn had received a proposal from a coach that included things like TV contracts, money from Nike, and compensation that went beyond salary. By then I was just starting to make a little money—I was in the $400,000 to $450,000 range, which in 1980 was not bad.

My attorney and good friend Nick Chilivis went with me and had the "laundry list" of things we had written down to talk about. Nick made one thing clear to me before the meeting: no matter how things went—good or bad—we were not going to make any kind of decision that day. He insisted that we come back and talk about it, which was very good advice. That was Nick's way of being an attorney, a friend, and also a Georgia Bulldog.

I was interested, and there was a lot of encouragement by some of the members of the committee. Unfortunately it got into the press that I had taken the job, which was absolutely not true. I later found out that a member of the committee had told a certain trustee from Montgomery that the situation looked good. That particular trustee was known to have a habit of enjoying libations after sundown. A media person from Montgomery always knew what time to call this trustee in order to get the best information. By the time that reporter called the trustee, he was convinced I was coming to Auburn. That's how the rumor got out that I was leaving Georgia to take the job at Auburn, but I can assure you I never told anyone at Auburn that I was coming. All I ever said was that I was interested.

For a couple of days I did a lot of soul searching. But in the final analysis, I just kept looking at the pictures of all the players I had coached at Georgia that were on the walls of our home. I told Barbara that I had too much invested in Georgia after 17 years. Besides, our children all grew up Bulldogs. I remember Derek, our youngest child, crying as I was going to the airport to visit Auburn. He said, "I hate Auburn!" I understood that because Georgia was all he had ever known. At that age (10) it is either love or hate.

When the Oklahoma opportunity came along, I hadn't been at Georgia long enough. When Auburn called, I had been at Georgia too long.

I have been asked if I would have coached in the Sugar Bowl if I had taken the job at Auburn. I don't think we ever got that far down the road, but I don't think it would have been fair to Georgia if I had stayed under those conditions. It also would not have been fair to Auburn for me to coach in the game. Thankfully, I never had to make that decision.

Georgia did some things to help me after I decided to stay. The administration didn't want to raise my salary, but they agreed to turn the house on Milledge Circle over to me over time with the promise of paying the maintenance and the utilities for as long I remained coach and/or athletic director. They felt like it was a very good bargain at the time. After all this time, when I look at what has happened to coaches' salaries, I would agree.

I was also given complete control as Georgia's athletic director. Before this, the job had been split. Forestry professor and former faculty chair Reid Parker had been the AD for administration, and I had been the AD for sports. That compromise was put together because Dr. Fred Davison, our president, didn't want me to be the football coach and the athletic director at the same time, and he had good reasons for that.

I don't think the administration understood how serious I was about being the athletic director. Back then a lot of veteran football coaches wanted the athletic director job merely for the control. I saw it as another challenge and something that I could do well if I put my mind to it. After that everything was in place. If I was going to turn down a great opportunity from my alma mater, chances were I was going to be at Georgia for the long haul. We would go on to win the Sugar Bowl and the national championship. We followed the championship by an expansion that put Sanford Stadium at over

82,000 capacity. The timing was perfect and all the signs seemed to point to my staying at Georgia for a long, long time.

Little did I know that a different kind of opportunity, one outside of athletics, would be just around the corner.

1985: Senator Dooley?

As long as I can remember I've been interested in politics. When I was earning my master's degree in history at Auburn, most of the papers I wrote were on Southern political demagogues like Jim Folsom of Alabama and Huey Long of Louisiana. The political process really fascinates me.

When I was a senior at Auburn, Fob James was a sophomore and my roommate. Fob went on to become the governor of Alabama. After I became coach at Georgia, he and I would go fishing together, or we would go duck hunting up in Canada. It seemed like every time we were together the conversation would eventually turn to politics. He knew I had an interest in public service, and he would always encourage me to seriously consider running for office one day.

In the spring of 1985 an opportunity presented itself that I felt I had to consider.

Fob and I were on one of our fishing trips when he introduced me to DeLoss Walker of Memphis. DeLoss had run a lot of successful campaigns, including Fob's run for governor. DeLoss felt the Senate campaign in Georgia would be a great opportunity for a newcomer because Matt Mattingly, a Republican who had beaten the legendary Herman Talmadge in 1980, was vulnerable.

I knew that if I were going to seriously consider the idea, I would have to make a very quick decision—football season was not that far away. I talked to an old friend, Jim Minter, the editor of *The Atlanta Journal-Constitution.* I had known Jim since his days as a sports writer, and I trusted him. He knew me well, and I knew he would deal straight with me. Jim was very enthusiastic and suggested that I talk to Bill Shipp, the well-known political writer at the newspaper. Bill thought it was a good idea too.

Bill wrote the story that I was considering running for the Senate. Since I had been the head football coach at Georgia for 20 years, I figured there would be some interest in the story. I didn't really figure on what happened next. The response was tremendous, and the calls from the media did not stop. We were getting ready to go on a European trip and decided we better have a press conference at the airport just before we took off.

When I boarded the plane for Europe, I was pleased to know that Senator Talmadge would be on the trip with his new bride "Lin-Da," as he called her. It turned out to be a great opportunity for me to learn from a true political master. I can still remember the senator talking to Barbara in his wonderful Southern drawl: "Now BOB-bor-RAH, if Vince is going to run, the first thing you have to do is take that makeup off. Then you have to take all those jewels off. Then you have to go down to Sears and get you a couple of dresses so you can get out there and campaign!"

We still laugh about that. We had a wonderful time listening to his stories and listening to him talk about politics in general. I also remember him talking about the difference between being a senator and being governor of Georgia. [Editor's note: Herman Talmadge was Georgia's governor from 1948 to 1955 and senator from 1957 to 1980.]

"You'd make a fine senator," he said. "But it has been the most frustrating thing I've ever done. When I was governor, I ruled the state with an iron fist. But in the Senate you are one of one hundred. You propose a bill and by the time it goes through the Senate and goes through the House, you don't even recognize it!"

Zell Miller, who was also a Georgia governor before he became a senator, told me the same thing: when you become a senator and you've been a governor, it is frustrating. The power you have just isn't the same. I filed that thought away for use at a later date.

When I came back from Europe there were an incredible number of letters, pro and con, about whether or not I should quit coaching and run for the Senate. I still have those letters somewhere in the house. I made it a point to answer all of them.

In the final analysis, I knew I had some unfinished business as a football coach. I knew this was a great opportunity, and I had a great chance to be a senator. I think the chances are good I would have won. But I also knew that I was not finished with what I wanted to do as a coach. To be perfectly honest about it, I thought another opportunity at politics would come along somewhere down the road. In fact, I was sure of it.

1989: Governor Dooley?

When I met with DeLoss Walker in the spring of 1985, he pointed to what he thought were two good opportunities in Georgia politics: the senate race in 1986 and the governor's race for the 1990 election. So when I decided not to run for the senate in 1985, I knew the governor's race would be looming out there. The same group of friends encouraged me to strongly consider this race as well.

When I announced my retirement as head football coach in December of 1988, my plan was to also resign as athletic director and throw myself into the campaign for governor. But early on I got the feeling that something was not right. Most political campaigns begin slowly and build up to a strong finish for the election. I was already well known, so the campaign felt like a volcano erupting right when we started. I thought there was too much attention, too early. If I weren't a football coach, I wouldn't have people chasing me.

I finally had to admit to myself that while my mind was in it, my heart was not. I would wake up in the morning, and I never felt good. I wasn't excited about what I was going to do that day. I felt like I was being pushed everywhere I went. Not only was my heart not in it, but my gut wasn't in it either. Maybe I was getting a real taste of politics, and I was deciding that I didn't like it.

I remember that I was tired of feeling bad, and there was only one way that I was going to feel good again. I called Georgia's president, Dr. Charles Knapp, and asked him how he would feel about my returning as athletic director. He didn't hesitate. "I'll call off the search right now," he said.

Then I had to tell all the people who had spent so much of their time helping me. I especially had to tell my longtime loyal friends, Nick Chilivis and Fob James, but they understood. They both agreed that if my heart wasn't 100 percent in it, that I should not make such a commitment. Hamilton Jordan, too, the former aide to President Jimmy Carter, was really very good in helping me. He spent so much time helping with strategy, even as far back as the Senate race in 1985. Hamilton was disappointed, but I feel certain he understood.

I felt particularly bad when I had to tell DeLoss. He had run a lot of successful campaigns, and he turned down other opportunities because he wanted to be with me. Based on our agreement, I wasn't obligated to pay him anything when I decided not to run, but I paid him $25,000 because I backed out on him. It was just the right thing to do.

Maybe if I had grown up in the land of politics, all of this would have been much easier. To me it is all a matter of what you are used to. As a football coach people ask about pressure, but you don't really think of it as pressure because that's all you know. It was the lifestyle of a football coach. I think it would be the same way if you grew up in politics. In politics, if you get 52 percent, you've had an overwhelming victory. I just couldn't relate to that mindset.

When I made the decision not to run for governor of Georgia, I had to face a sobering reality. I had said no to a senate race in 1985 and now I was saying no to a race for governor. I knew that this would, in all likelihood, be my last shot at politics. I thought about this long and hard because I was moved by the opportunity to go into public service. I felt I could provide leadership that at times had been sorely lacking in politics.

"You have to understand that if you turn this [the governor's race] down, there might not be another opportunity in politics for you," Hamilton Jordan told me. "It's one thing to say no once. But now you've said no twice. That sends a message."

I understood that and I accepted it. Regardless of the long-range consequences, I knew that staying out of politics was the right decision for me.

I have had no regrets.

8

A Series of Crises: From Chest Pains to Jan Kemp

If there is an overriding philosophy, or strong belief, that I have, it is that if you are in coaching or athletic administration, one thing is certain: in order to survive for the long term, you have to be prepared to deal with the inevitable crises that will come. If you go back through my career, that's exactly what it has been—one crisis after another. Whenever it's calm, you can be assured another storm is gathering, and you had better be ready for it.

During the period of time when I was a coach (1964–1988), we had a lot of crises both on and off the field. The key to survival is being able to address them in the proper way. When you're faced with a crisis, if you take definitive action to do something about the problem, then you have a chance to continue your career for a long period of time. If you don't, your career will be cut short.

Now, there is no question that the landscape of college football has changed since I became a head coach in December of 1963. Prior to that I think there was more of a tendency to be very patient if a coach was struggling. In my era people became a little less patient, and needless to say, there is even less patience now.

Take the situation with coach Wallace Butts before I became head coach at Georgia. In coach Butts' last eight seasons, he finished five of them with losing records. He had four straight losing seasons before winning an SEC championship in 1959. Coach Butts also had problems off the field that were kept very quiet even though a lot of people knew about them. He was able to go through that crisis for a long time before he was finally forced to resign as coach in 1960. No football coach would be allowed to struggle for that long today.

When we got to Georgia in 1963 the basketball program was in the middle of its 13th straight losing season. Today nobody could survive that, but Red Lawson did at Georgia. Why? The main reason was a "Who cares?" attitude. As the athletic director, coach Butts really didn't care. He had a coach with a great personality, and people loved to hear all of his stories about the wind factor at old Woodruff Hall. All of that changed when coach Joel Eaves became athletic director in 1963. Coach Eaves was a basketball man. I played basketball for him at Auburn. He was going to make sure that we had a competitive basketball program at Georgia.

The point I'm making is that people were much more tolerant about losing before my era as a head coach. When my era came along they were less tolerant. And after my era they are even less tolerant still. The bottom line is that as a coach, you have to understand that despite your best efforts there will be a crisis from time to time. How you handle those crises will ultimately determine how long you stay in the business.

In my 25 years as head football coach and later as athletic director, we certainly had our fair share of crises at Georgia. Each time we got to the other side I personally believed that not only were we able to survive, we used those opportunities to make the program better. As the German philosopher Friedrich Nietzsche said, "That which does not destroy me, makes me stronger."

1971: "A Very Important Year"

The first time we faced what could be called a crisis came after the 1970 season. We had won two SEC championships (1966, 1968) in our first five years at Georgia. Then we had two break-even seasons in 1969 (5-5-1) and 1970 (5-5). Coach Eaves wasn't one to beat around the bush. Prior to the 1971 season he called me into his office to talk and he said, "Vince, this is a very important year."

This was the reality of our situation despite the fact that we had won two SEC championships and posted a 38-13-3 record in our first five seasons. In coaching, the question is always: "What have you done for me lately?"

I didn't get all shook up about it, but I understood where coach Eaves was coming from. He felt it was important to him as athletic director because, after all, he brought me to Georgia. It was a pride thing with him.

For us to win a couple of championships and then let the program go down a little sent the message that things weren't headed in the right direction. And frankly, if we had had another mediocre year, I'm not sure I would have survived. But we bounced back in 1971 with a very good team. We were 11-1, beat North Carolina in the Gator Bowl, and finished No. 7 in the nation.

So after a little dip, we came back with a season that would put us in position to win the SEC championship. Over the years, that would become a familiar pattern.

1974: Struggling with Integration

If there was ever a rock bottom for me as head coach at Georgia, it had to come after the 1974 season, when we were 6-6. We finished the regular season with a terrible beating from Georgia Tech (34-14) at home. Then we went to the Tangerine Bowl, an invitation I never should have accepted, to play Miami of Ohio, which had a really good team. We played poorly and they beat us pretty badly as well (21-10). I was so distraught after that season that I made a promise to myself: if I couldn't do a better job of coaching the team, I was going to get out. That's how bad it was.

Many of the problems were my fault because I didn't fully understand how to handle our team after we integrated. We signed our first group of black players in 1971, and I didn't know how to handle the morale problems that came with that change. Those problems were caused by extreme responses from both races. Finding some solutions was my challenge.

I could feel that it was not a unified team, so I did two things. First, I got the team together for an open session of complaints. One white person would stand up and say a black person was an activist or a protester. Then the black player would accuse the white player of being a racist. Then each person would explain his side of it.

Everybody was given a chance to air their grievances, and then each side was given a chance to explain. Before that we had no communication, we just went out and played. I think that meeting brought the team together and gave us a better understanding of one another.

The second thing I did was quit thinking about black or white and just apply what I believed to everybody. In the beginning, I have to confess that I wasn't quite sure how to act because I had never coached black players before. I tried to be understanding and perhaps overly sensitive to their concerns because they were in a unique situation, but by doing that it was difficult to be consistent.

Once 1975 came we decided not to make race an issue any more. From that point on we were going to be colorblind—there were no white players and no black players. The only people we coached were football players on the Georgia football team. As a result, I think we were better coaches and ultimately it helped us survive that crisis. Surviving that crisis, I believe, led directly to the great seasons we had in 1975 (9–3, Cotton Bowl) and 1976 (10–2, SEC championship, Sugar Bowl).

1977: Our Only Losing Season

We had smaller crises on the field over the next few years. In 1977 we had our only losing season (5-6) in 25 years. But when that season was over we really took a hard look at ourselves as a coaching staff. I told our coaches that in any game or any season, the first thing that we have to do in analyzing the situation is to sit down and look at ourselves. We had to start by second-guessing ourselves and seeing how we could have done a better job. Then, after we were satisfied with that, we could make demands of our football team and make sure that they were doing their best job.

We came back in 1978 (9-2-1) with the "Wonder Dawg" team that won many close games. In 1979 we didn't have a tailback and finished 6-5, but we bounced back the next year by signing the greatest tailback of all, Herschel Walker, and winning the national championship. That put us on the track for our most consistent period at Georgia.

The only regret that I have in that entire period of the eighties was that we didn't take full advantage of our 1980 national championship when it came to recruiting. We should have brought in a great class that year, but we didn't. I believe that was the last year of the early signing period, and we had so many early commitments that we might have overextended ourselves. We had a lot of commitments from good, but not great, players. There were a lot of great players out there we couldn't pursue because we had so many commitments.

I guess if we didn't want to do things the right way, we could have withdrawn some of our scholarship offers and gotten some of those great players, but we weren't going to do something like that. It probably began to hurt us in 1984 and 1985, when that great freshman class of 1980 was gone.

But our biggest problems during that time were definitely off the field.

1984: The South Africa Decision

One of the things a coach must learn about being in the public eye is that you never quite know how your decisions are going to be perceived. This was never more true than in 1984 when I decided to make a personal trip to South Africa. I enjoyed traveling, and we had made Bulldog trips with boosters to a lot of places around the world. But I wanted to go to South Africa to learn about apartheid firsthand. Of course we all agreed that apartheid was wrong but, like a number of people, I had a natural curiosity and wanted to see for myself.

When word leaked out that I was contemplating the trip, some local groups began to protest, feeling my visit would somehow give legitimacy to the practice of apartheid. I totally disagreed with that point of view and, quite frankly, the criticism made me more determined than ever to make the trip. I even talked to Andrew Young, the former mayor of Atlanta and a U.N. ambassador. He encouraged me to go, with the rationale that I could become a better spokesperson against apartheid, as he had after his first trip to South Africa. I soon realized that as the head football coach at Georgia, any negative impact from the trip would not affect just me. It could potentially affect my team, so I met with them to explain my position.

It was very gratifying to learn that regardless of how the players felt about the situation in South Africa, they were completely supportive of my right to make the trip. As I told them in a letter later on, that show of support really touched me.

It also made me reconsider making the trip. I finally realized that the situation had become so emotional that we were running the risk of having people protest our team when we traveled. That was totally unacceptable, and regardless of my personal feelings on the subject, I could not in good conscience expose my players and their families to such treatment. They had been very loyal to me, and it fell upon me to return that loyalty.

So I decided not to make the trip to South Africa but promised myself I would someday visit when I was no longer the head football coach. Since then, of course, apartheid has come to an end in South Africa and several years ago I was finally able to visit. It was a learning experience but ultimately a gratifying one.

1986: The Jan Kemp Crisis

Off the field, we had had a few bouts with the NCAA during my time at Georgia, but none of them were major infractions, which often call for serious sanctions like being banned from TV or bowl games. However, in my last year as athletic director, we did have very serious violations in basketball, and we withdrew the team from the NCAA Tournament. It was the right, but painful, thing to do.

But always, when we were faced with those kinds of situations, we stepped forward right away and tried to do what was right. We never covered anything up. Because of the system, there were mistakes made, especially with a few overzealous alumni. We had some who bought the players' tickets or tried to help—in good conscience—only to have it backfire. This was all but solved when the NCAA passed legislation to remove alumni and boosters from the recruiting process. Any violations committed by alumni were unbeknownst to us, and when we did discover problems, we addressed them immediately. Because of that, I believe, we gained some respect from the NCAA's committee on infractions.

The biggest off-the-field crisis of all was the one involving Jan Kemp, an instructor in the remedial studies program at Georgia in the early eighties. She sued the university after she was dismissed as an instructor, and in the process she accused us of exploiting our athletes and not caring about whether or not they got an education. Needless to say the story made national news and opened us up to all kinds of criticism. Some of that criticism was justified and some of it wasn't. It was an incredible test of how strong our program really was.

This particular crisis came about for a lot of different reasons. It was a time when the NCAA athletic academic admission standards went from a relatively good standard—the old 1.6 formula—to almost no standard at all. The 1.6 formula was a combination of grade point average, test scores, and class rank.

There was also a mandate by the federal government that educational institutions had to make the effort to open their doors to minority students who had previously been denied access. It also required that once those students were in place, everything should be done to help them earn a degree. It was a noble and worthwhile goal, but in order to accomplish it, some changes had to be made. The old NCAA 1.6 formula standard was replaced by a simple 2.0 high school grade point average in any subjects—not the core subjects of math, science, and English like we have today—but all subjects. That let virtually 99 percent of all students into college and soon resulted in the biggest single problem in intercollegiate athletics and higher education. We certainly had our problems at Georgia trying to balance athletic competition and university standards with no help from the NCAA.

As I look back on it and analyze how I could have done things better, we simply would not have recommended as many marginally qualified athletes as we did. In a way we were misled because we had documentation of people coming in with incredibly low SAT scores who still got their degrees. We had admitted some students with SAT scores of 450 or 500 who got degrees. What no one realized, now that I look back on it, was those scores were not indicative of anything. To make a score of 400, someone just had to take the test. They didn't have to score anything, since the only requirement was to take the test and not worry about the score. So some just took the test and put anything down. We were convinced by the history of academic success achieved by students with low test scores that we could help them enough to get a degree. Maybe we were rationalizing the situation to ourselves, but as I remember it, I thought we were doing the right thing.

The other part of the problem came from the developmental studies program. The program was put in place to help marginally qualified students who needed assistance in some subjects prepare to enter the main student body. The head of the development studies program was Leroy Ervin, and Leroy, I believe, had his own agenda. Yes, he was getting funding for developmental studies from athletics because we wanted to provide that to help our athletes, but athletes were not the only people getting preferential help from developmental studies. Leroy was also taking care of the sons and daughters of influential people.

Every class in developmental studies had its own way of exiting individuals into the mainstream of the student body. It really depended on the professor. In some cases, when a professor chose not to exit somebody who had been in the same class for a couple of quarters, the case could be reviewed by the vice president for academic affairs, Virginia Trotter. She could choose to administratively exit someone out of the program, sometimes over the teacher's objections.

In December 1982 Virginia Trotter gave administrative exits to eight or nine football players as we were getting ready to play in the Sugar Bowl. She had done it in the past, but when it got into the press, people assumed that the only reason she did it was so they could play in the Sugar Bowl—which was not the case. But convincing people of that was a very hard sell.

Then it really hit the fan and we were investigated. Actually it triggered a bunch of investigations. I always said that our body was split wide open and everybody got a flashlight to take a look in every crack and crevice of our athletic anatomy. We were investigated by the attorney general, the NCAA, the faculty, and, on a daily basis, the media.

We finally adopted the philosophy that we couldn't stand up every day and answer everything that was being thrown at us. We said that if the program was on solid ground, we would survive. We just decided that if we saw the crisis as an opportunity to make the program better, then we would come out of it in the proper way. We might be bruised or have a black eye, but we would survive and be better for it, and that's exactly what we did.

I'm not trying to minimize the crisis. The president, Dr. Fred Davison, resigned. Virginia Trotter resigned. Leroy Ervin resigned. But people remember this crisis most because of Jan Kemp and her emotional charges that we were just using our athletes.

When the football players were exited from developmental studies, she went public with all kinds of charges that we were exploiting athletes in the program and giving them no chance to get an education. She eventually lost her job. The administration claimed she was fired for incompetence. She claimed she was fired for going public with her charges.

Obviously, I disagreed with her charges, but she was basically stonewalled by the administration. Nobody ever communicated with her or acknowledged her concerns. As a result she was very bitter and eventually sued the university and won a huge judgment. [Editor's note: In 1986 Jan Kemp won a $2.6 million judgment against the University of Georgia. The award was later reduced to $1.1 million.]

I can really only speak to my own contact with Jan Kemp. She wrote me a 15-page handwritten letter outlining all of the problems she had with what we were doing in the athletic department. There was no way I would respond to all that in a letter, so I picked up the phone and called her. I asked if we could just sit down and talk about it. She agreed, and we met at the Howard Johnson's restaurant. We sat down for an hour and 45 minutes and talked about everything.

About 70 percent of what she was talking about was baseless. The other 30 percent of her questions I couldn't answer but I promised to check them out. After checking them out, about half of those concerns had no basis either. But the remaining 15 percent of things she raised included some very legitimate problems that needed to be addressed. I think she always appreciated the fact that I visited with her.

In an essay that I would write afterward, I expressed my disappointment that all of it happened. It certainly wasn't good for the university, to be sure. Since we had not broken any rules and had acted in good faith, we didn't apologize—but we did regret it. But if I had to do it all over again, would I do it differently? Sure I would. What I would do differently is that I wouldn't sign as many academically high-risk football players, which certainly caused part of the problem. Again, that was done in good faith.

As part of our response to the crisis we raised our academic standards higher than the rest of the SEC, which hurt us in the short run, particularly when it came to signing big linemen. It hurt in some of those big games, like when we played Auburn, who had those same big linemen we couldn't sign. But in the long run it helped us because eventually the rest of the league adopted our standards.

And we learned something about how to operate in a crisis: don't spend a lot of time trying to defend what has gone wrong; instead spend most of your time trying to fix the problem and make it better. I think that attitude has helped us a lot over the years.

1980: A Scary Homecoming

Sometimes a personal crisis can affect your professional life. It was homecoming of 1980. We were undefeated and ranked very high (No. 6). It was Thursday night and Barbara and I had just picked up Derek after he had played in a recreation league football game. Barbara wanted to go look at the homecoming decorations.

In the seventies a lot of things were going on at Georgia. We thought maybe that the students had lost a little school spirit, so we formed the Spirit Committee, and they met at our house. Barbara was the chair of the committee. One of the traditions the committee started was to "paint the town" on homecoming. We were on our way to see how the students had painted the town. We had just crossed an intersection and WHAM!

We found out later that the guy had been drinking heavily and that he had run three red lights before he hit us. He hit us in the back and on the side where Derek was. Fortunately, he still had on his football uniform so he wasn't hurt. I can't say the same for Barbara and me.

My head went straight down on the steering wheel, and my lip broke open. I was bleeding everywhere. Barbara was slapped up against the front part of the car. It was one of those situations where you see lights and you see the ambulance, but you really don't know where you are. I went to the hospital that night and I probably should have stayed. I had a concussion, but I talked them out of making me stay. I guess that's a bad thing about being in the position I was in—head coach. I tended to be a little hard-headed and most people listened even when they shouldn't.

They didn't let Barbara go because they knew that she took a blow on the side of her lower back. Many times when someone is hit in that spot the spleen will fill up and burst, and that is exactly what happened. They had to take her spleen out, and she stayed in the hospital over the weekend. As usual, she was the smart one.

Dr. Happy Dicks, one of my old players, stitched me up at the hospital that night, and they released me. The next day I went in and saw the team while my lip was still swollen and hanging over my chin. I told them that it was the hardest lick I'd had since I was a junior quarterback at Auburn. I was running an option play and a defensive end from Mississippi State cracked me in the mouth. I bled for two days!

When I finally got to the stadium for the game on Saturday, the doctors gave me some kind of pill for the pain, and it basically put me in la-la land. Fortunately, Herschel was running all over the place against Vanderbilt, so it was an easy game to coach (Georgia won the game 41-0). It was a homecoming that none of us in the Dooley family will ever forget—it could have been a whole lot worse.

1987: Chest Pains and Another Close Call

It all began with something pretty funny. Or at least I thought it was kind of funny. We were playing Vanderbilt in Nashville. They were up 21–7 and the place was going absolutely crazy. At that moment I started feeling this pain in my chest. Sometimes in a crisis you have to laugh or you'll cry. Something struck me that made me laugh: wouldn't this be a heck of a way to end a coaching career? I'll get beat by Vanderbilt and then have a heart attack and be gone! Fortunately, we caught Vanderbilt and won the game (52–24) and my chest pain went away.

We had sandwiches on the plane back to Atlanta and they really gave me indigestion. By the time I did my television show and got back to Athens, I had only about an hour's sleep. That Sunday was the inauguration day of our new president, Dr. Charles Knapp, so I decided to walk up the hill from the student center to where they were having the ceremonies. By the time I got up the hill, I could not breathe! I thought, "Man, you are really in bad shape." I figured it was due to the lack of sleep.

I went back to the office later and worked all day, to about 9:00 P.M. I was really tired so I decided that what I needed was to work out. So I went to the swimming pool, and within 10 minutes I was feeling acute indigestion again. I just figured I was extremely tired, so I stopped and decided that I'd get up early the next morning and get in a good workout. But the next morning I started swimming and 10 minutes in I started having the indigestion again! So right there I said I was going to see the doctor. Instead I got to the office and forgot about it. I went to the staff meeting and got into my regular routine and didn't think about it again.

Later in the morning my secretary, Rosa Greenway, noticed that I had a lot of antacid pills on my desk. Then I remembered and asked her to call Dr. Ham Magill so he could check me out. Dr. Magill wanted to do a scan of my heart to see if there was any blockage. I said, "Fine, we have an open date in two weeks, and I'll come back then." Dr. Magill said he wasn't talking about two weeks—he was talking about now! I was supposed to go to Orlando to speak, but Dr. Magill made it very clear that I probably wouldn't be doing that.

Well, he did the procedure and found some blockage in the heart, and the rest of what he said was pretty much like a dream. He started talking about doing something called an "angioplasty" to open up the blockage. The next thing I knew I was wired up and headed to Atlanta in an ambulance! I remember getting rolled down the hallway of the hospital and hearing all these people say, "There's coach Dooley! There's coach Dooley!" It was kind of embarrassing.

It's a very common procedure now, but back then an angioplasty was something very few people knew about. A lot of people were interested in my procedure because Emory had not been doing it very long. And the fact that they were doing it on the head football coach at Georgia during the season brought out the reporters as well.

I stayed at Emory until Thursday morning, then went home and was at practice that afternoon. I wasn't sure if I was allowed to be on the sidelines that Saturday, but the doctor told me it was OK. We were playing Kentucky, and I was hoping that we would have one of those Vanderbilt-like games where things were easy. As it turned out, it was one of those games that went down to the wire.

What I remember most about the game was that an official on our side made a terrible call. Their left tackle moved prior to the snap, and everybody in the stadium saw it except the official, who was right in front of me. Kentucky threw a touchdown on the play, and I was really mad. There I was with this heart thing, and my blood was pumping pretty good. We were behind late but Lars Tate ran a sweep and scored with about a minute left, and we won the game 17–14. That was a pretty good test of my heart.

An angioplasty is an operation where doctors basically place a small balloon inside your blocked artery. They literally blow it open to unblock the artery. But about 30 percent of angioplasties re-close. On the day before the Liberty Bowl in Memphis I was swimming and that old familiar chest pain came back. Once you've had that feeling, you never forget it. So right after the game I had another angioplasty.

Three months later we were walking down the street in Japan, and I could feel it in my chest—I couldn't breathe again! Barbara had a really tough decision to make. She could bring me back to the States so I could be checked, or she could go to Hong Kong and finish all that shopping!

I always say she picked Hong Kong and that delayed our return home by a couple of days. When I finally got back home and into the hospital, I found out that my artery was 99 percent closed! Dr. John Douglas, a great cardiologist and pioneer of angioplasty at Emory, was also a former high school quarterback at North Augusta. I remember that he looked at me sternly and said, "Don't wait so long next time."

It was quite an experience. After that I became a heart counselor for all of the coaches in America. If anybody had a heart problem, they would always call me. I had heart brothers and sisters all over the country. I had some people tell me that what happened to me made them go get checked. If I helped in that regard, then what I went through was worth it. My good friend and great pro coach Dan Reeves later joined me as a heart brother.

1995: The Firing of Ray Goff

One of the things I took pride in as a head football coach was that I never fired an assistant coach. I may have reassigned them somewhere in the athletic department if things were not going well, but I wanted to keep them in our organization. I have always believed in the old saying about loyalty: it's a two-way street. If you expect people to be loyal to you, then you have to be loyal to them. Unfortunately, with the demands and high salaries of assistant coaches today, that is no longer practical. But back then it was the way I operated as a coach.

Things are different when you're an athletic director and a head coach is involved. You really can't reassign a head coach; there has to be a change. The decision to dismiss Ray Goff as head football coach in 1995 was one of the most difficult ones I have ever had to make. How could it not be difficult? He was one of my former players, one who had helped us win a championship in 1976. He was a player I had recruited. I had been in his living room, and I knew his momma and daddy. By then Ray's daddy, Jim Buck (a wonderful man), had passed away. Ray was ultimately the person who I had supported to be the next head coach when I retired in 1988. No matter how justified the decision may have been, it was far from easy.

In my opinion, we were not going in the direction we needed to in the football program. We had gotten very, very close in 1992 (a 10-2 season) when we went to the Citrus Bowl and beat Ohio State. We almost won the championship, but lost a close game to Tennessee (34-31) and a close game to Florida (26-24). At times Ray's teams were right there, but for whatever reason they could not get over the hump. In fact, after 1992, the program went in the opposite direction.

The next three years Ray's teams went 5-6, 6-4-1, and 6-6, losing to Tennessee and Florida three years in a row and Auburn twice. There was a lot of pressure from key people to make a change after the second mediocre year, especially after getting beat by Vandy at homecoming (43-30) and losing to Florida (52-14).

I fought that off and decided to give Ray one more year, but I set a "significant improvement" standard. I was hoping for a good year but the team did worse, going 6-6, losing to Auburn and Florida, both in Athens. We lost to Florida 52-17.

I think I went the extra mile to give Ray a good severance package. According to the contract, we were only obligated for his base salary, but I recommended that we give him his television plus his income from Nike. Then Larry Walker, his attorney, came in and negotiated an even stronger package than I had offered. We could have very easily said that the contract calls for the base salary only, but we didn't. We just thought it was the right thing to do.

It's a tough thing to lose your job, and I'm sure it has come back on Ray from time to time. I know it's been tough for him. My only regret now is that Ray has become somewhat estranged from the program at Georgia. I wish that he would come around a little more and participate more. But I understand why he feels that way. Ray and I have been cordial when we see each other, but I wish our relationship could be more than cordial. He has come to a few of the lettermen's barbecues and a few of the golf tournaments. I just hope that as time goes on, he'll feel that he is still a big part of Georgia and will come around a little more.

Christmas Day, 1995: Glen Mason Stays at Kansas

After interviewing the candidates to replace Ray as head coach, I settled on two men: Glen Mason, the head coach at Kansas, and Jim Donnan, the head coach at Marshall. Both were very good football coaches. I had been around Glen before at meetings of the American Football Coaches Association. He was an Ohio State man who had played for Woody Hayes, a coach for whom I have always had great admiration. Glen had done a very good job at Kent State before he went to Kansas, where he also had some success rebuilding that program. Jim Donnan was the quarterback on the North Carolina State team that beat us in the 1967 Liberty Bowl. He later coached for my brother at North Carolina, and then at Oklahoma during their great run. He had had tremendous success at Marshall, including a Division I-AA national championship.

Both were very good candidates, but I decided on Mason because he had had his success in Division I-A. I also thought he was more prepared for the public relations aspect of the job. But when I told Jim Donnan of my decision, I also said that if things didn't work out with Glen Mason, I would be back in touch. When I said that, I didn't know I was being prophetic.

I knew that coach Mason was divorced, but I did not know the custody situation with his children. His two children lived with him (they even came with him to the press conference), and he simply told me that he had joint custody and that he planned to bring them to Athens. I had no reason to question that, but in hindsight I should have. As it turned out his wife didn't mind him having custody as long as she could see the children anytime she wanted, but if he was going to move them out of the state, she wasn't going to go for that.

I really had no inkling that there was going to be a problem. But I do remember that, talking to him by phone after he went back to Kansas to coach the team in the bowl game, he just didn't seem as jovial or excited about things. I didn't think much about it at the time, but I think that was a prelude of what was to come. The phone call came at about 10:00 on Christmas morning. Barbara and I were in Birmingham visiting relatives. We were actually getting ready to go back to Athens, but had not really talked about exactly when we were going to leave.

Glen had taken his Kansas team to the Aloha Bowl in Hawaii, which was supposed to be his last official act before becoming head coach at Georgia. So when the call came it must have been about 4:00 or 5:00 in the morning out in Hawaii. He got right to the point. He just said, "Coach, I'm not coming. I'm going to stay at Kansas." At a time like that, you don't spend a whole lot of time arguing. Glen had obviously made up his mind, and by then I understood the circumstances. In my mind it was over, and I needed to immediately turn my attention to the next thing, which was how to address this crisis.

All I said was, "Are you sure?" When he said, "Yes," my final response was, "Good luck to you." I walked into the dining room where Barbara was having a bite to eat. I just said, "Let's go."

We got in the car and I told her what had happened. Of course back then we didn't have cell phones like we do now. I could have really used one that day because I had to stop every so often at different places along the way to use a pay phone. I called Claude Felton, our sports information director, and told him to set up a meeting with John Shafer, my senior associate athletic director. We would talk about our plan of action as soon as I got back to Athens.

When I got back to Athens we all sat down and talked about the situation. Jim Donnan was a close second in the process so I didn't hesitate to call him to see if he was still interested. Ironically, Jim was away from home working out when I called, but an hour later we did make contact. Needless to say he was very enthusiastic and very excited about the opportunity. We made the deal and the next day he was on his way to Athens with his staff.

I know it was a long day for me, but it was an even longer day for the Georgia people, I'm sure. Most of them found out Glen Mason's decision by watching television. I can just imagine that a bunch of them had an early Christmas meal and then turned on the TV to watch the

Aloha Bowl and the man they thought was going to be their new head coach. Then when the broadcast started, they announced that Mason was staying at Kansas. I know that had to be a shock.

By Christmas night, 1995, Georgia had a new coach, a man in whom I had a lot of confidence. And we had survived yet another crisis at Georgia.

Five years later we would have to let Jim Donnan go as football coach, but by then we had a new president in Michael Adams. That, as they say, is another story for another day.

9

New York, New York: Next Stop, the College Football Hall of Fame

A football coach doesn't have a whole lot of time for introspection. There is always another practice, another meeting, or another game to prepare for. By my nature, I don't spend a whole lot of time looking back. I was raised to always move on and focus on the next thing. But at certain times in your life, you can't help but stop and reflect on how you arrived at a certain point. You also think about all of the people who helped you get there.

One of those times came in December of 1994 when I was inducted into the College Football Hall of Fame. Georgia had a number of players already in the Hall of Fame when I was inducted, but I was fortunate to be the first Georgia coach to go into the Hall. I am proud that several years later (1997) coach Wally Butts (1949–1960) was inducted as well.

It's a long way from the tough side of Mobile, Alabama, to the Grand Ballroom at the famous Waldorf-Astoria Hotel in New York City. The Georgia delegation that came to see my induction was huge— and it was loud. In fact, there were so many Georgia people in the audience that night that it bordered between embarrassing and heart-warming. When my name was announced and the spotlight hit me, they were certainly the most vocal group of the night. They went on and on because they were proud Bulldogs and really fired up.

That's when the memories began to flood back. There were memories of people who were there, dressed in their finest for this black-tie dinner, and memories of those who could not be there. So many people played a role in getting me to the head table for the Hall of Fame dinner—as I have said many times, nobody accomplishes something like that on their own, and the recognition is a tribute to all who helped along the way.

So many memories came flooding back that night.

A "Values" Education

It all started with my parents, of course. I was a Depression baby, born in 1932. It was tough making ends meet, but I never knew it. In fact, I didn't know I grew up in poverty until I read about it 30 years later!

My dad, William, grew up as an orphan in Mobile. He was adopted by a couple named Dooley, but they both died when he was 12 years old. He then moved to New Orleans to live with an aunt. He never finished grammar school. In fact, I don't think he stayed in school beyond the fourth grade, but he came back to Mobile when he was 16 years old and became an electrician. Although he had very little formal education, he taught himself to read and acquired all the great intangibles of life experience. He worked until he became the chief electrician at the National Gypsum Company, and the man who eventually replaced him had to have an electrical engineering degree. He used that fact to impress upon me the need to get a college education. I was in summer camp in the Marine reserves when he died of cancer. He was only 67 years old.

My mother, Nellie, also dropped out of school in about the sixth grade.

She had heart problems and high blood pressure, but she never would spend any money on the medication the doctor ordered. She wanted to spend it on us—my brother, Billy, and my two sisters, Margaret (whom we called "Dede") and Rosezella.

When I went off to college, she made me buy a pair of dress pants for $5. I had one shirt, one tie, one sport coat, two pairs of khakis, and two pairs of dungarees. That was my wardrobe, and she wanted to be sure that I was dressed like the other students. But more importantly, she wanted me to have a coat and tie to wear to Sunday mass. I was a freshman at Auburn and we were getting ready to play Alabama when I got the word that she had died. She was only 52 years old.

Even though my parents had very little formal education, they gave me what I call a "values" education. They instilled in me some basic, fundamental beliefs that I have carried with me all of my life. Those beliefs came in the form of sayings that I am sure were heard by a lot of youngsters growing up during that time—sayings like: "If something is worth doing, then it's worth doing well." Or, "If you tell somebody you're going to do something, then do it."

My mother's favorite saying was: "Manners will take you where money won't." I will never forget that. There were many things like that and they were much more important than just a formal education.

That's Just What Families Do

Billy and Rosezella were in New York for the Hall of Fame dinner but my oldest sister, Dede, was not. She had died several years before. She was married with four children when her husband, a commercial pilot, was killed in a crash. So Dede and her four babies came back home to live with the family in Mobile. We didn't think much about it because that's just what families do. We all helped raise the babies. I first started learning to change diapers when I was 10! It was good early training for later.

Dede had two girls and two boys. When the boys were old enough, they moved to a Catholic boys orphanage until they graduated from high school. The girls stayed with us. When it came time for college, one of the boys, Archie, went to live with Billy and the other, Bud, came to live with me. We paid for them to attend college. Again, that is what families are supposed to do.

Bud still lives in Athens, where he worked for the university for more than 30 years. Bud has two sons, Vince and Billy.

One of the most fun things about that trip in 1994 was showing Rosezella around New York City. We had all been there together once before when Billy got married up in Vermont. On that occasion I packed my wife, Rosezella, and Dede into my car and we drove all the way to Vermont to watch Billy get married. On the way back we stopped in New York for a couple of days. I took them all to the theater to watch Robert Goulet in *Camelot*. We sat way up in the cheapest seats in the theater. Watching my sisters you would have thought that it was the greatest moment of their lives as we listened to Robert Goulet! They talked about it forever.

Not a lot of people know this, but I had another sister whom I never met. Little Mary Rita died when she was only two years old, which was before I was born. She contracted infantile paralysis (polio) and died before they could get the fever under control. Back then the mortality rate for children with fever was pretty high. I've been to her little grave at the Magnolia Cemetery in Mobile, where my parents are also buried, on several occasions.

The Coach Who Changed My Life

When I was young I went through a period when I really resented authority. I had run right off the beaten path and was hanging out with a rough crowd. At that time when so many things in my life didn't make sense, sports did. That's when Ray Dicharry came into my life.

Ray Dicharry (pronounced Da-Sherry) was from Baton Rouge, Louisiana, and was our coach at McGill High School in Mobile. At our school the head coach had to do everything—football, basketball, and baseball. In a seven-year period, coaching all three sports, Ray Dicharry had the greatest record of any high school coach in the country!

He was a person players really looked up to. He had the ability to shape kids' lives when they really needed it. He was what I always felt a high school coach should be.

Because of his commitment, when I was going through my toughest times, he pulled me to the side and talked to me pretty straight. He said, "If sports are important to you and you want to do well in sports, then you have to sacrifice. You have to give up some things. You have to learn how to say no." One of the things I had to give up was a group of buddies who were always getting into trouble. They thought I was going high-class on them, but I did it anyway.

He left McGill and went to Tampa, Florida, to be the head coach at Jesuit High School. When I was down there recruiting, I would always try to go by and see him. By the time we went down there to play Wisconsin in the Outback Bowl in 1997, Ray had died. So I took his wife, Dottie, out to lunch. Ray Dicharry is the reason I have always admired the great job that high school coaches do.

It was 1948, the summer before my junior year in high school, and my friend Bobby Duke came by my house to take me to football practice. I was asleep and I didn't want to go. I had made up my mind to give up football and to concentrate on basketball, which I really loved. Basketball was fun and I was good at it. I was the sixth guy on the McGill team as a sophomore, and I wasn't doing particularly well in football. But Bobby kept insisting, telling me I had a chance to start at quarterback. He talked me into getting out of bed that morning for practice and sticking with football. I'm glad he did. I try to go by and see Bobby every time I'm in Mobile.

I had no intention of signing a football scholarship. I was going to play basketball, but the coaches kept coming to my house, trying to get me to sign for football. Auburn, Alabama, Tulane, and even Georgia came by. Auburn put on the hard sell, saying that the education I was going to get was worth $4,000. Now, you have to understand that to my parents $4,000 was like $100,000 would be today. I was asking lots of questions, but my mother's only question was, "Where is the Catholic church?" That was her priority and her only concern.

I tried to put the football coaches off, but they just kept working on me. Every time I would leave the house for basketball practice, there they were. Finally one school really turned up the pressure to the point of offering me money to sign! I left that coach and went straight home and called the Auburn coaches, who were staying at the Admiral Semmes Hotel. I told them I was ready to sign. Bobby Duke and Ed Baker, two of my McGill teammates, signed with Auburn too.

Life After College

After I finished at Auburn, my life was pretty much laid out for me. The Korean War was going on, but I was in an NROTC training program that allowed me to stay in college and graduate. After graduation I had a two-year obligation to the Marine Corps. I was commissioned as a Second Lieutenant in the morning, graduated from Auburn in the afternoon, and then went to Chicago to play in the College All-Star Game. After the game I drove to Quantico, Virginia, to begin my two years of service.

I really enjoyed my time in the Marines and drew a lot of things from it that I applied to coaching. Many of the leadership and organizational principles are the same. After I got out I spent eight years in the reserves and had my own platoon in Auburn.

It's amazing how small the world is sometimes. In 1991 General Carl E. Mundy was named the Commandant of the Marine Corps. When he accepted the honor, he noted that Vince Dooley was his first commanding officer. As it turned out, he was the squad leader of my platoon in Auburn!

When my tour of duty was over, I had a big decision to make. I had enjoyed the structure of the Marines, and they were recruiting me to stay in the Corps. My colonel wanted me to go with him to his next duty station, in North Africa. He told me that on weekends I could fly to various places in Europe. The thought of being in Europe was kind of exciting. But I also had a chance to go back to Mobile and put my business degree to work by entering the banking business and working for an Auburn alumnus who had been involved in my recruiting. Then again, I had a chance to go back to my high school as a coach, and I also had an offer in Texas as a college assistant.

I wrote my college coach, Shug Jordan, to let him know my obligation to the Marines was finished. He asked me to come by and offered me a job as an assistant coach. The starting pay was $5,100. "I know that's not much," said coach Jordan, "but I made $3,600 when I started." The offer from Auburn convinced me that I needed to take a serious look at coaching and to give it a go. And that's what I did.

I came back to Auburn in 1956, and in 1957 I was a faculty adviser to students. That's when I met a freshman named Barbara Meshad in church. She was one of the students whom I thought needed some "extra" advising. It seems like we dated just once a year. We dated once when she was a freshman, and we just didn't hit it off. We dated once more when she was a sophomore, but nothing came of it. We finally dated again when she was a junior, and the third time it took.

I'm not sure what she was thinking. I guess the first two years she looked at me and figured I was just an old man, but we were both Catholic and we had the same values, so it was just a matter of time. We were married on March 19, 1960. That's about 45 years, 4 children, and 11 grandchildren ago.

Children Are Our Greatest Blessing

On a night like the Hall of Fame banquet you try to count all of your blessings, and for Barbara and me, there have been no greater blessings than our four children, Deanna, Denise, Daniel, and Derek. They are all grown up now with families of their own, and we continue to be blessed by the 11 beautiful grandchildren they have given us. It can be difficult being the child of someone who has been as visible as I have been over the years. Still, they all have good souls and good hearts, thanks primarily to Barbara.

Both of my daughters, Deanna and Denise, ended up in journalism and public relations. They are very good at what they do. Deanna is gritty, a real competitor who had to work at it a little harder than her sister. She gave us two grandsons—Patrick, the first born, and Chris—and the only granddaughter for 15 years, Catherine, whom Barbara calls "the princess."

Things came a little easier for Denise, who is kind of laid back and has a gentle soul. Her three boys, Ty, Joe, and Cal, are extremely active and challenging. But Denise and her husband, Jay, just go with the flow.

Daniel had to struggle the most and had to work harder than the others. It didn't come as easy for him in school, but because of a lot of grit and determination, he did very well. He and his wife, Suzanne, have two children, Michael and Matthew. Matthew was born with cerebral palsy. He is a real kick despite having special needs.

The Good Lord probably blessed Derek more than any of them. He's very gifted and competitive, too. He did very well in school, receiving his undergraduate degree from Virginia, where he played football, and then going on to Georgia's law school, where he served on the debate team. He is now a coach with the Miami Dolphins.

Derek was the baby. I would always call his brother and two sisters "the bunch," because they all arrived close together. Derek came five years later. I have always said that the bunch never did like Derek because he got to do things earlier than the rest of them. His mother called him "Precious" because he was the youngest. Barbara and Derek had five or six years together by themselves after the rest of the kids were gone.

Derek met his wife, Allison, at Virginia, and today she is a successful ob-gyn. Coincidentally, her father was a cheerleader at Auburn when I was coaching and her grandfather was the longtime Baptist minister there while I was in school. They have two boys, John Taylor and Peyton, and the last child is a girl, Julie Ann. That brings the count to nine boys and two girls.

I am also proud to say that all four of our children hold degrees from the University of Georgia. Deanna, Denise, and Daniel all received their undergraduate degrees from UGA. Derek graduated from Georgia's law school.

All four of our children are special, but they are special in very different ways. That adds to the strength of our family. They all have great inner qualities and I'm proud of them. We all get together every year during the week of the Fourth of July at our place on Lake Burton. In fact that, more than anything, is why Barbara wanted to build that place. If you build it, they will come—and they do. That's four kids and their spouses and 11 grandchildren; it's quite a gathering.

Georgia and Coach Eaves Come Calling

I thought I had a chance, though just an outside chance, at the Georgia job when Joel Eaves, my old Auburn basketball coach, was named the athletic director at Georgia in November of 1963. From my perspective

Georgia had gone through a lot of tough times. A lot of people questioned Georgia's program and whether or not things were being done the right way.

Coach Eaves took the job and when he would come back to Auburn to visit, we would sit down and talk. He kept saying that he would like to bring me to Georgia as assistant head coach. I knew he was thinking about me but just couldn't rationalize hiring an unproven freshman team coach from a rival school. What put coach Eaves over the edge was a call from Frank Broyles, the head coach at Arkansas. I had written coach Broyles because he was one of the two coaches (Darrell Royal at Texas was the other) whom I wanted to work for if I left Auburn.

So Frank Broyles called coach Eaves looking for me and told him he was prepared to offer me a job. Before coach Broyles could reach me, coach Eaves offered me the job of head coach at Georgia for the starting salary of $12,500. A housing allowance and my television show would up my compensation to $15,000!

"Oh, by the way," coach Eaves said, "Frank Broyles called and he wants you to be an assistant coach. So what do you want to be, a head coach or an assistant coach?" That was typical of coach Eaves. I asked him to give me five minutes so I could call Barbara. Barbara was excited and said that if we went to Georgia, she'd never complain about me being away from home again. Obviously, she didn't keep that promise. I got right back to coach Eaves and said, "If you're foolish enough to stick your neck out, I'm foolish enough to come."

On the day I was introduced as head coach at Georgia (December 4, 1963) Dan Magill came to pick me up. He told me to hide in the back seat of the car. I told him I could be walking down the middle of Broad Street and nobody would know who I was. Then he put me in the Holiday Inn, and told me not to answer the door or the phone. Finally, they came and got me and took me to the Continuing Education Center where I met the president (O. C. Aderhold) and the athletic board.

New Year's Eve, 1963: a night that I will never forget. We were all at the Holiday Inn in Athens. Deanna was two years old, Daniel six months old, and Barbara was pregnant with Denise. There was an ice storm and power to the hotel went out.

I think everybody was crying but me.

Barbara was crying because Auburn was playing in the Orange Bowl the next day, and all of our friends were down in Miami where it was warm and sunny. "What kind of place have you brought me to?" she said. So I told Barbara I would take Deanna and get out of her hair so she could tend to Daniel. Deanna and I had dinner by candlelight at the Holiday Inn restaurant.

The next day the power came back on and we had a chance to watch Auburn in the Orange Bowl. That was our old life and we were about to start something brand-new. There was certainly no guarantee of success.

On New Year's Day, 1964, the College Football Hall of Fame seemed light-years away, but on that night in New York, when I stood up to receive the honor, it seemed like those 30 years—filled with memories— had gone by in the blink of an eye.

10

Back on Top:
SEC Football Championship
Fills a Void

Very early in my coaching career I knew that I would someday want to be an athletic director. I knew there would come a time when I would have to step aside as a football coach. As I previously said, I didn't want to be like Bear Bryant and coach until I was dead. And logically, where do football coaches go?

Right here I should say that it was very important to me to avoid the stereotype of dumb football player. I wanted to do well in school when I got to Auburn. I wasn't a great student, but I was a good student. Education was important to me and still is.

So when I became a football coach I didn't want to be considered just another narrow-minded coach who only cared about winning games. I enjoy many other things in life: history, reading, traveling, and I have a real joy for learning. While I was coaching at Auburn I went to school in the off-season even though I already had a degree in business management. I enjoyed history and ended up taking 85 quarter hours of history courses to earn my master's degree. I can't tell you how many classes I've audited at the university just to satisfy my curiosity on something. I am proud that I recently received the Love of Learning Award from Phi Kappa Phi, a national honor society.

The bottom line is that whatever I do, I want to do it well, and it seemed like a natural fit to be a successful athletic director. I had always had a broad appreciation for other sports—I played basketball and football in college. When coach Joel Eaves stepped aside as Georgia's athletic director in 1979, I was excited to step up to the challenge.

We were about to enter one of the most difficult times in the history of intercollegiate athletics. Title IX, which guaranteed equal opportunities to female athletes, was just coming into effect, and we were having all sorts of problems with the women's basketball coach. We had a part-time coach who worked with us, but also spent half of her time working for the physical education department. It was obvious to me that we could not continue that kind of setup.

In fact, we had three or four coaches who were in that same type of situation—splitting their time with the physical education department. Coach Eaves was very frugal, and when he came to Georgia in November 1963, that kind of arrangement with some of our coaches might have been necessary to save money. But once we began to benefit from some successes, I knew that the situation had to be addressed.

The first thing I did was chair the committee to hire our first fulltime women's basketball coach. That turned out to be Andy Landers, who is still at Georgia today. He is one of the very best in his profession. This step was just the first to bring us in line with the new requirements. I saw Title IX as a challenge and an opportunity, and I was excited about it as I took over as athletic director in 1979.

Then we started adding women's sports. We had scheduled women's track in 1981, but Herschel Walker had a very talented sister, Veronica, who was a track star. So we decided to add women's track a year early so Veronica Walker could become the first women's track athlete that we ever signed to a scholarship. I thought it was a smart decision on two counts.

We had to drop some men's sports, like wrestling and gymnastics, and those were very tough, finance-driven decisions. But the goal was to have a very well-rounded program—for both men and women—where every sport could compete at the highest level. We finally achieved that goal during the eighties. In the Butts-Mehre Building there is a cube in the display area near the door. The cube is called "The Fabulous 80s." It took all of the things our department accomplished in the eighties—Men's Final Four in basketball, national championship and three SEC championships in football, and championships in many other sports—and compared them to the rest of the schools in the league. Based on a point system devised by the SEC at the time, we were number one in women's sports, number one in men's sports, and number one overall. That's how good and balanced our total athletic program became in the eighties.

In the nineties we continued to be strong and got even stronger. In the 1998 school year we had our greatest year ever, winning four team national championships. We finished second (behind Stanford) in the Sears Cup, which ranks schools on their overall athletic program for the academic year. In 2001 we finished third, and in 2004, my last year as athletic director, we finished fifth in the same competition, which had become known as the Director's Cup (it was sponsored by NACDA, the National Association of Collegiate Directors of Athletics).

I'm especially proud of our accomplishments because most of the schools that we competed against outside of the conference offered, in some cases, as many as 14 more sports than our total of 20. Since you get to count only 20 toward the award, the other schools were able to throw out a lot of sports, but we had to count all 20 of ours. There was no margin for error, and we weren't able to count equestrian, where we have won two national championships, because it is not yet a varsity sport recognized by the NCAA.

Our department has been recognized in a couple of other ways over the past 10 years. Texas A&M created the first Excellence in Athletics Cup, which evaluated schools on eight different categories. Among those were graduation rates and how well the school provided gender equity opportunities. The winners from the various conferences around the country were Duke (ACC), Stanford (Pac-10), Michigan (Big Ten), and Villanova (Big East). Georgia finished at the top of the Southeastern Conference.

The other recognition came a few years ago when the student newspaper at the University of Florida did an analysis of which schools got the biggest production from its athletic department based on the dollars spent. When all of the totals came in, the paper picked Georgia's

155

athletic department as the one that used its resources most efficiently. That was certainly a point of pride.

There have also been many other points of pride that our athletic department has been able to enjoy. During my tenure we had more than 100 Academic All-Americans and more than 50 NCAA postgraduate scholarship recipients. As a coach and then later as an athletic director, I believed that every meeting with a student-athlete should begin with a discussion of academics. I insisted on our football coaches doing that while I was head coach and encouraged all coaches to do the same while I was athletic director. I made a point to ask the student how things were going in each of his or her classes. The purpose of that was to let the student know up front how important academics are. I tried to set the tone early in their careers.

That is why we came up with the Director's Honor Roll, which gives certificates to every student-athlete who makes over a 3.0 grade point average. We also created a student-athlete academic awards dinner called the Round Table, where students invite their professors to come to dinner and be recognized for their help.

The sign as you walk into the bottom floor of the Butts-Mehre Building says it all: "If it is to be, it is up to me." This is my favorite sign because it shows a football player succeeding on the field *and* in the classroom.

We were one of the first athletic departments in the nation to come up with a mission statement. It came out of the adversity of the Jan Kemp situation. We decided that we had to use that disappointing time as an opportunity to make our program better. We met with Cohn & Wolfe (a public relations firm) and they suggested putting together a statement of our principles and what our department stood for. It took us a year and a half to finalize what we wanted to say, but we did it, and every year we have Mission Renewal Day, which is when we meet to recommit ourselves to those basic principles. Last spring we had the 17th annual Mission Renewal Day, and that long-term commitment

Coach Dooley (left), Herschel Walker (center), and Carmine Ragucci (of the
Downtown Athletic Club) in New York following the 1982 Heisman Trophy
presentation. PHOTO COURTESY OF CLATE SANDERS/UNIVERSITY OF GEORGIA.

Coach Dooley's movements along the sidelines became known as the "Dooley Shuffle."

Georgia athletic director Joel Eaves (left) hired Dooley in December 1963, when Dooley was only 31 years old.

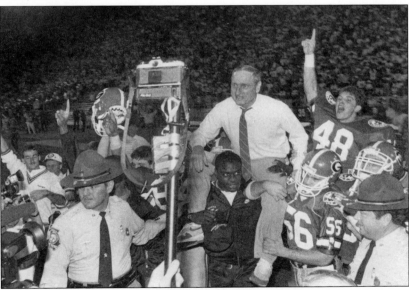

Coach Dooley is carried off the field after his final game—a 34–27 win over Michigan State in the Gator Bowl on January 1, 1989. It was Dooley's 201st victory.

Coach Dooley with Penn State coach Joe Paterno. Georgia and Penn State met in the Sugar Bowl for the 1982 national championship.

Vince Dooley with Florida State head coach Bobby Bowden.

Coach Dooley was inducted into the College Football Hall of Fame on December 6, 1994. He was the first Georgia coach to reach the Hall of Fame. PHOTO COURTESY OF DAN EVANS/UNIVERSITY OF GEORGIA.

Coach Dooley runs the Olympic torch through the UGA campus in 1996.

Coach Dooley with Georgia head coach Mark Richt (left) and Georgia governor Sonny Perdue. Perdue was a walk-on football player for Dooley in 1965. PHOTO COURTESY OF DAN EVANS/UNIVERSITY OF GEORGIA.

Coach Dooley waves to the Sanford Stadium crowd at the end of the Kentucky game on November 22, 2003. It was his last game as Georgia's athletic director. PHOTO COURTESY OF STEVE GUYER/UNIVERSITY OF GEORGIA.

President Michael Adams (left) did not grant Dooley's request for a contract extension, a decision that divided the university's fans and supporters. PHOTO COURTESY OF RICH ADDICKS/*THE ATLANTA-JOURNAL CONSTITUTION.*

Vince and Barbara relax in coach Dooley's garden. A professorship in horticulture has been established at Georgia in his name.

grew out of a difficult situation. The point is that these kinds of challenges should stimulate you. The Greek poet Horace said, "Adversity has the effect of eliciting talents which in prosperous circumstances would have lain dormant."

We instituted a drug education program four years before the NCAA did. In 1982 we found out that we had a drug problem when we caught one of our football players bombed out of his mind on the night before a big game. As coaches we just could not understand how anybody could do such a thing if they cared about themselves and their teammates. It forced us to study something that we knew absolutely nothing about.

We brought in a drug expert from the NFL, which was just getting into drug education. He spent three days with us and confirmed that we did have some problems. I took my coaching staff to hospitals where they were treating people for drug addiction. We were just astounded at what we learned!

Thanks to our success in athletics, we were able to donate $2 million to the academic side of the university. We first pledged $1 million, and when that was paid off we pledged $1 million more. I'm proud to say that the last thing I did as athletic director at Georgia was to pay off the second million-dollar pledge to the university.

In 1988 I personally pledged $100,000 to begin the Vincent J. Dooley Library Endowment Fund. I have always believed that academics should be at the forefront of what we do. But I knew that if I wanted to say that to the coaches and student-athletes, then I should be willing to step up to the plate and put my money where my mouth is. I picked the library because I'm interested in a lot of academic disciplines, but all of them have one thing in common: the library.

Each year the library takes the interest from the fund and uses it for things that are not covered in their regular budget. Our 1966 and 1968 SEC championship teams each raised more than $100,000 for the library fund. There is a plaque in a room at the library to honor them. Since reaching the initial goal of $1 million, it has continued to grow, and I'm happy to report that it has now grown to almost $4 million. I am also happy to say that of the 1,000-plus endowments on campus at Georgia, the library endowment is the fifth-largest.

I have always felt that to have a program that competes at the highest level, you have to do three things: 1) allow full scholarship allotments for every sport; 2) hire good coaches, and 3) give those coaches the resources they need to be successful. In order to be successful, coaches must have quality facilities, and I believe we have provided them at Georgia. These facilities and improvements include:

- Seven expansions to Sanford Stadium, raising its capacity to 92,746 plus 77 sky suites, giving us the fifth-largest stadium in the country.

- The $12 million Butts-Mehre Heritage Hall, which houses our athletic offices. We have since spent another $4.5 million on renovations.

- An athletic association contribution of $7.5 million toward the building of the $40 million Ramsey Center, which houses our nationally ranked swimming, gymnastics, and volleyball programs and serves the entire student body at Georgia.

- The $7.5 million Rankin M. Smith Sr. Student-Athlete Academic Center.

- The $2 million Spec Towns Track grandstand.

- The $3.5 million baseball stadium.

- The $3.5 million renovation to Stegeman Coliseum.

- The $8 million complex for our women's softball and soccer teams.

- A $29-million extension to the Coliseum that will include men's and women's basketball practice facilities, a gymnastics practice facility, and an Olympic weight room. That extension is now under construction after the athletic board approved a recent request by athletic director Damon Evans.

Fund-raising

Today fund-raising is an integral part of every athletic program in the country, but that was not always the case at Georgia. For many years we never had to do any fund-raising because football and the contributions from ticket priority took care of everything.

But as women's athletics emerged, and in order to compete across the board, we had to go into fund-raising. The first fund-raiser we ever did was for the Butts-Mehre building, a $12-million facility that became a model both as a facility and as a fund-raising project for college athletic departments around the country. The contributions of the Georgia people were just absolutely amazing. Thanks to the contributions from our supporters, we were able to pay off the $12 million that we had borrowed to build Butts-Mehre in just four years!

When we decided to get into fund-raising in a major way, the first person we hired was Kit Trensch, who was put in charge of endowing scholarships. When Kit came to Georgia, we had only one endowed scholarship. When she left about 12 years later, there were over 180 endowed scholarships. She then took on the role of director of fund-raising and had a great deal of success. Kit set a fine example as a fund-raiser by personally making a contribution of almost six figures. That included $25,000 to the Rankin M. Smith Student-Athlete Academic Center, where there is a study room in her honor.

The contributions for ticket priority that we receive from our supporters are also a very special point of pride. When I came to Georgia in 1964, there were 1,749 contributors for ticket priority who gave an all-time high of $76,488. Forty years later that number had grown to

159

about fifteen thousand contributors for a grand total of more than $25 million! Every year but 1 in the 41 years we were at Georgia there was an increase in the total contributions from our supporters. That is something of which I am very proud.

We had some Title IX consultants who came in from time to time to give us an assessment of our compliance. They told us that some schools might have better individual facilities, but as an overall program, nobody had better facilities than ours. I am very proud of that.

We also asked other experts to come in and give us their honest assessment of our program. After Dr. Adams arrived as president, he requested that we hire an outside consulting firm to take a thorough look at the department. I recommend Gene Corrigan and Chuck Neinas, who are two of the most respected people in all of college athletics. Chuck is a former commissioner of the Big Eight and a former director of the College Football Association (CFA). Gene was athletic director at Virginia and Notre Dame before he became the commissioner of the Atlantic Coast Conference. No one knows more about what it takes to run a successful athletic department than Gene and Chuck.

In 1998 they came to Georgia and I'm proud to say their report was very positive. I'm sure it didn't hurt that in that same year our teams won four national championships! [Editor's note: Contacted at his home in Boulder, Colorado, Neinas remembered giving Georgia's program high praise. "I told Vince that I didn't know if we should give him an A or an A+," said Neinas, "because there was not a sport at Georgia that didn't have the financial support and facilities necessary to win the SEC championship. And if you can win the SEC championship, you can win the national championship."]

As proud as I am of all the things we accomplished at Georgia during my time as athletic director, before 2002 there was still something missing: we had not won an SEC championship in football since 1982. You can do a lot of great things as an athletic director, but in the South, you'll ultimately be judged by the success of the football team. The fact that we had not won a championship in 20 years was a source of frustration for me.

I had heard the critics who said I really didn't want our coaches to win in football because "he doesn't want anybody to do better than him." How ridiculous! If people know me, they know that if I'm going to do something, I want to do it well. I knew that, as athletic director, if we didn't have a good football program, it reflected poorly on me. After all, I hired the coach.

Ray Goff won 10 games and got very close in 1992, just four years after I had retired. I had found out as coach that fans were willing to forgive a down season every now and then if you give them a championship once in a while. But, for whatever reason, Georgia had not been able to get over the hump for 20 years.

In 2002 I had the feeling that we might have a special team when we drove down the field and kicked a field goal late to beat Alabama 27–25 at Tuscaloosa. Alabama fought back and took the lead, but then our team just took the lead right back in a hostile environment. It looked like a team that had the intangible qualities of a champion.

Then we won the great game at Auburn 24–21, where we had been lucky enough to clinch five of our six championships. David Greene and Michael Johnson made a great play to win that game. I had almost given up.

I remember the feeling the night we beat Arkansas 30–3 in the Georgia Dome for the SEC championship. I knew how good I felt, but I also knew that it was an even greater feeling for our coach, Mark Richt. It is a wonderful feeling when, as athletic director, you watch one of your teams win a championship. I've seen our teams do it in swimming, tennis, basketball, baseball, softball, golf, gymnastics, and many other sports. But it can never replace the feeling you have when you win a championship as a coach. To be with your staff and your team in the locker room when it's over is one of the best feelings in the world. There is nothing like it and there never will be anything to equal it. I was very happy that Mark Richt and his players got to experience it. We all want to do it again, of course.

As we headed out of the Georgia Dome that night (December 7, 2002) a big void that had existed in the program for so long had finally been filled. I still had 18 months left on my contract at Georgia, and I'm sure no one would have blamed me if I had just taken it easy until my retirement in June of 2004. But that's not what I wanted to do. I was 70 years old, but I felt great and had a lot of energy. The athletic department was in the best shape ever, both competitively and financially, but we still had challenges, foremost among them a fund-raising campaign. In addition there were facility projects, including especially the Coliseum and the stadium, which needed to be completed. Also, several key people had asked me to stay on so that we could meet that challenge.

So as I looked down the road at what lay ahead I kept coming back to the same conclusion: I didn't want to retire.

11

President Michael Adams: The Controversy from My Perspective

A lot has been said and written about my disagreement with Dr. Michael Adams, the president of the University of Georgia, and his decision not to honor my request for a contract extension in 2003. My position on this issue has remained unchanged: I respect Dr. Adams' right, as the president of the university, to make the decision; I simply disagree with it. And I believe in my heart that, to this day, the vast majority of the Georgia people disagree with it as well.

When you look at the landscape of college athletics, it is generally accepted that someone who has remained at one institution as long as I did at Georgia (41 years) should be allowed reasonable input into his retirement date. Of course, I am thinking of people like Bobby Dodd at Georgia Tech, Bear Bryant at Alabama, Darrell Royal at Texas, and Dean Smith at North Carolina. I make no secret of the fact that being unable to do the same at Georgia, after four decades of service, is a profound personal disappointment.

Because I have such deep respect for the office of the president, and because Dr. Adams still sits in that office, I will limit my comments here to things that I know to be factual or that are a matter of public record. I do, however, have some strong personal feelings and opinions, not only about my situation but also about Dr. Adams and the university in general. I may share those feelings at a more appropriate time, but the well-being of the university takes precedent. Still, there are some aspects of this story that deserve some clarification and expansion.

I would first like to say that I had a very, very good working relationship with the other four presidents under whom I served.

Dr. O. C. Aderhold was president when I arrived in December 1963. Not a lot of people remember how tough it was when I became football coach and Joel Eaves became athletic director. Georgia was not really respected in the college athletics community and did not have the reputation that it now enjoys as a public institution. Dr. Aderhold was appreciative of the way that coach Eaves ran the department and was very grateful that we were not only winning, but winning the right way.

I knew Dr. Fred Davison before he became president because he was dean of the veterinary school. He was a true Georgia person who loved the university and who had a real appreciation for the role of athletics. We went through some great times together, but we also had some tough times. The Jan Kemp situation in the eighties resulted in Davison stepping down, but he was a great president for this university. [Editor's note: In 1985 Kemp, an instructor at the University of Georgia, charged that she was pressured to give UGA athletes passing grades they had not earned in order to allow them to continue playing. She sued the university and won a $2.6 million judgment.]

When Dr. Davison resigned, Dr. Henry King Stanford took over for only one year. But it was one of the best years we ever had. There were a lot of pots boiling over that year, both academically and athletically. He was able to keep a lid on all of them.

Dr. Charles Knapp came from Tulane, and when he got here he was suspicious of our athletic department. I understood why: Tulane had to shut down the men's basketball program because it had gotten so out of control. I knew he didn't want to go through something like that again. He was also naturally suspicious, taking over after the Kemp crisis. He told me that after a couple of years he came to appreciate how things were done at Georgia. He began to appreciate that the program was run efficiently and with integrity. I was able to work with him as well as any president we've had at Georgia. I would meet with him on a regular basis, just as I had with Presidents Davison and Stanford, because I always thought it was an extremely important and vital thing to do. And President Knapp always returned my calls promptly.

An Agent of Change

When Dr. Adams came in 1997, I tried my best to stick to the same formula and meet with him once a month, as I had done with the other presidents. I always felt that with the high visibility and passion associated with athletics, keeping the president informed was of vital importance. Most national NCAA administrators agree.

But it was obvious that he had a different approach when it came to organization and communication, and he did not want to meet on a regular basis. Ironically, the new athletic director, Damon Evans, has been appointed to the president's cabinet for the same communication reasons I outlined.

On those rare occasions when Dr. Adams and I did meet, it was almost always about his agenda.

When Dr. Adams arrived, it appeared that he may have been charged to be an agent of change, a role he did not hesitate to assume. Although change is beneficial in many instances, Dr. Adams seemed to feel that the only way to improve things was to change them, whether it was changing a dean or changing the food at the Georgia Center. It became clear to me early on that he wanted to do the same for athletics, and in order to accomplish that, he would have to do something with me.

In just his second year he told me that some key people (a phrase he used often, never identifying the individuals) were not happy with me as athletic director. I told him that in my job, just like his job as president, it was natural that some people would not be pleased. He said, "You've done a good job here, Vince, but you never want to stay too long. And you need to have something named after you."

My first thought was, "Now that's a crafty way to make a change! Is he thinking that I would want to resign in order not to stay too long and to have something named after me? Is he hoping that I will comply and gracefully retire on my own?"

I dismissed it because I have always felt that you need to go the extra mile to give someone new the benefit of the doubt—especially if that someone is the president. But in reality, I should have listened more closely.

The Rumors Begin

First of all, I have to say that Michael Adams is a very bright man and, at times, can be a very charming person. He has a wonderful family. And I also like his father, who is very much a gentleman. I like his wife, Mary, and their children.

But in December 2000 I started to hear the first rumors that Dr. Adams did not want to renew my contract. At first I dismissed the rumors, but when they became more frequent and came from reliable people—especially considering his previous "name something after me" tactic—I took it seriously. So on December 15, 2000, I wrote Dr. Adams a letter requesting that he extend my contract as athletic director for four years.

While flying down to Tallahassee, Florida, to interview Mark Richt for the job of head football coach, Dr. Adams and I discussed the matter. I said, in the spirit of compromise, that I would settle for three years as athletic director and two more as a consultant after I retired. I thought it was a reasonable request. We did not discuss the issue further on that trip.

Adams wrote a letter back to me on January 29, 2001, offering two years as athletic director and two years as special assistant to the president. I didn't understand his reasoning, particularly given what had happened in December when we both interviewed coach Richt. During the course of that interview, coach Richt specifically asked me how much longer I planned to be athletic director. I told him that my plans were to help him get his program going for at least the next three years. After that, I told him, I might be in another capacity with the university.

If Dr. Adams disagreed with my answer at the time, I certainly didn't expect him to say anything in front of coach Richt. But he did not say anything to the contrary on our trip back to Athens. Therefore, I drew the conclusion that he was comfortable with my staying on for three more years. I felt like we had made a commitment to coach Richt when he took the job and that Dr. Adams should allow me to keep that commitment.

In response to Dr. Adams' letter of January 29, offering me two years as athletic director and two years as a consultant, I wrote to Dr. Adams on February 1, stating my rationale for wanting three years, especially citing my commitment to coach Richt.

In a meeting on February 6, 2001, he offered me a contract extension of two and a half years. That meant I would have to retire in the middle of the 2003–2004 academic year.

When I asked him why he gave me half of a year, Dr. Adams said it was not uncommon with faculty appointments. When I reminded him that this was not at all a common practice in athletics, he basically said, "Take it or leave it."

I told him that I was going to take it, but I also said, "I'm going to take the high road publicly, but I'm going to tell you that I disagree with you and your decision. I don't think you're treating me fairly."

The next day there was a press release about the two-and-a-half-year contract. Publicly, I just said that I was grateful because it would give me three more football seasons and that I would be able to keep my commitment to coach Richt. But privately, I was not happy and was very disappointed, and Dr. Adams knew it.

I understand that Adams heard from many people that he was being very petty and vindictive by giving me "a half year," or six months less than I had requested. A few months after the announcement, he sat down for a Q&A with Tim Tucker of the Atlanta Journal-Constitution. Adams was asked if he would be willing to give me six more months to make it three years. Adams said he would not have a problem with that.

I was surprised when Adams called and told me about the interview and him saying he would not have a problem with giving me an additional six months if I asked. I thought to myself, "That is a change!" And I told him, "You must have had a problem with it or you would not have been so adamant about the half year in our contract discussions." Then I told him that if he wanted to give me six more months, I would be happy to take it. But I was not going to ask him for it. It would have to be his decision and his announcement.

In June, six months were added to my contract. I was grateful for the six-month addition, but I wish he had come to me directly and told me he would like to add the half year instead of using the media to accomplish the mission.

Donnan Paid Under the Table

The 1997 season was a very good one for our football coach, Jim Donnan. We had gone 10-2 and had beaten Florida for the first time in many years. But after that season, North Carolina pursued Donnan and we began negotiations on a new contract.

I never wanted to negotiate through an agent because I didn't think it was appropriate or fair to the university. An agent has an expertise in negotiation; I'm an athletic administrator. So I decided that the negotiations would be between coach Donnan's representative, Richard Howell, and our attorneys at King & Spalding. It did slow things down.

We got to a point in the negotiations where Donnan's side kept asking for more and more. When we got to about the last two things, I just said no after saying yes to everything else. I said we had gone as far as we were going to go, and the negotiations came to a standstill. Then, all of a sudden, the problems seemed to be solved, and Donnan was ready to sign. I didn't understand why at the time.

Later I found out that Adams had secretly arranged for Donnan to receive an additional $250,000 in severance pay. Their agreement was without my knowledge and wasn't authorized by the athletic board. Adams told Jim Nalley, the board chairman of the University of Georgia Foundation, to take care of it. [Editor's note: In the summer of 1998, with Nalley serving as mediator, Adams agreed to pay Donnan an additional $255,350 in severance pay should he be fired with three years or more left on his contract.]

I'm not sure why Adams did it. Maybe he thought the secret agreement would never see the light of day. But the secret deal eventually became very public when the decision was made to fire Donnan at the end of the 2000 season.

In January 2001 Howell wrote Dr. Adams a letter outlining the details of their secret agreement. Howell then called Ed Tolley, the attorney who represents the athletic association.

Tolley showed up in my office and asked, "Are you aware of this secret deal?" I had no idea what he was talking about. Then he proceeded to tell me the details. I simply could not believe it.

After being summoned by then-chancellor Stephen Portch to discuss the issue, Adams came to my office to explain why he had done it. He realized that he had made a mistake. So we had to have a meeting to decide exactly how we were going to handle the situation that, at that time, had not become public.

Adams was not there but sent his good friend, university attorney Steve Shewmaker, who came with him from Kentucky (where Adams had been president of Centre College). I was there with my personal attorney, Nick Chilivis. Floyd Newton was there from King & Spalding, the firm that represents the UGA Foundation, and Tolley was there to represent the athletic association.

When we first started talking, Shewmaker said we should just absorb the money through the athletic association budget and not bring the matter before the board, thus avoiding public exposure. I assumed he was speaking on his own initiative, but when I first heard his idea I thought that it would be like Watergate—a cover up. The unanimous reaction around the room was very negative to that idea.

Finally, we agreed that the only way the money could be authorized was through the athletic board. So the issue was brought before the board, and I spoke on behalf of Dr. Adams. I told the board that Dr. Adams told me he regretted the decision and acknowledged that if he had to do it over again, he would do it differently. I said I accepted Dr. Adams' position and that I would like for the board to authorize the additional money for coach Donnan. They did. [Editor's note: On April 17, 2001, the executive committee of the UGA Athletic Association authorized an additional $255,350 in severance pay for Jim Donnan.]

Certain aspects of that episode still bother me today. The University of Georgia Foundation authorized a forensic audit by the accounting firm Deloitte & Touche, because the foundation had concerns regarding certain expenditures of its funds by President Adams. This incident was discussed as part of that audit.

In the administrative response to the audit, Shewmaker denied that he had originally suggested that the money for Donnan be absorbed into the athletic association budget to avoid bringing the matter before the board, thus avoiding public exposure of the situation. I thought maybe I hadn't heard him right. So I called the three attorneys who had been in the room when Shewmaker allegedly made the suggestion—Chilivis, Tolley, and Newton. All three said they remembered the same thing. Shewmaker is a very congenial fellow, but in this case I wondered about his memory.

In retrospect, I wish the president had just come to me and said, "Vince, I understand what you're talking about. But I really want to get this done, and I want you to go ahead and give Donnan what he wants."

I would have disagreed with Dr. Adams but, of course, I would have done it.

The Jim Donnan Firing

After the way the 2000 season ended (a 7-4 record that included a 27-15 loss to Georgia Tech), it was obvious that Donnan was in trouble as our head football coach.

I met with him and told him that I was going to recommend that he get one more year. But I also told him I wasn't sure how the president might react.

My thinking was that if I could get Donnan one more year, I could go back to him and tell him that I knew it wasn't going to work because of how the president felt about him. I would tell him that it was in his best interest to start looking for another job as soon as possible and that he had one year to find one. This plan would allow Donnan to exit gracefully and save face.

Obviously, Dr. Adams decided otherwise. In respect to him, you have to say the decision worked out well because we hired coach Richt, who has had great success at Georgia. I wanted to get to the same end, but in another way. I was disappointed but respectful of the president's right to make the decision to fire Donnan. I just thought my way of addressing it was better. I guess, being a coach myself, I try not to embarrass another coach if possible.

When we got to the press conference to announce the decision, I did not want to appear to be mad. I wasn't. I wanted to appear to be supporting the president, though it was not my recommendation, and I wanted to make that clear. It would have been misleading on my part if I had said that not only did I support the decision, but that I was in 100 percent agreement with it. That would have been untruthful on my part. The president can ultimately overrule the athletic director, which is what Adams did in this case.

There was another thing about the Jim Donnan firing that really concerned me. Adams decided that he didn't want Donnan to coach in the bowl game in Hawaii after he was fired. It became my job to tell Donnan. I did not like the idea, and I told Adams it was a mistake—that a coach ought to be allowed to coach his team in his last game. Adams insisted he did not want Donnan to go to Hawaii and coach the team and wanted me to name an interim coach.

Shortly after I told Donnan, the captains and several of the team leaders came to me and were very upset, and I understood why. I could tell from the conversation that it could be a serious problem if Donnan was not allowed to coach the team in the bowl game.

I called Adams to tell him the story, and I was firm in supporting the team. He was not happy, but I told him there could be serious problems if he stuck with his decision. He said he would let me know later.

Adams ultimately acquiesced and let Donnan coach the team. Adams decided that he would not make the trip to the bowl game, though every president in my memory has attended our bowl games.

Donnan took the team to Hawaii—and won.

The Hiring of Jim Harrick

We were looking for a new men's basketball coach after we had to fire Ron Jirsa in 1999.

I thought we had a pretty good system in place for hiring coaches. We had used it to hire Tubby Smith, who is now a great coach at the University of Kentucky. In our system, Dick Bestwick, a former senior associate living in Athens, was quietly hired as a consultant for a meager $3,000. He had many connections in the college sports industry, and he would quietly make calls, working behind the scenes. He would gather the information and pass it along to a small in-house committee that included Claude Felton, Avery McLean, and Damon Evans.

We got the prospects down to a short list that included Mike Brey of Delaware, Buzz Peterson from Appalachian State, Fran Fraschilla of New Mexico, and a few others. Jim Harrick was not on that list.

Dr. Adams called me. He said he knew Harrick and that he was a really good coach.

I told him that I didn't know Harrick, but obviously he was a good coach. I also said that because of past transgressions at UCLA, we did not have him on the list.

Adams said, "I know him, and I think we need to take a look at him."

So I told Adams that I would take his recommendation, since I did not know Harrick, and I put him on the list.

I can say this now: Brey was the guy I wanted. He had a great background at Duke and knew how to win and win the right way. I thought he was exactly what we needed.

But Adams went to the Final Four in Tampa with me, and we interviewed Harrick, along with the other candidates. I have to admit that I liked Harrick in the interview and liked him even more when I met his wife in the second interview. He certainly convinced me that he was sincere when he explained that he had made some mistakes at UCLA but had learned from them.

Still, I liked Brey. That's who I wanted. Notre Dame was his priority, and I understood that. But they didn't hire him. They hired Matt

Doherty. Brey eventually decided to stay at Delaware, despite knowing what the opportunity was here.

So when Brey pulled out, we turned to Harrick, and the rest, as they say, is history.

The Jim Harrick Crisis

Every coach, at some time or another, recruits athletes who are high-risk—academically, personally, or both. As a coach you accept that risk, but it should only be on rare occasions. There have been many success stories of high-risk student-athletes making good. But when you recruit a high-risk athlete and it's obviously not going to work out for him, the team, and the university, then you have to step up and say that the athlete will no longer be part of your program. You just have to admit that you made a mistake and cut your losses so as not to endanger the entire program.

That's where Harrick made his mistake. In hindsight it's easy for us to sit back and say, "You never should have recruited a kid like Tony Cole." But the key is the management of high-risk individuals after you recruit them and bring them to your campus. If they are not manageable, you compound the error by keeping them. That is when I have a problem.

I saw some of the things that Cole was doing on the bench. I started hearing things about how undisciplined he was. But when the ESPN story broke, the really shocking thing was the classroom business. [Editor's Note: On February 27, 2003, ESPN reported that former Georgia basketball player Tony Cole claimed to have received cash and other benefits from head coach Jim Harrick and his son, assistant coach Jim Harrick Jr. The report also said that Cole and several other Georgia athletes received an A in a basketball class taught by Harrick Jr., despite the fact that they did not attend class.]

Coaches have been teaching classes for as long as I can remember. I used to teach a football class. Is there a potential conflict of interest? Yes, if the class is not managed right. It became obvious that Jim Harrick Jr. was not responsibly managing the basketball class.

173

I thought the administration overreacted when it made an initial rule that no athletic association employee could teach a class in the future. That was an extreme overreaction. Ron Courson, our trainer, is one of the best in the country. Why would you not take advantage of his expertise? We had others in the department who were equally qualified to teach, but those potential conflicts had to be managed well. Now they are, with some strict guidelines.

When the ESPN story told of payments and other benefits to Cole, I met with Harrick. He told me that he thought we could get through the controversy. I told him I wanted to get through it—but to do it the right way. I wanted to find the truth.

As more facts were reported me to by our attorney, Ed Tolley, it became clear that there were some serious problems facing our university and there was no way we were going to get through it without making some difficult decisions.

We had the first meeting about this situation, which had now become public and very serious, in Dr. Adams' office. After the meeting Adams pulled me aside and said, "We both have a stake in this situation—your legacy and my national reputation."

I was a little taken aback by that remark. Although I didn't say anything, I did think it was an interesting observation at a time when the university's reputation was being challenged.

I sent a note to Dr. Adams stating my intention to withdraw the team from the SEC and the NCAA tournament. He endorsed my recommendation, though he did not like the fact that I took the initiative in writing the letter.

Then we told Harrick Jr. that we would not renew his contract.

Then came the matter of Harrick Sr.

We had another meeting in the president's office to discuss how to proceed with Harrick because it was obvious that he could not be retained. Adams had several of his top aides there. Claude Felton and Damon Evans were there with me.

Adams was adamant about how he felt about Harrick and how he wanted the situation handled. He strongly emphasized that he wanted to make it tough on Harrick. Ultimately, we decided to suspend

Harrick until we completed our own investigation. Only then would we know if we had grounds to dismiss him. Fortunately, Harrick left of his own accord and we didn't have to face that decision.

We received a lot of criticism for taking the team out of postseason play. There is no question that it was hard for the players. As a coach, it is difficult to tell a group of players that their season is done early. But I don't think it was a hard decision, because it was the right one.

After our internal investigation into the basketball program, we self-imposed a number of penalties. In addition to pulling our team from the NCAA tournament, we released four of Harrick's signees from their commitment to Georgia. We felt these self-imposed penalties were sufficient. The NCAA disagreed, which was very disheartening. [Editor's note: On August 5, 2004, the NCAA placed the Georgia men's basketball program on four years probation, as well as eliminating three scholarships for unethical conduct, academic fraud, and for giving extra benefits not permitted by NCAA rules. Georgia had to vacate all of the wins from its 2002 and 2003 seasons in which the six players had participated.]

Damon Evans wanted to appeal the decision, and I agreed. But it was, of course, his decision because I had passed the torch to him before the NCAA's ruling.

The appeal turned out to be a good decision, because on June 3, 2005, the NCAA reinstated the three scholarships it had previously taken away. It restored our faith in the system because the NCAA appeals committee recognized all the work we had done and therefore modified the harsh penalties.

My Contract Extension Denied

I have to admit that when 2003 began things were going well and I felt very good. We had just won our first SEC football championship in 20 years. Spirits were high. There was a lot going on, and it was all very positive.

I still had a year and a half left on my contract as athletic director, but already many Georgia people were telling me privately that I shouldn't retire, encouraging me to still head the program. I thought about that and came to several conclusions. I felt good. My health was good. The athletic department was in good shape, but there were some additional projects, especially relating to the stadium and the Coliseum, that I wanted to address. Most of all, I wanted to finish the fund-raising campaign that had just gotten off to a great start.

And, to top it all, I just wasn't ready to retire.

I told several close friends and Georgia supporters about the situation, seeking their thoughts on how best to approach Adams on the subject.

That spring there was a seminar at the Classic Center in Athens that Dr. Adams and I were both scheduled to attend. Dr. Adams said that he would like to take some time to catch up because he had something on his mind. I assumed he had gotten wind of my conversations with a few confidants about staying on as athletic director.

After Dr. Adams introduced the seminar, we went off into the corner of the hallway and had a cup of coffee. [Editor's note: This meeting took place on March 26, 2003.]

"Is there anything on your mind?" he said. Obviously, that was the opening for me.

I said, "As a matter of fact, there is."

Then I told him that I had been thinking about my contract for a good while. I also told him that a number of Georgia people had come to me, encouraging me to stay on.

"I am just not ready to retire," I finally said.

He asked me how long, and I said four years—the approximate length of the capital campaign.

"I thought we had a deal," he said. He was obviously upset.

I explained that we did have a contractual agreement, but, after 40 years at Georgia, I felt that I had earned the right to reconsider and ask for an extension to my contract. I listed some things I wanted to do, which included, among other things, expansion projects to the stadium and Coliseum and seeing the upcoming capital fund-raising campaign to its conclusion.

He just said, "I'll get back to you on this."

Now, I want to set the record straight on something right here. It was portrayed by some that I had violated an ironclad or solemn promise to retire as athletic director after my contract was up on June 30, 2004. That was not the case at all. Over the years I had several contracts, and it was never assumed that each contract would be my last.

Back in December 2000 I originally asked for four years. After some negotiation, I said I would settle for three, but Dr. Adams would give only two and a half. He later gave me the additional six months.

That was the best deal I could get at the time, though I did think I might be ready to retire in three years, which was stated in the letter exchange about the issue. Regarding my request for a contract extension, the president stated that he understood my request for an extension and had no problems with it. In a letter written on June 5, 2003, Dr. Adams said, "I appreciate and respect your personal decision to approach me with this request."

After that meeting on March 26 with Dr. Adams, I did not hear from him on this matter for almost two months. It appeared in retrospect that he may have been using those two months to build a case with "key people" for not granting me an extension.

During that time I got media calls because it had started to leak out that I had asked to stay on. I could also sense that the issue was starting to create discord among Georgia supporters. I thought it was bad for the university to have this controversy going on.

Billy Payne, one of my former players, said he had spoken to a member of the UGA Foundation who suggested that I go to Adams and offer a compromise. I thought that was a good idea, but Billy was not so sure.

I called Adams' office to set up a meeting. My plan was to tell him of my concern for the university and to offer a compromise in the best interest of the institution. I would ask for two years as athletic director and two years as a consultant and fund-raiser. I wanted that many years in order to be of service throughout the upcoming Archway to Excellence capital campaign.

All of my ideas and efforts proved to be moot. When I arrived at Dr. Adams' office on June 5, 2003, and immediately after I pleaded my

The University of Georgia

Public Affairs
News Bureau

Thursday, June 5, 2003

Coach Vince Dooley
Athletic Director
Butts-Mehre Heritage Hall
Campus

Dear Vince:

You will recall that you brought up the issue of another four year contract extension at a brief meeting with me on March 26. I told you at that time that I needed to think about the question you raised.

I appreciate and respect your personal decision to approach me with this request. I have come to the conclusion, however, to honor the contract and agreement that we reached in 2001. The contract that we ultimately signed extended your time as Athletic Director through June 30, 2004. At the same time, I committed to continue your employment as a Special Assistant for Athletic Development at the same annual pay for one additional year. That contract and agreement represented an extension of three years as Athletic Director and one year as Special Assistant.

When we had our final discussion concerning your contract extension over two years ago, I tried very hard to frame the arrangement so that you would end your tenure as Athletic Director on a positive note, and so that we could undertake a transition to new leadership that could take advantage of your input and continued presence. I took into account specifically your February 1, 2001, letter where you indicated that if you were allowed to retire as Athletic Director three years from June 30, 2001, you would feel that you had been treated fairly. I believe this was the right course then, and is the right course now as well.

While we have faced some challenges together in the past, the current state of our athletic program is strong and the future is bright. Two excellent new coaches in our principal revenue sports have been hired, and the programs in the other sports areas are stable and possess great potential. While we have certain future challenges, including further attention to the NCAA probe into our men's basketball program, our people have the skill and right mindset to meet those challenges.

Your remaining year as Athletic Director and a year as a Special Assistant in fundraising can give you the opportunity to continue a personal involvement with the University. Please know also that I am open to additional years of involvement in that capacity if we mutually agree that such would be in the best interest of the University.

On more than a few occasions in the past, I have shared with you my belief that with our positions in the public and media spotlight, it is often the case that our relationship is perceived as being tense. To the contrary, we have been in agreement far more times than not. Let me assure you that I value your friendship and welcome your continued involvement in the life of the University.

Sincerely,

Michael F. Adams
President

case for a compromise in what I thought was in the best interests of the university, he handed me a letter and informed me that he had already made his decision. He said, "We will stick to the original contract." My retirement date would still be June 30, 2004. He was in the process of releasing this information to the media.

Not only was Adams denying my request for a contract extension, but in the same breath he informed me that he had already put together a search committee to find the new athletic director. His intention was to bring the new athletic director into the department six months before I was scheduled to retire!

Nobody brings in a new athletic director or a dean or a department head that early when there is already somebody in the position. And to have a search committee and an advisory committee for the hiring of a new athletic director—and to not be included in either one—was pouring salt on the wound, as I would write to him on June 27.

At that point, there was not a whole lot to say. I told him I was disappointed, but I did acknowledge that, as president, it was his decision to make. I shook his hand. I shook the hand of Tom Landrum, his assistant, who was obviously there as a witness.

Then I left and went back to my office. I told Claude Felton and Damon Evans what had happened. Then I had to prepare my response to the press. Privately, I could not help but feel that Dr. Adams handled this matter in a short-sighted manner.

The Fallout Begins—and Continues

Obviously, I was disappointed with Adams' decision. But the reaction from a lot of the Georgia supporters surprised me. They sensed that something was not right, and the ones who spoke out publicly, and privately to me, expressed their unhappiness with the way the situation was handled.

The reaction by the Georgia supporters was two-fold. A large majority of them who had never had any dealings with Adams simply thought that his treatment of me was very shabby, considering my 40 years of loyal and productive service to the university.

UNIVERSITY of GEORGIA ATHLETIC ASSOCIATION

<u>PERSONAL AND CONFIDENTIAL</u>

June 27, 2003

Dr. Michael F. Adams
President
The Administration Building
Campus

Dear Dr. Adams:

As I told you when we met on Thursday, June 5, in your office in the presence of Tom Landrum, I was disappointed with your decision not to honor my request to extend my contract. At the same time, I did acknowledge to you the fact that it was, of course, your decision to make.

As you recall, I had requested the meeting in hopes that we could come to some resolution regarding my request for you to extend my contract for another four years. Two months had passed since we had that discussion and my private request had become public and was stirring a controversy that was not good for anyone, especially the University. Because of this, I asked you to consider a two-year extension as athletic director and two years as a consultant fund raiser which could carry me through the all-important "Archway to Excellence" capital campaign.

As it turned out, of course, asking for this consideration was moot since you had already made the decision not to honor my request and had chosen to abide by my existing contract that expires June 30, 2004, plus the agreement to serve as a consultant fund raiser for one year.

As you stated in your letter to me of June 5, 2003, you took into account my letter of February 1, 2001. That letter was in response to an earlier one from you that offered me a two-year extension at the time as a counter proposal to the new four-year contract I had requested. As a compromise, I did propose three years and indicated in my letter, as you mentioned, that if you accepted my three-year compromise proposal that carried me through June 30, 2004, I "would feel I had been treated fairly."

At the same time, you acknowledged the fact that I was within my rights to ask for an extension by stating in your June 5, 2003 letter that you "appreciated and respected my personal decision to approach you with this request."

Office of the Director of Athletics
Butts / Mehre Heritage Hall · 1 Selig Circle · Athens, Georgia 30602
P.O. Box 1472 · Athens, Georgia 30603-1472
(706) 542-9037 · (706) 542-9100 fax
www.georgiadogs.com

continued

Letter to Dr. Adams
June 27, 2003
Page Two

I am naturally disappointed that you did not honor my request, but I became more than just disappointed when you told me almost in the same breath that you had already appointed a search committee with a mission of bringing in a new athletic director by January, 2004—six months before my scheduled retirement date. The rationale, as I understand it, was to promote "a smooth transition." Since I will still be at the University for the following year in a fund raising capacity and housed at the Smith Academic Center thanks to your approval, a six-month transition period of having two athletic directors at Georgia serving simultaneously was not necessary.

Forming a search committee with a year and a month left for any position at the University and having a replacement on board six months prior to the retirement date of a long tenured employee is unprecedented I would imagine for any official on campus including the president, vice presidents, deans and directors. I know that a standard search procedure in the industry of intercollegiate athletics is the model followed by Tennessee in replacing Doug Dickey. A formal search committee was formed after the new year in the final six months of Doug's contract and the successor was chosen in mid-May providing an ample six week window for a smooth transition.

I realize that you have every right to decide how the search process should be conducted, but I would be remiss if I did not convey to you that the decision regarding the search process has not only been poorly perceived by the public, it has had the effect of "pouring salt on the wound" . . . an unnecessary personal insult to me.

In conclusion, I realize that I was not asked to serve either as a member of the search committee or as a consultant to the search committee; however, I would be negligent if I did not offer for your consideration exclusively the names of certain individuals whom I think would be the best candidates to fill the position of Director of Athletics at the University of Georgia at this time.

I will communicate in confidence to you my feelings on replacements at a future date. Meanwhile, thank you for listening to my thoughts. If you so desire, I will be willing to meet with you at any time to discuss all of these issues.

Sincerely,

Vincent J. Dooley
Director of Athletics

VJD/rbs

Another group of Georgia people, primarily those on the University of Georgia Foundation who had ongoing issues with Adams over his spending of the foundation's money, saw his actions toward me as a symptom of a much larger problem. That problem was the foundation's frustration with the leadership and the spending habits of the president. That frustration resulted in an audit commissioned by the foundation.

Adams wisely drew on his education and experience in political communications to paint the reaction as one of "academics versus athletics," even though the UGA Foundation trustees maintained that their differences with Adams had to do with spending and leadership and long preceded the decision he made about me. His decision regarding me no doubt poured fuel on the fire, or, to say it another way, brought to a head the sores that had been festering.

I was really irritated at the "academics versus athletics"spin because nothing could be further from the truth. I finally had to issue a public statement asking the people who had been so vocally against Adams that if they had an issue with the president, not to bring my name or the athletic department into it. The story was being portrayed as academics versus athletics (Adams even said publicly that the issue was about who was going to run the university, academics or athletics), and for the sake of the university I just couldn't let that go on.

Some critics thought I should have taken this stand earlier. But to my way of thinking, the controversy was triggered by the short-sighted manner in which Adams handled my request for a contract extension. When it became obvious to me that it was hurting the university, I knew I had to step forward. I issued a statement, saying, among other things, that "academics must always be at the forefront" of what we do at the University of Georgia.

After my statement, Dr. Adams immediately issued the following statement: "Now is the time for all of us to come together and move the University of Georgia forward. I want coach Dooley's advice as we do so, and I intend to sit down with him as soon as possible."

Several days later Dr. Adams and I did meet. We talked on a number of topics, and finally he asked, after all that had happened, what would make me happy.

First of all, I told him it wasn't a matter of making me happy. I told him that the most important thing we could do was to send some kind of signal that would allow the Georgia people, who were bitterly divided on this issue, to begin some kind of healing process. I told Dr. Adams that if he would give me just one more year as athletic director, it would show our supporters that he was trying to be flexible and reasonable. I also asked him to put the search for a new athletic director on hold and that I would be willing to work with him to find a suitable replacement in the future.

Given what I know about the Georgia people, I honestly believed that most of them would accept this as a reasonable compromise.

He told me that he would think about it, but he first wanted to know about the audit that he heard was being conducted by the foundation.

He, in essence, said that the audit should stop.

I told him that was beyond my control. I really did not know any details about the audit, and some of my friends told me up front that it was none of my business. They did not want me to know, and I accepted what they said without question. That basically ended the meeting with Dr. Adams.

A few weeks later we met again and he said no to my second attempt to compromise in the best interests of the university. He certainly had the right to make that decision. Perhaps he thought that was best for the university.

In the final analysis, he said publicly that he wanted my advice, but privately, he obviously chose not to take it.

As I said at the beginning of this chapter, while I respect the office of the president and his right to make personnel decisions, I neither understand nor agree with his decision not to renew my contract. I am glad to have this opportunity to share my feelings with the Georgia people and to set the record straight.

The following are some final thoughts concerning Dr. Michael Adams.

Damon Evans

I was very happy to recommend Damon Evans to replace me as athletic director, but there is more to the story. In my June 27, 2003, letter to Dr. Adams I explained my disappointment over his decision not to renew my contract. In the original version of that letter, I included a section supporting Damon and expressing confidence that he was ready to assume the duty despite, in essence, his youth and inexperience.

I was confident because he would have working with Claude Felton, who had great expertise in public relations. I thought the two working together would be a powerful team. But fearing at the time that my recommendation might hurt Damon, I omitted that section from the final version of the letter that I sent to Dr. Adams. I told Damon why I did it.

The paragraph that was omitted from the letter said:

> One of the brightest, most capable young administrators in the country is already in place in our athletic department. Damon Evans is a loyal Bulldog who has all of the leadership qualities to not only sustain the great program we have, but also to take it to new heights. In fact, I had considered Damon as a worthy successor, and part of that succession plan was for me to stay on a few more years to give him more time to develop his skills. Despite the fact that the plan fell through, I am convinced that Damon is ready, especially considering that he would have working with him as his top associate Claude Felton, a loyal Georgia grad and the most respected sports communications director in the country. The one-two punch of Evans and Felton would be the basis of a powerful team to lead Georgia athletics into the future.

The original letter, which was still in my files, became public after the *Atlanta Journal-Constitution* filed an open records request. Writer Jeff Schultz ran the story in December 2003, prior to Adams making his decision to hire Damon. I did talk to Adams by phone when he boiled the list of candidates down to three, and, of course, I supported Damon. Unfortunately, my recommendation regarding Claude did not work out, but that was an administrative decision.

Public Comments

The controversy surrounding my situation has apparently irritated Adams from time to time, and I suppose that is understandable. Occasionally, he would show that irritation in public.

As an example, at a press conference someone pressed him about his decision not to grant my contract extension request. He said something to the effect of, "We'd be better off three years" after I was gone. Needless to say, that made the newspaper.

I really felt that the remark was totally unnecessary. Even if one feels this way, one doesn't say it publicly.

Here is another occasion when his irritation was played out publicly. In May 2003 nine of our football players sold their SEC championship rings. Nobody felt worse about it than I did, but, as I said at the time, I have great confidence in our head coach, Mark Richt, and I knew he would handle it judiciously.

Obviously, there was a lot of negative press, and many people believed that Adams used the incident to take a shot at me in a statement he released to the press: "My patience, the patience of the faculty, and the patience of most of our supporters is exhausted over this continuing improper behavior by athletes. I am disappointed, and I expect corrective actions to be taken."

The fact is that we had been at a retreat up in the mountains the day before the story broke, and I told him there were going to be some things in the paper the next day about the players selling their rings. I didn't think he thought it was going to be as big a story as it was.

Using the phrase "continuing improper behavior by athletes" definitely made it seem as if he was laying all of this at the feet of the athletic director. The media certainly interpreted his remarks as a slap at the athletic director. They called and asked for my response. I gave none, of course.

After the end of spring practice in 2005, two of our starting football players were arrested, and the story made the headlines on the front page of the Sunday *Athens Banner-Herald*. I couldn't help but reflect back on what had happened with Dr. Adams in 2003 and think that he could have easily made the charge again, especially when the paper reported that nine football players had been arrested or cited since July 1, 2004, the date of my retirement. But this time, of course, he would have to direct his criticism at someone else.

Adams did express "disappointment" at the behavior but said that the situation would best be addressed by the coaches, who should decide what happens to the athletes.

Political Strength

Michael Adams' greatest strength is politics. He is knowledgeable and has great experience in the political arena. After receiving his master's and doctorate in political communications (a relatively new discipline), he served as chief of staff for Senator Howard Baker and later as an aide to Senator Lamar Alexander. Adams even ran (albeit unsuccessfully) for political office in a congressional race in Tennessee. All of these experiences have served him well in certain aspects of higher education. He is smooth-tongued and generally says all the right things. He also has a great ability to court and smooth talk the power base, as he has done so well with several people in key alumni, political, and higher education positions.

He values the importance of politics in higher education so much that three of his top cabinet members came to the university from the political arena. When not distracted, he has used his political background to great advantage for the university.

Other Conflicts

I was certainly not the only administrator at Georgia to get into conflicts with Dr. Adams. It is a fact that the Franklin College of Arts and

Sciences, the largest college at Georgia, gave him an overwhelming vote of no confidence in March 2004. Nearly 70 percent of the Franklin faculty voted that they had no confidence in his leadership. Only 15 percent supported Adams, and another 15 percent did not express a preference. The faculty no-confidence vote not only negates the academics versus athletics spin, but it also creates an academics versus administration issue.

There was the audit released by the University of Georgia Foundation about Adams' use of the foundation's money. I thought the audit called for a lot of concerns to be addressed, but the board of regents chose not to act upon those concerns—primarily, I presume, because they saw the audit as a threat to the authority of the board.

We annually set aside money in our athletic budget for the president to travel, entertain, and take part in athletic events. In 2001 $25,000 was set aside for Adams, a rounded number that has been constant for many years for the various presidents, with periodic increases for inflation. By 2003, in just two years, that amount had tripled to $75,000, with $25,000 allocated to each of the following items: president's travel, president's special occasions, and president's entertainment. In essence, the $50,000 increase requested by the president's office over the two-year period became a part of his discretionary fund.

I was never privy to the foundation's concerns regarding the president's spending as articulated in the audit. But the foundation's decision to have such an audit of Dr. Adams' spending raised a question in my mind. I often wondered if there was any correlation between the foundation's scrutiny of and insistence on more accountability for the president's spending and the dramatic increase in his expenses paid by the athletic association.

Just as I was completing this book, the news broke that the university would be severing its ties with the UGA Foundation, a body of distinguished Georgia alumni who have done an outstanding job in managing our $475-million endowment. The separation comes after a series of conflicts between the foundation members and the board of regents and, of course, Dr. Adams. I do not want to get into my personal feelings on that matter here, but I will say this: when a highly respected and distinguished individual like Jim Blanchard informs the president that he will no longer serve on the university's Archway to Excellence capital campaign, it gives me pause.

Blanchard has served as chairman and CEO of Synovus, a multi-billion-dollar financial services company. *Fortune* magazine named his company "The Best Company to Work For" in America in 1999. *Georgia Trend* magazine honored him as the "Georgian of the Year" in 2003. By any measure, he is one of the most outstanding business leaders in the United States. There is no one I respect more for his leadership, character, and love for the university than Blanchard. It is impossible to measure his true contributions to the University of Georgia. I'm sure that the great majority of the people in this state feel the same way. When someone of his stature considers separating himself from the university in any capacity, it has to be due to a very real concern.

Another real concern might be the statement Blanchard made about the regents when they made the decision to end the board's relationship with the foundation: "Consider me an adversary rather than an ally. The system of governance of our university system is broken, and I intend to be a part of the effort to fix it." Furthermore, he called the regents' action "an abomination and the act of a bully." That's strong language from a person who is known as an enthusiastic but mild-mannered leader.

Speaking of the regents, it has been said by a few people that I took issue with that body over their decision to support Adams' decision regarding my contract extension. Nothing could be further from the truth. In fact, in a letter published in the *Athens Banner-Herald* (February 4, 2005) and the *Atlanta Journal-Constitution* (February 6, 2005), I said in part that, "If I had been a regent at the time I would have supported President Adams in his decision (despite privately not agreeing with that decision). The president has a right to make those personnel decisions, and therefore I would expect all the regents to support the decision—which they did—including several friends of mine."

No matter what spin might be put on this issue, the fact remains that the university's Archway to Excellence capital campaign has been badly damaged by the divisiveness among the Georgia people.

The divisiveness certainly had its effect on the campaign's timetable, with the public kickoff delayed by approximately six months, as the campaign had not yet raised $250 million, or 50 percent of the campaign goal. This 50 percent figure is the industry standard for when a campaign normally goes public.

When the public campaign was then kicked off in April 2005, with a lavish black-tie affair in Atlanta, it was poorly attended. The staff and the student hosts outnumbered the donors by 2-to-1.

The most recent action against the UGA Foundation, which resulted in the resignation of such high-profile leaders as Blanchard, will take an added toll on the campaign. In addition, there are still many potential donors who have not given and will not give as long as the current leadership is in place.

Through June 30, 2005, $342.1 million had been received in gifts, commitments, and deferred gifts toward the university's $500 million campaign goal. Of that amount, $111.8 million was raised by athletics, which represents 32.6 percent, or approximately one-third, of the campaign's overall goal.

Despite it all, however, I am confident and pleased that the university will eventually reach its goal of $500 million. This goal will be reached in no small part due to the role of athletics. As in many campaigns across the country, the University of Georgia is counting the monies contributed by donors for their athletic ticket priority but which does not meet specific campaign objectives.

In summary, the university eventually will meet its $500 million goal, with athletics playing a significant role. This is especially true now that the revised ticket priority for Georgia football is in place, which through its increased rates of contribution will mean significantly more dollars raised each year for athletics and ultimately for the overall goals of the campaign throughout the fund-raising effort.

Unfortunately, because the Georgia people are now divided, the campaign will never reach its full potential. That division has harmed and will continue to greatly harm many areas of the university that are relying more and more on much needed private support in order to maintain the high quality of education that has come to characterize the University of Georgia.

We will never know how much President Adams' approach cost the university in charitable giving and in goodwill with the UGA alumni, faculty, and staff.

I have been asked why, in my opinion, President Adams decided not to honor my request for a contract extension. Only he, of course, can truly answer that question. But as stated earlier, I believe that from early on he wanted his own man in my place—someone totally beholden to him, with unquestioned loyalty and support. Had Dr. Adams honored my request, it would have been my duty to be loyal and to support the president, but that loyalty would not have been unquestioned, and I would not have been totally beholden to him.

Some believe that now that I am no longer athletic director, the conflict that has divided the Georgia people will simply go away. Others close to Dr. Adams thought these issues would be over after Damon Evans, one of my top assistants, replaced me as athletic director. I supported Damon for the position and think that he will do a wonderful job—though I was hopeful that the maturity of Claude Felton would be better utilized. But I can say that I feel that the Georgia people will never completely come back together and once again realize the university's full potential under the present circumstances. Leaders should unite people, not tear them apart.

Furthermore, almost every news story that has been reported about the university in the past few years is over some controversy, as opposed to the previous years when the university was looked upon nationally as a first-class academic institution on the rise. Almost all of the media stories then were positive. This shift in attitude is unfortunate, but it is a fact.

When the day does come that Dr. Adams completes his term as president, I would like to be able to say to him that I appreciate his contributions to the university. I really mean that. But, his tenure as president has been unnecessarily divisive so far.

As I said at the beginning of this chapter, I have the utmost respect for the office of the president at the University of Georgia. But never in my 40-plus years has there been such divisiveness among the Georgia people. We all look forward to the day when those who proudly wear the Red and Black are once again united in serving and supporting this great university that we all love so much.

12

Still So Much to Do

In the 40-plus years I have spent at Georgia I can now say that the two busiest years were my first as head football coach (1964) and my last as athletic director (2003–2004).

When you're a first-year football coach, everybody wants to see you. You get a lot of invitations to do things because people want to see the new coach and check him out.

My last year as athletic director was sort of like that, but in reverse. I got an incredible amount of invitations. All of the Bulldog clubs wanted me to come by and say farewell. I told them all that I really wasn't going anywhere. I still had another year to serve Georgia as a fund-raiser and consultant, and my office was just moving across the street to the Smith Center. (It is interesting that in four decades at Georgia, I only moved my office three times, all within a one-block area. I began at the Coliseum, moved one block to the Butts-Mehre Building, and then three-quarters of a block back to the Smith Center.) Because it was my last year as athletic director, the media demands also increased. Each reporter wanted an individual session, and I understood that.

Then on top of that, our teams were doing great. Our baseball team reached the College World Series. In June I flew out there (to Omaha) twice and in between I received the Corbett award, which is the highest honor an athletic director can receive. It is presented by the National Association of Collegiate Directors of Athletics (NACDA). Any time you are honored by your peers, it is very humbling. I also received several other awards, including the Toner in New York, the

Bagnell in Atlantic City, and the Contribution to Football award given by ESPN in Orlando. Without question, it was my busiest year since I was a rookie head coach.

There were so many things I wanted to get done during my final year as Georgia's athletic director.

One thing I did was write to all of my All-Conference and All-American players and my captains. I have a picture of each one framed and hanging in my house. I told each that I would like for them to come by, so that I could give them the picture and we could visit for a while. It's amazing how many of them came by the office and how much they appreciated the gesture. Guys like Tim Morrison, Scott Woerner, Andy Johnson, Jim Wilson, and Mack Guest. I even had a picture of Leroy Dukes, who played on my first team in 1964. Those were great visits, and I hope it meant as much to them as it did to me. I am still waiting to see a few who haven't picked up their pictures yet.

I made it clear to the staff that I did not want any kind of big, organized sendoff. Damon Evans and the senior staff wanted to do something for the Kentucky game, which would be my last home football game as athletic director, but I just didn't think that was appropriate, particularly with the controversy over my retirement. Besides, I didn't want to give anybody the impression that I was going to be fading into the sunset. I was going to be across the street for another year. Maybe at some point and time down the road, something like that might be appropriate, but not then. I thought the focus should be on the team and on the game because we were still in the hunt for the championship.

But some things you can't stop. The staff wanted me to be the speaker on Mission Renewal Day. I didn't want to but they tricked me into it. They gave a very nice video presentation and a nice good-bye ceremony, and I appreciated it.

I believe that the best way to handle things like that is to be spontaneous. If something happens, fine, but I just don't think it is appropriate to plan things. I'm just not a fanfare kind of guy. Some of the very nice things that happened at the Bulldog Club meetings I couldn't do anything about, so I decided to just enjoy them.

I was chairing the committee that picked our Circle of Honor, as I had since its inception 15 years ago. I thought I had it planned so there was no way I could be chosen in my last year as athletic director. But somebody pointed out that my interpretation of the rule was flawed and the committee overruled me. I had no choice but to accept. A lot of people wanted to do nice things and I had to understand that I couldn't resist all of them, especially since it would please those who sponsored the gesture.

One thing I didn't expect that was very gratifying was the nice reception Barbara and I received during our trips around the SEC during that final season. Skip Bertman, the athletic director at LSU, came to me first and said they wanted to honor me when we went to Baton Rouge in September. At first I said no, I just didn't want the fanfare, but Barbara said she didn't think it was courteous to say no. Of course, she was right. These gestures were genuine, and I knew I should accept them in the spirit in which they were given.

The LSU people did their tribute between quarters, and I had no idea what the response would be, especially with rival fans in a hostile place. In the presentation, they talked about the fact that I was the chairman of the football rules committee, and that I had a lot to do with the rule change that allowed LSU to wear their traditional white jerseys at home. The rule used to be that you *had* to wear your dark jerseys at home. Needless to say, I got a pretty warm response from the LSU people.

There was another great moment at the home game with Auburn. Claude Felton told me before the game that the Auburn band was going to do a tribute. He said, "So be in your box and don't be in the bathroom when it happens." Claude thinks of everything. I was standing there in the box when the Auburn band played "Glory, Glory to Old Auburn" which actually is the same tune as our fight song "Glory, Glory to Old Georgia"—another tie between these great old rivals. When the song began a handful of people waved. Then another group waved. It must have caught on because then the whole stadium started waving and then it was put on the video box.

Somebody told me that they saw through a pair of binoculars to the president's box, and he was just standing there, looking. Nobody was clapping, but I never noticed. As an Auburn grad and a Georgia man, it was a wonderful moment and I appreciated the gesture.

There were other nice tributes. Before we went to Tennessee their athletic director, Mike Hamilton, called. Doug Dickey, their retired athletic director and a former coaching adversary, presented me with a nice glass piece. I got a nice response from the Tennessee people, but they weren't as nice after we beat them 41–14.

Jeremy Foley, the Florida athletic director, wanted to do something at the Georgia-Florida game in Jacksonville, so he presented me with a nice plaque on the field. Even though the competition on the field is always very intense, I felt like we always had a good relationship with Florida and that there was an element of mutual respect.

Dave Braine, the athletic director at Georgia Tech, gave me a plaque that he presented on the field in Atlanta prior to our game with the Yellow Jackets. I was happy to receive such a warm reception from our longtime in-state rival.

There was a wonderful and spontaneous moment during the Kentucky game on November 22, 2003, my last home game as athletic director. Actually, the whole weekend was great. On Friday I went out to the equestrian facility and rode horses with Herschel Walker. That night I spoke to the Wesley Foundation, a commitment I had made to Jerry Varnado, one of our former players who is now a Methodist minister. After that I went to our basketball game because I wanted to visit with Dominique Wilkins, our former great All-American player. I didn't realize I was going to cause such a commotion but the Felton Fanatics were really, well, fanatical.

The Saturday morning of the game was routine. The Athens paper had somebody following me to record the events of the day. I decided not to go down on the field before the game in order to keep a low profile.

A lot of friends were up in the box: Fran Tarkenton, Herschel, and Frank Ros, the captain of our 1980 national championship team. I had made a commitment to the equestrian team to be with them at halftime, so I went down to the field for that. I remember getting a very nice reception from the crowd. I went back to my box and stayed there during the third quarter. Then I went up to some of the sky suites and visited with some people. After we went ahead for good, I started saying some of my good-byes.

With about five minutes left, I thought I'd go on down to the field, which is what I always do. I always go through the crowd quickly, and I figured I could slip down the aisle, and, before anyone saw me, I'd be down to the field. Of course, that wasn't the case. As soon as I started down the aisle people stopped me to say hello, shake my hand, or give me a high five. It was amazing and very moving. Some people wanted autographs, but I knew I couldn't stop to do that or I'd never get to the field. So I asked them to mail something to me so I could sign it and mail it back.

Once I got down to the field, the photographers started taking pictures with their backs to the game. I gave them a hard time because I've learned over the years that you never turn your back on the action in practice, scrimmage, or in the game. That's a good way to get wiped out! Then one side of the crowd started to chant "Vince" and the other chanted "Dooley." I was both amazed and moved by the reaction, but if had to happen, that's the way I like it—spontaneous.

After the game I went to see the team as I always do. I sat with coach Richt as I usually did while he did his radio show. They gave out the game balls. One went to our kicker, Billy Bennett, who broke the SEC scoring record. The next game ball went to Dr. Gerald Thomas, who had been our team optometrist for 38 years and was retiring. He was very emotional. I was happy for my good friend, who did great work and was a loyal Bulldog. The third game ball they gave to me. I expressed my thanks just as I had done that morning in the newspaper. Then I reminded them that there is nothing like being a Bulldog on Saturday night after a victory but that on Sunday morning they needed to start thinking about the Georgia Tech game, which was the following Saturday. Because of the SEC tiebreaker rule, the Tech game was going to have a bearing on the conference championship. We had to win to have any chance of going to the SEC championship game.

I reminded them how big the rivalry was to the Georgia people. It was a wonderful moment.

The response from our competitors was very gratifying, but I think it had something to do with a statement I've made many times before. Always handle yourself in such a way as to gain the respect of people. Compete hard, do your job well, but also treat people with respect. I have always tried to show the proper respect for people, competitors or not. If you treat people right, then you earn their respect. The old golden rule is very powerful and will bring great rewards in the long run. I would like to believe that philosophy was rewarded in the responses that all those people gave to me.

We got some more good news on June 28. Thanks to the performance of our baseball team, Georgia finished fifth in the Director's Cup, which goes to the top-performing athletic department in the nation. Ours was the highest finish of any SEC institution and any program in the entire South. It was our third top-five finish in the past six years. It was a great tribute to our coaches and athletes.

I think it is appropriate that on June 30, my last day as athletic director, I wasn't even at my office in Athens.

I went to Canada to see Claude Felton receive the Arch Ward award, which is the highest honor that a sports information director can receive. Claude was the first person I hired when I became athletic director in 1979, and he remains the most important hire I ever made. He has withstood the test of time. I can't think of a more appropriate place for me to have been on my last day on the job.

People have continually asked me how I felt about the final days, and I tell them I honestly don't know. I really haven't thought about it because I have been so busy. There is a stack of letters that have not been opened over there in a scrapbook. And I won't open them until I'm done.

My goal was to be as busy on my last day at Georgia as I was on my first. I feel confident that I accomplished that.

On July 3, 2004, a very nice honor came my way when the athletic board authorized the funding for the Vincent J. Dooley professorship in horticulture. There are only two in the horticulture department and my primary teacher, Michael Dirr, has the other one. I call him the Herschel Walker of horticulture. I was able to raise a good portion of the money ($250,000) for his professorship. I am proud to say that I am also helping to raise funds for the Allen Armitage professorship in horticulture, which will be completed in the very near future. I also took classes under Dr. Armitage, who is internationally known as the guru of herbaceous (annual and perennial) plants; Dr. Dirr is the guru of woody plants (shrubs and trees).

Gardening is something that I developed a passion for later in life, and I'm proud to say that my garden is not just a spring flower garden but has been described by Armitage and Dirr as a "mini botanical" garden. I like to call it a garden for all seasons. At times I've had many groups tour my garden and at one time had more than 500 people go through it. It doesn't matter when you go through my garden, something is always going on.

On July 8, 2004, I returned from a vacation at our lake home to spend my first day at my new office in the Smith Center. The staff moved all of my stuff from my old office at Butts-Mehre. You collect a lot of things over 40 years.

Let me take a moment and say something about Jennifer Kilcrease, who became my administrative assistant when I came to the Smith Center. I have been fortunate to have good administrative help through the years, and I am especially appreciative of the good work of Becky Stevens, who was with me for the last 13 years I served as athletic director. Jennifer, however, made a real sacrifice to work with me, leaving her position as travel coordinator of the athletic department. She knew that her assignment with me would be for only one year but was hopeful, as was I, that it might be longer. There is no way I could have gotten through this transitional year without her help. I was hoping she could be with me for another year or two, but President Adams and Damon Evans decided not to honor my request for an additional year with Jennifer as my assistant. It will be a real handicap trying to fill her shoes. She truly filled a void created when Becky left and did a wonderful job handling numerous requests by phone and mail and assisting me with public relations and fund-raising responsibilities this past year.

As I look back on this past year I would be remiss if I did not express the concerns I had regarding the decision not to retain some employees who served the university and the athletic association so well for many years.

I was in England on July 16, 2004, when Damon dismissed four people who had been longtime members of my staff: Freddy Jones, the ticket manager; Avery McLean, the promotions director; Kit Trensch, a very valuable member of the development office; and Hoke Wilder, who had done a number of jobs for us, including serving as director of NCAA rules compliance.

The fact is that Damon had said all along that he was going to make some changes. I told him that it would be appropriate to let me know about his plans. He did let me know, but it was the day before I was scheduled to leave for London. I told him that while it was his decision, I obviously didn't agree with it because I had hired those people. I wanted to support him, as I promised I would, but I also tried to inform him of the consequences of making those decisions.

Ultimately, Damon's dismissal of these longtime employees put me in a very awkward situation. Yes, he told me what he was going to do, but he didn't tell me how he was going to do it. It came out in the paper that he basically brought them into his office with Frank Crumley, his senior associate, and Andy Brantley, the university's human resources director. Damon told them of his plans, and told them to clean out their desks now. I thought it was an inappropriate way to treat people who had been in their positions as long as they had. They were all Georgia graduates and had served the university well.

In our next meeting I told Damon that while I would not argue with his decision, and I did support it, I disagreed with the manner in which he had carried it out. He told me that he felt he had to treat them all the same way. I assume that feeling was based on some corporate legal advice. I told him that such treatment might be OK in some cold, modern-day business, but these employees were part of an organization that thrived on family. After all, the sole function of athletic administration is to serve the student-athletes, who are trained by their coaches to operate within a team—or family—concept.

I was disappointed that he didn't come to me and tell me of his decision and ask my advice on the best way to handle the situation. I thought the appropriate thing would have been to tell the individuals in question that they could stay on staff through the football season but that they would need to have another job lined up at some point thereafter. That would have been a much better and more humanistic way to treat people who had been on the staff for so long, who had served so well, and who were all loyal Bulldogs.

Some may respond that coaches are not given that kind of consideration when they are dismissed. The circumstances surrounding coaches and athletic administrators are obviously quite different, especially since coaches work with student-athletes to build seasonal teams. I suppose that when athletic administrators start making the money coaches do, there will be a better argument for equal treatment.

When the media called to get my reaction, I was careful to be supportive of Damon, but also to make it clear that I did not support the way things were handled. I thought the situation was handled poorly, but at the time I didn't come right out and say that directly. Now that some time has passed, I have accepted Damon's decision and my rationale is that it stemmed from him being a young athletic director who, in my opinion, got some poor advice. It will be a lesson for him and he will grow from that experience and others. I did, of course, support Damon for the job and I am sure he will grow in the position and become a top athletic administrator. I am grateful that he took the initiative to recommend to the athletic board that I retain my office in the

Smith Center, our family end-zone box at Sanford Stadium, and the car that I had under my contract.

I respect Damon, but I also realize that he is under his own set of pressures. I rather suspect it has been suggested to him that he needs to be his own man so that he will be perceived as being his own athletic director—to prove that he is not being influenced by me. I understand his job and to whom he reports. I have tried my best to stay out of the way but yet be available to help when called. In recent months I have stayed even further away to avoid even the slightest chance that it might seem that I am trying to influence Damon in any way.

On September 2, 2004, I issued a statement saying that I was not interested in the vacant job of athletic director at Auburn. It was an intriguing idea, going back to my alma mater this late in my career, but it was not meant to be.

There were a couple of columns by Paul Finebaum in the Mobile newspaper suggesting that I might be a good fit for the position. Prior to that I took a few calls from some key Auburn people asking if I had any interest. I even had an Auburn trustee come to me and ask about my interest. I told them basically that I had been here in Georgia a long time and, even though I had stepped aside as athletic director, my plans were to still stick around the university. At the same time, I said that if there was real interest from Auburn's standpoint, then I would listen. I pretty much left it at that.

In the final analysis, I think they would have had to talk me into it. If I had been called to duty to help my alma mater in a time of need, then I would have seriously considered it. But basically their interim president, Ed Richardson, had other ideas, and if he had other ideas, then certainly I had absolutely no interest in Auburn.

One of the nice things about my final two years at Georgia was that some really wonderful honors came my way. A lot of attention had to do with the fact that I was fortunate enough to have a long and reasonably successful career in coaching followed by a long and reasonably successful career in administration. When you are able to do both, it lends itself to being recognized as I have.

Early in 2004 I received the James J. Corbett award, presented by NACDA, which is the highest honor that an athletic administrator can receive. Then in December came the Toner award at the College Football Hall of Fame dinner in New York. That goes to an individual who has made significant contributions to the sport of football, and it was very gratifying to receive it. Also in December I went to Orlando to receive the ESPN Contribution to Football award. The only other two men who have received it are Keith Jackson and Darrell Royal, so that put me in some pretty good company.

There were a couple of other honors that came along that transcended athletics, and those were very special. Early in 2005 I was named to the *Georgia Trend* magazine Hall of Fame. I was inducted along with Tom Cousins, the internationally known real estate developer. The *Georgia Trend* Hall of Fame is mostly composed of people who have been very successful in business, and to be the first sports person named, and to go in with Tom Cousins, was really very special. Then in March Barbara and I went to Atlantic City to receive the Francis J. "Reds" Bagnell award from the Maxwell Foundation. I found out that I was only the third college football coach to receive the award. Joe Paterno and Eddie Robinson were the other two. I later received the Frank Sinkwich award from the Touchdown Club of Atlanta and the Bob Woodruff award from the Knoxville Quarterback Club.

All these honors were special occasions, but the greatest event of all took place on April 22, 2005, when the football lettermen hosted a "Thanks, Coach" celebration in honor of my 25 years of coaching and my 40 years of service to the university and its athletic association. This affair was restricted to Georgia lettermen, and over 500 came back for the reunion celebration. Football lettermen's club president Mack Guest and his cohorts and volunteers did a wonderful job of planning and exe-cuting this celebration for the old coach. They will never know how much I appreciated it.

For some of the players this was the first time they had returned to Athens and the university since they left 20 or 30 years ago. It was fun for me to see how they just picked right up with their old teammates as if no time had passed. In fact, I told the players that the greatest thrill I had that night—and I had many—was seeing the players coming together as teammates, telling stories, and literally hugging each other in jubilation. There is nothing like that special bond between players on a football team.

The bottom line on all of these honors is that they are actually wonderful tributes to the university. It reflects well on the university, the staff, and everybody who feels a sense of pride in Georgia. Ultimately it is Georgia that is being honored the most.

Even now that I am officially no longer an employee of the University of Georgia, there is still so much to do. Back in March I represented the university in the St. Patrick's Day Parade in Savannah. People still come by almost every day with something for me to sign. Right now I have stacks and stacks of football memorabilia that people want auto-graphed. I still have 40 years of files that I need to go through at some point, and I continue to make regular appearances on sports radio and television. I still get numerous requests for appearances, not to men-tion the fact that I still chair the NCAA Football Issues Committee, though that duty will soon come to an end.

The good news is that I have been given the office at the Smith Center to use for as long as I see fit. I appreciate the fact that Damon went before the athletic board and made the request. I know that took some gumption, given the fact that I had previously received a letter saying I would *not* have this office after July 1, 2005.

I appreciate Damon going before the board, but I also believe that it was the right and fair thing to do. If you look at a comparable situation—Dean Smith at North Carolina or Darrell Royal at Texas, for example—someone in my position can be an asset to the university. And that's what I want to be for as long as I can.

I guess everything I really want to say at this point was included in a letter I wrote to our fans that was published in newspapers around the state. I also think it is the best way to conclude this book.

Vince Dooley's Final Letter to Georgia's Fans and Supporters

My career in athletics has been a marvelous and rewarding journey.

I have truly wonderful memories of all the individuals I have had the privilege of being associated with over a 52-year period—the student-athletes, coaches, staff, fans, and supporters.

I have had the great privilege of being involved in intercollegiate athletics for more than five decades—four years as a student-athlete, eight years as an assistant football coach, 25 years as a head football coach, and 25 years as an athletic director, all in the Southeastern Conference.

Such a long tenure obviously afforded me the opportunity to observe many changes in intercollegiate athletics, all for the better.

As a head coach, I saw the integration of intercollegiate athletics in the South. In fact, the first black student-athlete to compete for Georgia was Maxie Foster, who walked on for the track team in 1968, later earned a scholarship, and became the first black student to graduate with a degree in health and physical education. He and some other special individuals, especially in football and basketball, were real pioneers for Georgia athletics and the Southeastern Conference.

Likewise, there have been great strides in the hiring of African-American coaches and administrators. At UGA, we hired Tubby Smith in 1995 to head our men's basketball program, and currently we are fortunate to have Dennis Felton in the same capacity. And I am proud that our new athletic director, Damon Evans, will be taking over in July. He not only will be a great administrator first and foremost, but is also an African-American football letterman and a graduate of UGA.

Another dramatic change was the passage of Title IX, which certainly had the greatest influence in reshaping athletics programs and providing enormous opportunities for women to participate in sports. I became athletic director just as the tidal wave of the integration of women into intercollegiate athletics was having its greatest impact.

My first job as athletic director was to hire our first full-time women's basketball coach. That person was Andy Landers, and he is still our basketball coach today after 25 years, and is recognized as one of the truly great coaches in the country. It has been a rewarding experience to watch the increased participation of women in sports at Georgia and all over the country, providing the opportunities for them to follow their dreams.

I also have watched the increased proficiency of coaches in all sports around the country through professional associations, detailed study, and work habits. There is no comparison between the coaches of today in all of our sports as opposed to those of just 20 years ago. I have seen it particularly in football and especially in the passing game, though the basic fundamentals of the game are just the same today as they were 48 years ago when I began coaching. The fundamentals will always remain the same.

There is one good attribute I believe I have and that is the ability to hire good people. I have been blessed, with rare exceptions, with a quality and talented group of coaches and administrators.

I always speak in terms of rewards as opposed to achievements. Over a period of 40 years at Georgia, there are a lot of things to feel good about. The thrill of victory and winning championships certainly has provided special memories. The construction of excellent facilities over a long period of time also is rewarding. Hiring coaches, giving them the resources to succeed, and watching them succeed at the highest level has also been rewarding.

Watching athletic teams, some of which I coached, and our administrative teams work together in a cooperative effort toward common goals is a special reward.

There are so many, but what becomes increasingly more important than the victories, the championships, and the facilities is the association with student-athletes, coaches, and administrators.

Perhaps the greatest reward of all, which is particularly special to coaches and teachers, is when one of your student-athletes at some point in time down the road, says to you two meaningful words: "Thanks, Coach."

I am proud to have served and as always is the case, you get so much more than what you give from the experience. All of my experiences have helped me grow as a teacher, coach, and administrator. The great part of it all is that it is not over yet. I am still excited, motivated, and optimistic about the future, and I intend to continue to be active and serve where I can to still reap the rewards of being part of intercollegiate athletics.

—Vincent J. Dooley
Athens, Georgia

Appendix I

Chronology

- 1932: On September 4, Vincent Joseph Dooley is born in Mobile, Alabama.

- 1949: With Vince Dooley at quarterback, McGill High School wins Mobile City championship in football. He captains two city basketball championship teams, and his teams finish second and third in the state tournament, where he sets a state scoring record.

- 1950: Vince Dooley graduates from McGill in Mobile. Dooley accepts a football scholarship to Auburn University.

- 1951: As a sophomore, Dooley starts at defensive back for Auburn and is named second-team All-SEC. He is also the starting guard on the Auburn basketball team.

- 1952: Dooley becomes the starting quarterback at Auburn as a junior. He leads the team to a 13–7 upset of Maryland in the season opener. Dooley injures his knee which curtails his playing time.

- 1953: As captain, Dooley leads Auburn to a 7–2–1 record and a berth in the Gator Bowl, where he is named the game's most valuable player.

- 1954: Dooley graduates from Auburn with a bachelor's degree in business management and plays in the College All-Star Game in Chicago. After the game, he reports for duty at the United States Marine Corps base in Quantico, Virginia. After training in Quantico, Dooley is assigned to Parris Island, South Carolina. He plays for the football team at Quantico and coaches at Parris Island.

He serves eight years in the Marine Corps reserves, attaining the rank of captain before becoming head football coach at Georgia.

- 1956: Dooley returns to Auburn after two years of military service. For the next five years he serves as quarterbacks coach for Ralph "Shug" Jordan.

- 1960: On March 19, Dooley marries the former Barbara Meshad of Birmingham, Alabama.

- 1961: Hoping that it will move him a step closer to becoming a head coach, Dooley becomes the head freshman coach and director of scouting. In three years Dooley coaches two undefeated freshman teams.

- 1963: On December 4, Dooley is named the new head coach at Georgia, replacing Johnny Griffith. At 31 years old, he is the nation's youngest head coach. He also earns his master's degree in history that year.

- 1964: On September 26, Dooley records his first victory as head coach, 7-0 over Vanderbilt in Nashville; on December 26, Georgia defeats Texas Tech 7-0 in the Sun Bowl to give Dooley a 7-3-1 record in his first season as coach.

- 1965: On September 18, Georgia upsets Alabama, the defending national champions, 18-17 in the season opener.

- 1966: On November 12, Georgia wins its first SEC championship under Dooley by beating Auburn 21-13 at Auburn.

- 1968: On November 16, Georgia wins its second SEC championship under Dooley, again by winning at Auburn (17-3); in December, Bill Stanfill is named Georgia's first-ever Outland Trophy winner.

- 1971: On December 31, Georgia defeats North Carolina 7-0 in the Gator Bowl to give the Bulldogs an 11-1 season. It is the only meeting between Dooley and his brother, Bill, the head coach at North Carolina.

- 1975: The "Junkyard Dawgs" defense is born, and it leads Georgia to a 9–2 regular season and a berth in the Cotton Bowl.

- 1976: After shaving their heads as a show of solidarity, Georgia goes 10–1 during the regular season to win Dooley's third SEC championship.

- 1977: On September 24, Dooley wins his 100th game as Georgia defeats South Carolina 15–13 in Columbia.

- 1978: Georgia posts a 9–2–1 season, including four victories by a total of six points. Because of their ability to win close games, this team is tagged the "Wonder Dawgs."

- 1979: On July 1, Dooley becomes Georgia's athletic director in addition to his duties as head football coach.

- 1980: On Easter Sunday, running back Herschel Walker of Wrightsville signs with the University of Georgia; after beating Florida 26–21 with a miracle play in Jacksonville, Georgia beats Auburn 31–21 to give Dooley his fourth SEC championship; on November 29, a 38–20 win over Georgia Tech makes Georgia the nation's only unbeaten, untied team at 11–0; Dooley is named NCAA National Head Coach of the Year.

- 1981: On January 1, with President Jimmy Carter looking on, Georgia defeats Notre Dame 17–10 to give the Bulldogs their first consensus national championship; on November 14, Georgia defeats Auburn 24–13 to give Dooley his fifth SEC championship.

- 1982: On November 13, Dooley wins his sixth SEC championship with a 19–14 victory at Auburn. After a 38–18 victory over Georgia Tech on November 27, Georgia is 11–0 and ranked No. 1 in the nation. On December 4, Herschel Walker wins the Heisman Trophy.

- 1983: On January 1, No. 2 Penn State defeats No. 1 Georgia 27-23 in the Sugar Bowl for the national championship.

- 1984: On January 2, Georgia upsets No. 2 Texas 10-9 in the Cotton Bowl to give the Bulldogs a 10-1-1 record. Georgia completes the best four-year run in its history, going 43-4-1 from 1980 to 1983.

- 1985: In January, Dooley is named president of the American Football Coaches Association after serving for nine years as AFCA Ethics Committee Chairman.

- 1988: On November 26, Dooley wins his 200th career game, beating Georgia Tech 24-3 in Sanford Stadium. On December 14, Dooley announces that he is retiring as head coach after 25 seasons.

- 1989: On January 1 in Jacksonville, Dooley records his 201st and last victory, a 34-27 win over Michigan State in the Gator Bowl. Dooley completes his career with a record of 201-77-10. The next day, Ray Goff is named Georgia's new head coach.

- 1994: On December 6, Dooley becomes the first Georgia head coach to be inducted into the College Football Hall of Fame; earlier that year he is named chairman of NCAA Football Issues Committee.

- 1995: Dooley is named President of the NCAA Division I-A athletic directors.

- 1996: Georgia's Sanford Stadium becomes the women's soccer venue for the 1996 Summer Olympics.

- 1997: Dooley is named to Honors Court, National Football Foundation, and College Hall of Fame. The Court selects each year's class into the Hall of Fame.

- 1999: Dooley is named president of the National Association of Collegiate Directors of Athletics (NACDA); Georgia's athletics department finishes second in the Sears Cup, which goes to the nation's best overall athletic program. Georgia's teams win four national championships in the 1998-1999 academic year.

- 2001: Dooley receives Amos Alonzo Stagg award for lifetime achievement in college football; he is named NACDA Division I-A Southeast Regional Athletic Director of the Year.

- 2002: On December 7, Georgia defeats Arkansas 30-3 to win its first SEC football championship since 1982 and its first since Dooley retired as coach.

- 2004: Dooley receives James J. Corbett Memorial award, the highest honor given by NACDA; on June 30, Dooley officially retires as Georgia's athletic director; in December, Dooley receives the John L. Toner award from the National Football Foundation and College Hall of Fame for his contributions to football.

- 2005: In January Dooley is inducted into the *Georgia Trend* magazine Hall of Fame; on March 4, Dooley receives the Francis J. "Reds" Bagnell award from the Maxwell Foundation in Philadelphia; on March 5, Dooley receives the Frank Sinkwich award from the Touchdown Club of Atlanta; on April 15 Dooley receives the Bob Woodruff award from the Knoxville Quarterback Club. After serving as a consultant and fund-raiser for one year, June 30 was Vince Dooley's last day on the payroll at the University of Georgia. He will retain an office at the Smith Center for as long as he wants it.

Appendix II

Vince Dooley's Top 10 Wins at Georgia

10. Georgia 28, Georgia Tech 24
November 25, 1971, in Atlanta
Georgia trailed 24–21 and had the ball on its own 35-yard line with just 1:29 to go. That's when sophomore quarterback Andy Johnson engineered one of the most famous drives in Georgia history. To do it, Johnson had to complete a fourth-down pass to Mike Greene, which gave Georgia a first down at Tech's 25-yard line with 48 seconds left. After a pass down to the 1-yard line with time running out, running back Jimmy Poulos jumped over the top of the Tech defense for the winning score with only 14 seconds left.

9. Georgia 29, Georgia Tech 28
December 2, 1978, in Athens
This is considered by many to be the best game ever played between these two old state rivals. Georgia Tech jumped out to a 20–0 lead at Sanford Stadium only to see Georgia rally to take a 21–20 lead after Scott Woerner's punt return for a touchdown. Georgia Tech's Drew Hill then returned the ensuing kickoff 101 yards for a touchdown and Tech led 28–21 after a successful two-point conversion. But freshman quarterback Buck Belue threw a touchdown pass on fourth down and Amp Arnold ran for a two-point conversion to give Georgia the dramatic win.

8. Georgia 21, Auburn 13
November 12, 1966, at Auburn
Georgia needed just one more victory to give Dooley his first SEC championship but trailed Auburn 13–0 at halftime. Georgia dominated the second half with three long touchdown drives to win the

game and Georgia's first SEC title since 1959. Georgia would go on to face SMU in the Cotton Bowl.

7. *Georgia 41, Florida 27*
November 6, 1976, in Jacksonville
Florida was in position to win its first-ever SEC championship as it led the Bulldogs 27-13 at halftime. Florida was still leading 27-20 when it went for a fourth down on short yardage deep in its own territory. Georgia stopped the fourth down play and went on to roll over the Gators. The next week Georgia beat Auburn to clinch the SEC championship.

6. *Georgia 15, Michigan 7*
October 2, 1965, in Ann Arbor, Michigan
Georgia was given no chance against the bigger, stronger Wolverines, who played at home before more than one hundred thousand fans. But the Bulldogs proved to be quicker and tougher than Michigan, the defending Rose Bowl champions. More than ten thousand people came to the Athens airport to welcome the team back home.

5. *Georgia 18, Alabama 17*
September 18, 1965, in Athens
With a national television audience looking on, Georgia trailed the defending national champions 17-10 late in the game. Dooley called the famous flea flicker play as Kirby Moore threw to Pat Hodgson, who lateralled back to Bob Taylor, who ran for the touchdown. Dooley immediately called for the two-point conversion attempt, which Georgia made to upset the Crimson Tide. It was Dooley's first major upset as Georgia's head coach.

4. *Georgia 21, Alabama 0*
October 2, 1976, in Athens
Alabama was the dominant program in college football in the seventies, but when they came to Sanford Stadium, the Crimson Tide was dominated by the Bulldogs. The victory touched off one of the wildest celebrations in school history and launched Georgia to the SEC championship.

3. *Georgia 26, Florida 21*
   November 8, 1980, in Jacksonville

Georgia was undefeated and ranked No. 2 when it went to Jacksonville to play the Gators. The Bulldogs trailed 21–20 and had the ball on their 7-yard line with a little over one minute left. On third down Buck Belue threw to Lindsay Scott in the middle of the field, and Scott never stopped running until he scored. The next Monday Georgia was ranked No. 1 and then went on to win the national title.

2. *Georgia 10, Texas 9*
   January 1, 1984, Cotton Bowl

Georgia trailed the entire game until it recovered a fumbled punt in the final minutes. On third down, John Lastinger ran 17 yards for a touchdown to give the Bulldogs a huge upset and deny No. 2 Texas the national championship.

1. *Georgia 17, Notre Dame 10*
   January 1, 1981, Sugar Bowl

The national media gave undefeated Georgia little chance against the Fighting Irish, but Herschel Walker recovered from a dislocated shoulder suffered early in the game to run for 150 yards and two touchdowns. Scott Woerner intercepted two passes to stop Notre Dame scoring threats while Georgia turned a blocked field goal and two other turnovers into 17 points. With the win, Georgia finished its season 12–0 and gave Dooley his only national championship.

Appendix III

Vince Dooley's All-SEC Players and All-Americans

All-SEC Players

1964
T	Jim Wilson, AP, UPI Second Team
DB	Wayne Swinford, AP
OT	Ray Rissmiller, AP Second Team, UPI Second Team
DT	George Patton, AP Second Team
E	Barry Wilson, AP Second Team

1965
DT	George Patton, AP, UPI
DB	Lynn Hughes, AP, UPI
E	Pat Hodgson, AP Second Team

1966
OT	Edgar Chandler, AP, UPI
C	Don Hayes, AP
E	Larry Kohn, AP
DT	George Patton, AP, UPI
DB	Lynn Hughes, AP, UPI
RB	Ronnie Jenkins, AP Second Team, UPI
DT	Bill Stanfill, AP Second Team

1967
OT	Edgar Chandler, AP, UPI
FB	Ronnie Jenkins, AP
DT	Bill Stanfill, AP, UPI
DB	Jake Scott, AP
OG	Don Hayes, AP Second Team

1968

E	Dennis Hughes, AP
OT	David Rholetter, AP, UPI
DE	Billy Payne, AP, UPI
DT	Bill Stanfill, AP, UPI
DB	Jake Scott, AP, UPI
P	Spike Jones, AP
QB	Mike Cavan, AP Second Team
FL	Kent Lawrence, AP Second Team
PK	Jim McCullough, AP Second Team
LB	Happy Dicks, AP Second Team

1969

DG	Steve Greer, AP, UPI
LB	Chip Wisdom, AP Second Team
P	Spike Jones, AP

1970

OG	Royce Smith, AP
DB	Buzy Rosenberg, AP
C	Tommy Lyons, AP Second Team, UPI
PK	Kim Braswell, AP Second Team
DE	Chuck Heard, AP Second Team
T	Larry Brasher, AP Second Team
LB	Chip Wisdom, AP Second Team
OT	Tom Nash, UPI

1971

OT	Tom Nash, AP, UPI
OG	Royce Smith, AP, UPI
C	Kendall Keith, AP
DB	Buzy Rosenberg, AP, UPI
QB	Andy Johnson, AP Second Team
DE	Mixon Robinson, AP Second Team, UPI
DT	Chuck Heard, AP Second Team
LB	Chip Wisdom, AP Second Team, UPI

1972

C   Chris Hammond, AP Second Team

1973

OG   Mac McWhorter, AP

DG   Danny Jones, AP Second Team

1974

OT   Craig Hertwig, AP, UPI

RB   Glynn Harrison, AP

WR   Gene Washington, AP Second Team

TE   Richard Appleby, AP Second Team

RB   Horace King, AP Second Team

E   David McKnight, AP Second Team

LB   Sylvester Boler, AP Second Team

OG   Randy Johnson, UPI

1975

OG   Randy Johnson, AP, UPI

RB   Glynn Harrison, AP, UPI

OT   Mike Wilson, AP Second Team

RB   Kevin McLee, AP Second Team

LB   Ben Zambiasi, AP Second Team

DB   Bill Krug, AP Second Team

1976

OT   Mike Wilson, AP, UPI

OG   Joel Parrish, AP, UPI

QB   Ray Goff, AP, UPI

RB   Kevin McLee, AP, UPI

PK   Allan Leavitt, AP

LB   Ben Zambiasi, AP, UPI

DB   Bill Krug, AP, UPI

WR   Gene Washington, AP Second Team

DE   Dicky Clark, UPI

1977
DT   Ronnie Swoopes, AP
LB   Ben Zambiasi, AP, UPI
OG   George Collins, AP Second Team, UPI
DB   Bill Krug, AP Second Team, UPI

1978
G   Mack Guest, AP
RB   Willie McClendon, AP, UPI
LB   Ricky McBride, AP
G   Matt Braswell, AP Second Team, UPI
PK   Rex Robinson, AP Second Team, UPI

1979
OG   Matt Braswell, AP, UPI
C   Ray Donaldson, AP
PK   Rex Robinson, AP, UPI

1980
OT   Tim Morrison, AP, UPI
QB   Buck Belue, AP
RB   Herschel Walker, AP, UPI
DB   Jeff Hipp, AP, UPI
PK   Rex Robinson, AP, UPI
DB   Scott Woerner, AP, UPI
DG   Eddie Weaver, AP
OG   Nat Hudson, AP Second Team, UPI
DT   Jimmy Payne, UPI

1981
WR   Lindsay Scott, AP, UPI
QB   Buck Belue, AP, UPI
RB   Herschel Walker, AP, UPI
DT   Jimmy Payne, AP
OT   Jimmy Harper, AP Second Team
C   Joe Happe, AP Second Team
RB   Ronnie Stewart, AP Second Team
PK   Kevin Butler, AP Second Team, UPI

1981, cont.
- DG   Eddie Weaver, AP Second Team, UPI
- LB   Tommy Thurson, AP Second Team

1982
- C   Wayne Radloff, AP, UPI
- RB   Herschel Walker, AP, UPI
- DE   Freddie Gilbert, AP, UPI
- LB   Tommy Thurson, AP, UPI
- DB   Terry Hoage, AP, UPI
- DB   Jeff Sanchez, AP, UPI
- OG   Guy McIntyre, AP Second Team
- PK   Kevin Butler, AP Second Team
- OT   Jimmy Harper, UPI
- DT   Jimmy Payne, UPI

1983
- OG   Guy McIntyre, AP, UPI
- PK   Kevin Butler, AP, UPI
- DE   Freddie Gilbert, AP, UPI
- DB   Terry Hoage, AP, UPI
- TE   Clarence Kay, AP Second Team
- OG   Winford Hood, AP Second Team
- LB   Knox Culpepper, AP Second Team
- LB   Tommy Thurson, AP Second Team, UPI

1984
- PK   Kevin Butler, AP, UPI, Coaches
- LB   Knox Culpepper, AP, UPI, Coaches
- DB   Jeff Sanchez, AP, UPI, Coaches
- C   Pete Anderson, AP
- DT   Kenny Sims, AP Second Team

1985
- C   Peter Anderson, AP, Coaches
- DE   Greg Waters, AP, Coaches
- DB   John Little, AP, UPI, Coaches
- DB   Tony Flack, UPI

1986

OT	Wilbur Strozier, AP, UPI, Coaches
DB	John Little, AP, UPI
RB	Lars Tate, AP Second Team, UPI
DT	Henry Harris, AP Second Team, UPI
LB	John Brantley, AP Second Team
P	Cris Carpenter, AP Second Team

1987

OG	Kim Stephens, AP, Coaches
LB	John Brantley, AP
RB	Lars Tate, AP Second Team, UPI

1988

C	Todd Wheeler, AP, UPI, Coaches
RB	Tim Worley, AP, UPI, Coaches
TE	Troy Sadowski, AP Second Team
OT	Scott Adams, AP Second Team
RB	Rodney Hampton, AP Second Team
LB	Terrie Webster, AP Second Team
OLB	Richard Tardits, AP Second Team, UPI
DB	Ben Smith, AP Second Team, Coaches
DT	Bill Goldberg, UPI, Coaches

All-American Players

Jim Wilson, T, Pittsburgh, Pennsylvania
1964 (AP, NEA, FWAA-Look, Helms, Sports Extra)

Ray Rissmiller, T, Easton, Pennsylvania
1964 (Time, Sporting News)

George Patton, DT, Tuscumbia, Alabama
1965 (AP, FWAA, Look, FB News)

Edgar Chandler, OG, Cedartown, Georgia
1966 (NEA)
1967 (AP, UPI, NEA, CP, FWAA, Look, Coaches, Time,
    Sporting News, FB News)

Lynn Hughes, SAF, Atlanta, Georgia
1966 (Playboy)

Bill Stanfill, DT, Cairo, Georgia
1968 (AP, UPI, CP, FWAA-Look, Coaches, Sporting News,
    FB News, NY News, Walter Camp, Time, Playboy, Kodak)

Jake Scott, SAF, Arlington, Virginia
1968 (AP, UPI, NEWS, FWAA-Look, Coaches, FB News,
    NY News, Walter Camp, Playboy, Kodak)

Steve Greer, DG, Greer, South Carolina
1969 (FB News, Sports Extra)

Tommy Lyons, C, Atlanta, Georgia
1969 (Sports Extra)
1970 (Sports Extra)

Royce Smith, OG, Savannah, Georgia
1971 (AP, UPI, NEW, CP, FWAA, Coaches, Walter Camp,
    Sporting News, FB News, Time, Playboy, Kodak)

Craig Hertwig, OT, Macon, Georgia
1974 (AP)

Randy Johnson, OG, Rome, Georgia
1975 (AP, UPI, Coaches, Walter Camp, Family Weekly, Kodak)

Mike "Moonpie" Wilson, OT, Gainesville, Georgia
1976 (AP, NEA)

Joel Parrish, OG, Douglas, Georgia
1976 (UPI, FWAA, Coaches, Walter Camp, FB News, Kodak,
    Playboy)

Ben Zambiasi, LB, Macon, Georgia
1976 (Family Weekly)

Allan Leavitt, PK, Brooksville, Florida
1976 (FB Digest)

George Collins, OG, Warner Robins, Georgia
1977 (Sporting News)

Bill Krug, ROV, Washington, D.C.
1977 (Playboy)

Rex Robinson, PK, Marietta, Georgia
1979 (Playboy)
1980 (UPI, FWAA, Playboy, FB News, NEA, Walter Camp)

Scott Woerner, CB, Jonesboro, Georgia
1980 (UPI, Kodak, Walter Camp, FB News)

Herschel Walker, TB, Wrightsville, Georgia
1980 (AP, UPI, Kodak, FWAA, Walter Camp, FB News,
    Sporting News, NEA)
1981 (AP, UPI, Kodak, FWAA, Walter Camp, FB News,
    Sporting News, NEA, Playboy)
1982 (AP, UPI, Kodak, FWAA, Walter Camp, FB News,
    Sporting News, NEA, Playboy)

Terry Hoage, ROV, Huntsville, Texas
1982 (AP, Kodak, Walter Camp, Sporting News, NEA, UPI)
1983 (NEA, UPI, Kodak, FWAA, Walter Camp, FB News,
    Sporting News, Playboy)

Jimmy Payne, DT, Athens, Georgia
1982 (Playboy, Walter Camp)

Freddie Gilbert, DE, Griffin, Georgia
1983 (UPI)

Kevin Butler, PK, Stone Mountain, Georgia
1983 (FB News)
1984 (Kodak, UPI, FWAA, Walter Camp, FB News, Sporting
    News, NEA)

Jeff Sanchez, SAF, Yorba Linda, California
1984 (Kodak, UPI, FWAA, Walter Camp)

Peter Anderson, C, Vineland, New Jersey
1985 (AP, UPI, Kodak Sporting News)

John Little, SAF, Lynn Haven, Florida
1985 (Football News)
1986 (Walter Camp, FB News)

Wilbur Strozier, OT, LaGrange, Georgia
1986 (Football News)

Tim Worley, TB, Lumberton, North Carolina
1988 (Kodak, Walter Camp, FWAA)

Troy Sadowski, TE, Chamblee, Georgia
1988 (Walter Camp)

Appendix IV

Year-by-Year Scores

1964 (7–3–1)   Captain: Barry Wilson, DE

9/19	3	Alabama	31	Tuscaloosa, AL
9/26	7	Vanderbilt	0	Nashville, TN
10/3	7	S. Carolina	7	Columbia, SC
10/10	19	Clemson	7	Athens
10/17	14	Florida State	17	Athens
10/24	21	Kentucky	7	Athens
10/31	24	N. Carolina	8	Athens
11/7	14	Florida	7	Jacksonville, FL
11/14	7	Auburn	14	Auburn, AL
11/28	7	Georgia Tech	0	Athens

Sun Bowl

12/26	7	Texas Tech	0	El Paso, TX

1965 (6–4–0)   Captain: Doug McFalls, DB

9/18	18	Alabama	17	Athens
9/25	24	Vanderbilt	10	Athens
10/2	15	Michigan	7	Ann Arbor, MI
10/9	23	Clemson	9	Athens
10/16	3	Florida State	10	Tallahassee, FL
10/23	10	Kentucky	28	Lexington, KY
10/30	47	N. Carolina	35	Chapel Hill, NC
11/6	10	Florida	14	Jacksonville, FL
11/13	19	Auburn	21	Athens
11/27	17	Georgia Tech	7	Atlanta

1966 (10–1–0, SEC Champions) Captain: George Patton, T

9/17	20	Miss. State	17	Jackson, MS
9/24	43	VMI	7	Roanoke, VA
10/1	7	S. Carolina	0	Columbia, SC
10/8	9	Ole Miss	3	Athens
10/14	6	Miami	7	Miami, FL
10/22	27	Kentucky	15	Athens
10/29	28	N. Carolina	3	Athens
11/5	27	Florida	10	Jacksonville, FL
11/12	21	Auburn	13	Auburn, AL
11/26	23	Georgia Tech	14	Athens

Cotton Bowl

12/31	24	SMU	9	Dallas, TX

1967 (7–4–0) Captain: Kirby Moore, QB

9/23	30	Miss. State	0	Athens
9/30	24	Clemson	17	Clemson, SC
10/7	21	S. Carolina	0	Athens
10/14	20	Ole Miss	29	Jackson, MS
10/21	56	VMI	6	Athens
10/28	31	Kentucky	7	Lexington, KY
11/4	14	Houston	15	Houston, TX
11/11	16	Florida	17	Jacksonville, FL
11/18	17	Auburn	0	Athens
11/25	21	Georgia Tech	14	Atlanta

Liberty Bowl

12/16	7	N.C. State	14	Memphis, TN

1968 (8–1–2, National Champions, SEC Champions)   Captain: Bill Stanfill, T

9/14	17	Tennessee	17	Knoxville, TN
9/28	31	Clemson	13	Athens
10/5	21	S. Carolina	20	Columbia, SC
10/12	21	Ole Miss	7	Athens
10/19	32	Vanderbilt	6	Athens
10/26	35	Kentucky	14	Lexington, KY
11/2	10	Houston	10	Athens
11/9	51	Florida	0	Jacksonville, FL
11/16	17	Auburn	3	Auburn, AL
11/30	47	Georgia Tech	8	Athens

Sugar Bowl

1/1/69	2	Arkansas	16	New Orleans, LA

1969 (5–5–1)   Captain: Steve Greer, DG

9/20	35	Tulane	0	Athens
9/27	30	Clemson	0	Clemson, SC
10/4	41	S. Carolina	16	Athens
10/11	17	Ole Miss	25	Jackson, MS
10/18	40	Vanderbilt	8	Nashville, TN
10/25	30	Kentucky	0	Athens
11/1	3	Tennessee	17	Athens
11/8	13	Florida	13	Jacksonville, FL
11/15	3	Auburn	16	Athens
11/29	0	Georgia Tech	6	Atlanta

Sun Bowl

12/20	6	Nebraska	45	El Paso, TX

1970 (5–5–0)   Captain: Tommy Lyons, C

9/19	14	Tulane	17	New Orleans, LA
9/26	38	Clemson	0	Athens
10/3	6	Miss. State	7	Jackson, MS
10/10	21	Ole Miss	31	Athens
10/17	37	Vanderbilt	3	Athens
10/24	19	Kentucky	3	Lexington, KY
10/31	52	S. Carolina	34	Athens
11/7	17	Florida	24	Jacksonville, FL
11/14	31	Auburn	17	Auburn, AL
11/28	7	Georgia Tech	17	Athens

1971 (11–1–0)   Captain: Royce Smith, OG

9/11	56	Oregon State	25	Athens
9/18	17	Tulane	7	Athens
9/25	28	Clemson	0	Clemson, SC
10/2	35	Miss. State	7	Athens
10/9	38	Ole Miss	7	Jackson, MS
10/16	24	Vanderbilt	0	Nashville, TN
10/23	34	Kentucky	0	Athens
10/30	24	S. Carolina	0	Columbia, SC
11/6	49	Florida	7	Jacksonville, FL
11/13	20	Auburn	35	Athens
11/25	28	Georgia Tech	24	Atlanta

Gator Bowl

12/31	7	N. Carolina	3	Jacksonville, FL

1972 (7–4–0)   Captain: Robert Honeycutt, FB

9/16	24	Baylor	14	Athens
9/23	13	Tulane	24	New Orleans, LA
9/30	28	N.C. State	22	Athens
10/7	7	Alabama	25	Athens
10/14	14	Ole Miss	13	Jackson, MS
10/21	28	Vanderbilt	3	Athens
10/28	13	Kentucky	7	Lexington, KY
11/4	0	Tennessee	1	Athens
11/11	10	Florida	7	Jacksonville, FL
11/18	10	Auburn	27	Auburn, AL
12/2	27	Georgia Tech	7	Athens

1973 (7–4—1)   Captain: Bob Burns, FB

9/15	7	Pittsburgh	7	Athens
9/22	31	Clemson	14	Athens
9/29	31	N.C. State	12	Athens
10/6	14	Alabama	28	Tuscaloosa, AL
10/13	20	Ole Miss	0	Athens
10/20	14	Vanderbilt	18	Nashville, TN
10/27	7	Kentucky	12	Athens
11/3	35	Tennessee	31	Knoxville, TN
11/10	10	Florida	11	Jacksonville, FL
11/17	28	Auburn	14	Athens
12/1	10	Georgia Tech	3	Atlanta

Peach Bowl

12/28	17	Maryland	16	Atlanta

1974 (6–6–0)   Captain: Keith Harris, LB

9/14	48	Oregon State	35	Athens
9/21	14	Miss. State	38	Jackson, MS
9/28	52	S. Carolina	14	Athens
10/5	24	Clemson	28	Clemson, SC
10/12	49	Ole Miss	0	Athens
10/19	38	Vanderbilt	31	Athens
10/26	24	Kentucky	20	Lexington, KY
11/2	24	Houston	31	Athens
11/9	17	Florida	16	Jacksonville, FL
11/16	13	Auburn	17	Auburn, AL
11/30	14	Georgia Tech	34	Athens

Tangerine Bowl

12/20	10	Miami (Ohio)	21	Orlando, FL

1975 (9–3–0)   Captain: Glynn Harrison, RB

9/6	9	Pittsburgh	19	Athens
9/20	28	Miss. State	6	Athens
9/27	28	S. Carolina	20	Columbia, SC
10/4	35	Clemson	7	Athens
10/11	13	Ole Miss	28	Oxford, MS
10/18	47	Vanderbilt	3	Nashville, TN
10/25	21	Kentucky	13	Athens
11/1	28	Richmond	24	Athens
11/8	10	Florida	7	Jacksonville, FL
11/15	28	Auburn	13	Athens
11/27	42	Georgia Tech	26	Atlanta

Cotton Bowl

1/1/76	10	Arkansas	31	Dallas, TX

1976 (10–2–0, SEC Champions)   Captain: Ray Goff, QB

9/11	36	California	24	Athens
9/18	41	Clemson	0	Clemson, SC
9/25	20	S. Carolina	12	Athens
10/2	21	Alabama	0	Athens
10/9	17	Ole Miss	21	Oxford, MS
10/16	45	Vanderbilt	0	Athens
10/23	31	Kentucky	7	Lexington, KY
10/30	31	Cincinnati	17	Athens
11/6	41	Florida	27	Jacksonville, FL
11/13	28	Auburn	0	Auburn, AL
11/27	13	Georgia Tech	10	Athens

Sugar Bowl

1/1/77	3	Pittsburgh	27	New Orleans, LA

1977 (5–6–0)   Captain: Ben Zambiasi, LB

9/10	27	Oregon	16	Athens
9/17	6	Clemson	7	Athens
9/24	15	S. Carolina	13	Columbia, SC
10/1	10	Alabama	18	Tuscaloosa, AL
10/8	14	Ole Miss	13	Athens
10/15	24	Vanderbilt	13	Nashville, TN
10/22	0	Kentucky	33	Athens
10/29	23	Richmond	7	Athens
11/5	17	Florida	22	Jacksonville, FL
11/12	14	Auburn	33	Athens
11/26	7	Georgia Tech	16	Atlanta

1978 (9–2–1)   Captain: Willie McClendon, TB

9/16	16	Baylor	14	Athens
9/23	12	Clemson	0	Athens
9/30	10	S. Carolina	27	Columbia, SC
10/7	42	Ole Miss	3	Athens
10/14	24	LSU	17	Baton Rouge, LA
10/21	31	Vanderbilt	10	Athens
10/28	17	Kentucky	16	Lexington, KY
11/4	41	VMI	3	Athens
11/11	24	Florida	22	Jacksonville, FL
11/18	22	Auburn, AL	22	Auburn
12/2	29	Georgia Tech	28	Athens

Bluebonnet Bowl

12/31	22	Stanford	25	Houston, TX

1979 (6–5–0)   Captain: Gordon Terry, DE

9/15	21	Wake Forest	22	Athens
9/22	7	Clemson	12	Clemson, SC
9/29	20	S. Carolina	27	Athens
10/6	24	Ole Miss	21	Oxford, MS
10/13	21	LSU	14	Athens
10/20	31	Vanderbilt	10	Nashville, TN
10/27	20	Kentucky	6	Athens
11/3	0	Virginia	31	Athens
11/10	33	Florida	10	Jacksonville, FL
11/17	13	Auburn	33	Athens
11/24	16	Georgia Tech	3	Atlanta

1980 (12–0–0, National Champions, SEC Champions) Captain: Frank Ros, LB

9/6	16	Tennessee	15	Knoxville, TN
9/13	42	Texas A&M	0	Athens
9/20	20	Clemson	16	Athens
9/27	34	TCU	3	Athens
10/11	28	Ole Miss	21	Athens
10/18	41	Vanderbilt	0	Athens
10/25	27	Kentucky	0	Lexington, KY
11/1	13	S. Carolina	10	Athens
11/8	26	Florida	21	Jacksonville, FL
11/15	31	Auburn	21	Auburn, AL
11/29	38	Georgia Tech	20	Athens

Sugar Bowl

1/1/81	17	Notre Dame	10	New Orleans, LA

1981 (10–2—0, SEC Champions) Captain: Buck Belue, QB

9/5	44	Tennessee	0	Athens
9/12	27	California	13	Athens
9/19	3	Clemson	13	Clemson, SC
9/26	24	S. Carolina	0	Athens
10/10	37	Ole Miss	7	Oxford, MS
10/17	53	Vanderbilt	21	Nashville, TN
10/24	21	Kentucky	0	Athens
10/31	49	Temple	3	Athens
11/7	26	Florida	21	Jacksonville, FL
11/14	24	Auburn	13	Athens
12/5	44	Georgia Tech	7	Atlanta

Sugar Bowl

1/1/82	20	Pittsburgh	24	New Orleans, LA

1982 (11–1–0, SEC Champions) Captain: Wayne Radloff, C

9/6	13	Clemson	7	Athens
9/11	17	Brigham Young	14	Athens
9/25	34	S. Carolina	18	Columbia, SC
10/2	29	Miss. State	22	Starkville, MS
10/9	33	Ole Miss	10	Athens
10/16	27	Vanderbilt	13	Athens
10/23	27	Kentucky	14	Lexington, KY
10/30	34	Memphis State	3	Athens
11/6	44	Florida	0	Jacksonville, FL
11/13	19	Auburn	14	Auburn, AL
11/27	38	Georgia Tech	18	Athens

Sugar Bowl

1/1/83	23	Penn State	27	New Orleans, LA

1983 (10–1–1) Captain: Freddie Gilbert, DE

9/3	19	UCLA	8	Athens
9/17	16	Clemson	16	Clemson, SC
9/24	31	S. Carolina	13	Athens
10/1	20	Miss. State	7	Athens
10/8	36	Ole Miss	11	Oxford, MS
10/15	20	Vanderbilt	13	Nashville, TN
10/22	47	Kentucky	21	Athens
10/29	31	Temple	14	Athens
11/5	10	Florida	9	Jacksonville, FL
11/12	7	Auburn	13	Athens
11/26	27	Georgia Tech	24	Atlanta

Cotton Bowl

1/2/84	10	Texas	9	Dallas, TX

1984 (7–4–1)   Captain: Knox Culpepper, LB

9/8	26	Southern Miss.	19	Athens
9/22	26	Clemson	23	Athens
9/29	10	S. Carolina	17	Columbia, SC
10/6	24	Alabama	14	Birmingham, AL
10/13	18	Ole Miss	12	Athens
10/20	62	Vanderbilt	35	Athens
10/27	37	Kentucky	7	Lexington, KY
11/3	13	Memphis State	3	Athens
11/10	0	Florida	27	Jacksonville, FL
11/17	12	Auburn	21	Auburn, AL
12/1	18	Georgia Tech	35	Athens
Citrus Bowl				
12/22	17	Florida State	17	Orlando, FL

1985 (7–3–2)   Captain: Peter Anderson, C

9/2	16	Alabama	20	Athens
9/14	17	Baylor	14	Athens
9/21	20	Clemson	13	Clemson, SC
9/28	35	S. Carolina	21	Athens
10/12	49	Ole Miss	21	Jackson, MS
10/19	13	Vanderbilt	13	Nashville, TN
10/26	26	Kentucky	6	Athens
11/2	58	Tulane	3	Athens
11/9	24	Florida	3	Jacksonville, FL
11/16	10	Auburn	24	Athens
11/30	16	Georgia Tech	20	Atlanta
Sun Bowl				
12/28	13	Arizona	13	El Paso, TX

1986 (8–4)   Captain: John Little, SAF

9/13	31	Duke	7	Athens
9/20	28	Clemson	31	Athens
9/27	31	S. Carolina	26	Columbia, SC
10/4	14	Ole Miss	10	Athens
10/11	14	LSU	23	Baton Rouge, LA
10/18	38	Vanderbilt	16	Athens
10/25	31	Kentucky	9	Lexington, KY
11/1	28	Richmond	13	Athens
11/8	19	Florida	31	Jacksonville, FL
11/15	20	Auburn	16	Auburn, AL
11/29	31	Georgia Tech	24	Athens

Hall of Fame Bowl

12/23	24	Boston College	27	Tampa, FL

1987 (9–3)   Captain: Kim Stephens, OG

9/5	30	Virginia	22	Athens
9/12	41	Oregon State	7	Athens
9/19	20	Clemson	21	Clemson, SC
9/26	13	South Carolina	6	Athens
10/3	31	Ole Miss	14	Oxford, MS
10/10	23	LSU	26	Athens
10/17	52	Vanderbilt	24	Nashville, TN
10/24	17	Kentucky	14	Athens
11/7	23	Florida	10	Jacksonville, FL
11/14	11	Auburn	27	Athens
11/28	30	Georgia Tech	16	Atlanta

Liberty Bowl

12/29	20	Arkansas	17	Memphis, TN

1988 (9–3)   Captain: Todd Wheeler, C

9/3	28	Tennessee	17	Athens
9/10	38	TCU	10	Athens
9/17	42	Miss. State	35	Starkville, MS
9/24	10	S. Carolina	23	Columbia, SC
10/1	36	Ole Miss	12	Athens
10/8	41	Vanderbilt	22	Athens
10/22	10	Kentucky	16	Lexington, KY
10/29	59	Wm. & Mary	24	Athens
11/5	26	Florida	3	Jacksonville, FL
11/12	10	Auburn	20	Auburn, AL
11/26	24	Georgia Tech	3	Athens

Mazda Gator Bowl

1/1/89	34	Michigan St.	27	Jacksonville, FL

Index

A

Adams, Mary, 166
Adams, Michael, 7, 8, 58, 142, 160, 163, 165–77, 179, 181–87, 189–91, 199
Adams, Scott, 224
Aderhold, O. C., 151, 164
Akers, Fred, 105
Alabama Sports Hall of Fame, 50
Alexander, Charles, 101
Alexander, Lamar, 186
Allen Armitage Professorship in horticulture, 199
Aloha Bowl, 141, 142
American Football Coaches Association, 59, 140, 212
Amos Alonzo Stagg Award, 213
Anderson, Peter, 12, 13, 223, 227, 239
Andrews, William, 101
Appleby, Richard, 37, 67, 98, 99, 221
Arch Ward Award, 58, 198
Archer, David, 102
Archway to Excellence capital campaign, 177, 188, 189
Armitage, Allen, 199
Arnold, Amp, 101, 102, 215
Athens Banner-Herald, 186, 188
Atlanta Falcons, 44, 115
Atlanta Journal-Constitution, 117, 120, 167, 185, 188
Auburn University, 3, 16, 43, 44, 45, 47, 49, 50, 53, 54, 56, 57, 62, 76, 79, 81, 82, 84, 86, 89, 91, 94, 95, 96, 97, 101, 102, 104, 107, 112, 117–20, 126, 134, 135, 139, 145, 147–53, 161, 195, 196, 202, 209, 210, 211, 215, 216, 229–41
Ayers, Doc, 15, 39, 41

B

Bagnell Award, 194
Baker, Ed, 147
Baker, Howard, 186
Baldowski, Clifford, 117
Bass, Marvin, 61
Bauman, Charlie, 60
Baylor University, 66, 91, 101, 233, 236, 239
Beasley, Terry, 95, 96
Belue, Buck, 13, 30, 50, 85, 88, 89, 102, 215, 217, 222, 237
Bennett, Billy, 197
Bertman, Skip, 195
Bestwick, Dick, 73, 172
Bishop, Bob, 110
Blackledge, Todd, 92
Blanchard, Jim, 188, 189
Bob Woodruff Award, 203, 213
Boler, Sylvester, 221
Boston College, 240
Bowden, Ann, 53
Bowden, Bobby, 53
Brantley, Andy, 200
Brantley, John, 224
Brasher, Larry, 220
Braswell, Kim, 220
Braswell, Matt, 222
Brey, Mike, 172, 173
Brigham Young University (BYU), 14, 90, 91, 238
Brown, James, 54
Brown, John, 89

Broyles, Frank, 48, 151
Bryant, Paul W. "Bear," 54, 55, 56, 57, 79, 107, 109, 153, 163
Buck, Jim, 139
Buckey, Dave, 60
Buckey, Don, 60
Burson, Joe, 93, 94
Busbee, George, 56
Butler, Kevin, 13, 14, 22, 54, 88, 90, 104, 105, 222, 223, 227
Butts, Wallace, 63, 125, 126, 143
Butts-Mehre Heritage Hall, 154, 156, 158, 159, 193, 199

C

Camelot (play), 146
Carlen, Jim, 45
Carpenter, Cris, 224
Carter, Jimmy, 123, 211
Castronis, Mike, 41, 42
Cavan, Mike, 14, 15, 42, 77, 78, 79, 85, 220
Centennial Olympic Park, 69
Centre College, 169
CFL (Canadian Football League) Hall of Fame, 36
Chandler, Edgar, 36, 219, 225
Charles, Prince of Wales, 69, 70
Chilivis, Nick, 56, 118, 123, 169, 170
Chilivis, Patti Tumlin, 56
Circle of Honor, 42, 195
Citrus Bowl, 14, 53, 139, 239
Clark, Dicky, 42, 98, 221
Clemson University, 14, 35, 47, 60, 61, 84, 88-91, 229-40
Cloer, Billy, 94
Cohn & Wolfe, 156
Cole, Tony, 173, 174
Coliseum. See Stegeman Coliseum
College All-Star Game, 68, 148, 209

College Football Association (CFA), 160
College Football Hall of Fame, 13, 20, 32, 63, 88, 143, 152, 203, 212, 213
College of William & Mary, 241
College World Series, 193
Collegiate Tennis Hall of Fame, 65
Collins, George, 15, 21, 222, 226
Contribution to Football Award, 194, 203
Cooper, Ken, 43
Copas, Dick, 43
Corbett Award, 193, 203, 213
Corrigan, Gene, 160
Cotton Bowl, 19, 21, 23, 26, 54, 76, 80, 100, 104, 105, 128, 211, 212, 216, 217, 230, 234, 238
Courson, Ron, 174
Cousins, Tom, 203
Cribbs, Joe, 101
Crumley, Frank, 200
Culpepper, Knox, 15, 16, 223, 239
Culpepper, Knox, Sr., 16
Curci, Fran, 70
Curry, Bill, 52

D

Daniels, Lee, 36
Davison, Fred, 58, 119, 133, 164
Dean, Charlie, 103
Deloitte & Touche, 170
Denney, Jimmy, 12
Denver Broncos, 25, 44
Detroit Lions, 22
Dicharry, Dottie, 147
Dicharry, Ray, 146, 147
Dickey, Doug, 81, 196
Dicks, Happy, 36, 76, 135, 220
Director's Cup, 155, 198. See also Sears Cup

Director's Honor Roll, 156
Dirr, Michael, 199
"Dixie" (song), 62
Dodd, Bobby, 55, 56, 57, 163
Doherty, Matt, 172-73
Donahue, Terry, 103
Donaldson, John, 39, 44, 222
Donnan, Jim, 35, 140, 141, 142, 168,
    169, 170, 171
"Dooley's Junkyard Dawgs," 54
Dooley, Barbara (née Meshad), 1, 2, 6,
    7, 53, 55, 60, 63, 68, 72, 84, 87,
    97, 99, 108, 109, 115, 117, 118,
    121, 134, 135, 138, 141, 149-52,
    195, 203, 210
Dooley, Bill, 39, 43, 44, 61, 66, 96,
    144, 145, 146, 211
Dooley, Daniel, 149-52
Dooley, Deanna, 1, 149-52
Dooley, Denise, 149, 150, 152
Dooley, Derek, 99, 118, 134, 135, 149,
    150
Dooley, Margaret (Dede), 97, 144, 145,
    146
Dooley, Mary Rita, 146
Dooley, Nellie, 144
Dooley, Rosezella, 97, 144, 145, 146
Dooley, Vincent J.
    as athletic director, 2, 3, 58, 63, 119,
        153-57, 160, 161, 162, 193, 206,
        211
    coaching at Auburn, 47, 49, 50, 54,
        117, 148, 149, 151, 210
    considering run for office, 6, 107,
        108, 109, 113, 115, 120-22
    hiring as head football coach, 1, 4,
        39, 50, 72, 151, 193, 210
    as a Marine, 6, 49, 71, 144, 148,
        210
    retirement as athletic director, 162,
        163-91, 193-207

retirement as head football coach,
    16, 51, 107-14, 122, 212
winning 200th game, 108, 212
Dooley, William, 144
Dorsett, Tony, 98
Douglas, John, 138
Duke, Bobby, 147
Duke University, 52, 155, 172, 240
Dukes, Leroy, 36, 194
DuPree, Sterling, 39, 44

E

East Tennessee State University, 14, 42
Eaves, Joel, 40, 55, 66, 78, 79, 103,
    126, 127, 150, 151, 154, 164
Edwards, Lavell, 90
Ellis, Alphonso, 37
Ellis, Elmo, 116
Emory University, 137, 138
Ervin, Leroy, 132, 133
ESPN, 173, 174, 194, 203
Etter, Bobby, 36
Evans, Damon, 58, 159, 165, 172, 174,
    175, 179, 184, 185, 190, 194,
    199-202, 204, 205, 206
"Excellence in Athletics Cup," 155

F

Felton, Claude, 58, 64, 141, 172, 174,
    179, 184, 185, 190, 195, 196,
    198
Felton, Dennis, 206
Fiesta Bowl, 104
Finebaum, Paul, 202
Flack, Tony, 92, 104, 223
Florida State University, 14, 47, 94,
    229, 239
Foley, Jeremy, 196
Folsom, Jim, 120
Ford, Danny, 14
Foster, Maxie, 205

Francis J. "Reds" Bagnell Award, 203, 213
Frank Sinkwich Award, 203, 213
Franklin College of Arts and Sciences, 186–87
Fraschilla, Fran, 172

G

Garrity, Gregg, 92
Gaston, Bobby, 86
Gator Bowl, 44, 60, 93, 94, 96, 109, 112, 113, 127, 209, 210, 212, 232, 241
Georgia Dome, 161, 162
Georgia Southern University, 48, 51, 58, 88, 109
Georgia Student Educational Fund, 46
Georgia Tech, 13, 20, 23, 37, 49, 55, 56, 57, 70, 76, 80, 82, 84, 86, 91, 94, 96, 97, 99, 101, 102, 104, 108, 127, 163, 170, 196, 197, 211, 212, 215, 229–41
Georgia Trend magazine Hall of Fame, 203, 213
Gibbs, Alex, 44, 46, 105
Gilbert, Freddie, 16, 27, 223, 226, 238
Gilbert, Paul, 14
Goff, Ray, 16, 28, 45, 48, 51, 80, 81, 82, 100, 112, 113, 138, 140, 161, 212, 221, 235
Goldberg, Bill, 17, 224
Golden, Don, 95
Goulet, Robert, 146
Graning, Chick, 57
Greene, Mike, 20, 96, 161, 215
Greenway, Rosa, 136
Greer, Steve, 17, 18, 19, 45, 47, 220, 225, 231
Griffith, Jim, 98
Griffith, Johnny, 210
Guest, Mack, 36, 194, 203, 222

H

Haffner, George, 45, 51, 85, 105, 112
Hamilton, Mike, 196
Hammond, Chris, 221
Hampton, Rodney, 18, 224
Happe, Joe, 222
Harper, Jimmy, 222, 223
Harrick, Jim, 172–75
Harrick, Jim, Jr., 173, 174
Harris, Henry, 224
Harris, Keith, 234
Harris, Ronnie, 89
Harrison, Bob, 45
Harrison, Glynn, 18, 19, 221, 234
Hartman, Bill, 45, 112, 113
Hayes, Don, 219
Hayes, Woody, 59, 71, 140
Hayley, Lee, 73, 118
Heard, Chuck, 36, 95, 220
Heisman, John, 4
Heisman Trophy, 76, 96, 211
Henderson, Johnny, 81
Hertwig, Craig, 19, 221, 225
Hill, Drew, 102, 215
Hipp, Jeff, 222
Hoage, Terry, 19, 20, 25, 29, 103, 223, 226
Hodge, Mark, 102
Hodgson, Pat, 46, 93, 216, 219
Hollis, Joe, 46
Holt, Darwin, 57
Holtz, Beth, 60
Holtz, Lou, 60
Hood, Winford, 223
Horace, 157
Howard, Frank, 60, 61
Howard, Happy, 54
Howell, Hornsby, 46, 47, 168, 169
Hudson, Nat, 222
Hughes, Dennis, 47, 220

Hughes, Lynn, 34, 219, 225
Hunnicutt, Lynn, 96

I

Indiana University, 59
Ingram, Hootie, 39, 47
Inman, Frank, 24, 47
Ivery, Eddie Lee, 102

J

Jackson, Andrew, 5
Jackson, Bo, 91
Jackson, Jerome, 95
Jackson, Keith, 203
James, Fob, 117, 120, 123
James, Lionel, 91
Japan Bowl, 60
Jefferson, Thomas, 5
Jenkins, Ronnie, 94, 219
Jirsa, Ron, 172
Johns Hopkins University, 24
Johnson, Andy, 20, 34, 49, 95, 96, 194, 215, 220
Johnson, Michael, 161
Johnson, Randy, 21, 221, 225
Johnson, Wayne, 113
Jones, D. J., 104
Jones, Danny, 221
Jones, Freddy, 200
Jones, Gomer, 116
Jones, Harry "Squab," 61, 62, 99
Jones, Spike, 220
Jordan, Hamilton, 123
Jordan, Shug, 54, 55, 57, 62, 63, 76, 107, 148
Joyce, Edmund, 115

K

Kasay, John, 21, 47, 49
Kasay, John David, 21, 22, 47
Kay, Clarence, 104, 223

Keith, Kendall, 220
Kelley, Mike, 102
Kemp, Jan, 125, 130–34, 156, 164
Kent State University, 140
Kilcrease, Jennifer, 199, 200
Kinard, Billy, 79
King & Spalding, 168, 169
King, Horace, 22, 221
Knapp, Chuck, 65, 109–12, 122, 136, 164, 165
Knoxville Quarterback Club, 203, 213
Kohn, Larry, 219
Korean War, 148
Krug, Bill, 22, 25, 82, 221, 222, 226

L

Landers, Andy, 154, 206
Landrum, Tom, 179
Lastinger, John, 23, 89, 103, 105, 217
Lawhorne, Tommy, 23, 24, 25
Lawrence, Kent, 17, 18, 24, 47, 93, 220
Lawson, Red, 126
Leavitt, Allan, 82, 221, 226
Leebern, Betsy, 63
Leebern, Don, 63, 64
Lewis, Bill, 19, 29, 48
Liberty Bowl, 22, 137, 140, 230, 240
Little, John, 25, 223, 224, 227, 240
Long, Huey, 120
Louisiana State University (LSU), 30, 101, 195, 236, 240
"Love of Learning Award, The," 153
Lowder, Bobby, 118
Lyons, Tommy, 25, 220, 225, 232

M

Magill, Dan, 18, 58, 64, 65, 66, 72, 99, 137, 151
Magill, Ham, 136, 137
Majors, Johnny, 49, 66
Marino, Dan, 3, 4, 89

Marshall University, 140
Mason, Glen, 140, 141, 142
Matthews, Jimmy, 97
Mattingly, Matt, 120
Maxwell Foundation, 203, 213
McBride, Ricky, 222
McClendon, Brian, 26
McClendon, Willie, 25, 26, 100, 101, 222, 236
McCullough, Jim, 79, 220
McDuffie, Wayne, 48, 49
McFalls, Doug, 93, 94, 229
McIntyre, Guy, 223
McKnight, David, 221
McLean, Avery, 172, 200
McLee, Kevin, 221
McMickens, Donnie, 84
McWhorter Hall, 43
McWhorter, Mac, 21, 221
Memphis State University, 238, 239
Miami Dolphins, 32, 150
Miami University of Ohio, 127
Michigan Stadium, 93. *See also* University of Michigan
Michigan State University, 113, 212, 241
Mike Castronis Award, 42
Miller, Zell, 121
Minter, Jim, 120
Mission Renewal Day, 156, 194
Mississippi State University, 66, 76, 98, 135, 230, 232, 234, 238, 241
Mitchell, Sam, 49, 98
Moore, Kirby, 37, 77, 93, 216, 230
Morris, Warren, 87
Morrison, Tim, 194, 222
Mrvos, Sam, 49
Mundy, Carl E., 148
Munson, Larry, 28, 66, 67, 91, 101
Murphey, Liz, 65

N

Nalley, Jim, 168
Nash, Tom, 36, 220
National Association of Collegiate Directors of Athletics (NACDA), 155, 193, 203, 212, 213
National Gypsum Company, 144
NCAA basketball tournament, 130, 174, 175
NCAA Football Issues Committee, 204, 212
Neinas, Chuck, 160
Neuheisel, Rick, 103
New Jersey Generals, 92, 103
New Orleans Saints, 31
New Orleans Superdome, 86, 87
Newton, Floyd, 169, 170
Nietzsche, Friedrich, 126
Nike, 53, 60, 118, 139
Norris, Carnie, 84
North Carolina State University, 60, 91, 111, 140, 230, 233

O

Ohio State University, 46, 59, 139, 140
Oklahoma State University, 116
Ole Miss. *See* University of Mississippi
Olympics, 27, 67, 68, 69, 212
    Atlanta (1996), 27, 68, 69, 212
    Barcelona (1992), 69
    Los Angeles (1984), 68
    Montreal (1976), 67
Orange Bowl, 57, 76, 79, 89, 152
Oregon State University, 29, 91, 232, 234, 240
Outback Bowl, 147
Outland Trophy, 32, 210

P

Pace, Bill, 28, 49, 98
Paige, Satchel, 72

Pancoast, Fred, 49, 52
Parker, Reid, 119
Parrish, Joel "Cowboy," 15, 221, 225
Paterno, Joe, 68, 92, 203
Paterno, Sue, 68
Patton, General George S., 59
Patton, George, 26, 27, 77, 219, 224, 230
Payne, Billy, 3, 27, 30, 68, 69, 76, 93, 177, 220
Payne, James, 27
Payne, Jimmy, 27, 222, 223, 226
Peach Bowl, 111, 233
Penn State University, 68, 92, 212, 238
Peterson, Buzz, 172
Pittsburgh Steelers, 35
Pollack, David, 32
Pont, John, 59
Portch, Stephen, 169
Poulos, Jimmy, 21, 37, 49, 95, 96, 97, 215
Prince Charles. See Charles, Prince of Wales
Principles of Football, The (Heisman), 4
Pyburn, Jeff, 50
Pyburn, Jim, 41, 50

R
Radloff, Wayne, 223, 238
Ramsey Center, 158
Rankin M. Smith Sr. Student-Athlete Academic Center, 158, 159, 193, 199, 202, 204, 213
Reeves, Dan, 138
Rhodes Scholarship, 24
Rholetter, David, 220
Richardson, Ed, 202
Richt, Mark, 7, 161, 162, 166, 167, 171, 185, 197
Ridlehuber, Preston, 93, 94
Rison, Andre, 113

Rissmiller, Ray, 34, 219, 224
Robinson, Eddie, 203
Robinson, Matt, 16, 28, 80, 81
Robinson, Mixon, 36, 95, 220
Robinson, Rex, 22, 28, 67, 101, 222, 226
Rodgers, Pepper, 70
Rogers, George, 28
Rogers, Kenny, 65
Rogers, Marianne, 65
Rogers, Steve, 100
Ros, Frank, 37, 196, 237
Rose Bowl, 94, 103, 216
Rosenberg, Buzy, 28, 29, 220
Round Table, 156
Royal, Darrell, 151, 163, 203, 205
Russell, Erk, 22, 39, 41, 48, 50, 54, 56, 78, 84, 88, 97, 109–12
Russell, Jean, 51
Russell, Rusty, 51

S
Sadowski, Troy, 29, 224, 227
Saia, Claude, 53
Salvadori, John, 82, 83
Salvadori, Mary, 83
Samford University, 53
Sanchez, Jeff, 29, 91, 223, 227
Sanford Stadium, 81, 101, 103, 119, 158, 162, 176, 202, 212, 215, 216
Schembechler, Bo, 60, 71
Schultz, Jeff, 185
Schwak, David, 99
Scott, Jake, 17, 29, 30, 34, 35, 78, 93, 219, 220, 225
Scott, Lindsay, 30, 85, 101, 217, 222
Sears Cup, 155, 213. See also Director's Cup
Seiler, Cecelia, 71
Seiler, Charles, 71

Seiler, Frank W. "Sonny," 71, 72
Seiler, Swann, 71
Sellers, Terry, 76
Shafer, John, 73, 141
Sheridan, Dick, 111, 112
Sherman, Ray, 18, 45, 51
Shewmaker, Steve, 169, 170
Shipp, Bill, 120, 121
Shirer, Jimmy, 96
Simpson, Bill, 72
Sinkwich, Frank, 25, 26, 101, 203, 213
Smith, Ben, 224
Smith, Camille, 72
Smith, Dean, 163, 205
Smith, Kent, 72
Smith, Loran, 72, 87
Smith, Myrna, 72
Smith, Rankin, Jr., 115
Smith, Royce, 21, 31, 220, 225, 232
Smith, Tubby, 172, 206
Southern Methodist University (SMU),
    14, 21, 26, 42, 76, 216, 230
Spivey, Dan, 17
Spurrier, Steve, 45, 52, 76
Stanfill, Bill, 27, 31, 32, 76, 93, 210,
    219, 220, 225, 231
Stanford University, 2, 155, 236
Stanford, Henry King, 164
Stegeman Coliseum, 2, 17, 18, 40, 159,
    162, 176, 193
Stegeman Hall, 40
Stephens, Kim, 224, 240
Stevens, Becky, 199, 200
Stewart, Ronnie, 222
Still, Art, 70
Strahm, Dale, 48, 51, 112
Strozier, Wilbur, 224, 227
Sugar Bowl, 3, 20, 28, 35, 59, 66, 68,
    79, 80, 83, 86, 89, 91, 117, 119,
    128, 132, 212, 217, 231, 235,
    237, 238

Sullivan, Pat, 95, 96
Sun Bowl, 56, 66, 210, 229, 231, 239
Super Bowl, 20, 32
Superdome. See New Orleans
    Superdome
Swinford, Wayne, 219
Swoopes, Ronnie, 222

T
Talmadge, Herman, 120, 121
Tangerine Bowl, 127, 234
Tardits, Richard, 32, 33, 224
Tarkenton, Fran, 196
Tate, Lars, 137, 224
Taylor, Bob, 29, 93, 94, 216
Temple University, 237, 238
Tereshinski, Joe, III, 22
Tereshinski, Joe, Jr., 22
Tereshinski, Joe, Sr., 22
Tereshinski, Wally, 22
Terry, Gordon, 236
Texas A&M, 85, 91, 155, 237
Texas Christian University (TCU), 237,
    241
Texas Tech, 94, 210, 229
Thilenius, Ed, 66
Thomas, Gerald, 197
Thurson, Tommy, 223
Title IX, 65, 154, 160, 206. See also
    University of Georgia: integra-
    tion of women in athletics
Tolley, Ed, 169, 170, 174
Toner Award, 193, 203, 213
Touchdown Club of Atlanta, 203, 213
Trensch, Kit, 159, 200
Trotter, Virginia, 132, 133
Tucker, Tim, 167
Tulane University, 147, 164, 231, 232,
    233, 239

U

UCLA, 70, 91, 103, 172, 238
UGAs I-III (mascots), 71
University of Alabama, 23, 26, 28, 40,
    41, 47, 52, 54, 55, 57, 59, 79,
    81, 84, 92, 93, 94, 101, 107,
    145, 147, 161, 163, 210, 216,
    229, 233, 235, 239
University of Arizona, 239
University of Arkansas, 22, 48, 49, 80,
    100, 151, 161, 213, 231, 234,
    240
University of California, 91, 235, 237
University of Cincinnati, 235
University of Florida, 16, 19, 31, 36,
    37, 44, 49, 52, 62, 76, 79, 81,
    82, 85, 86, 89, 91, 94, 98, 99,
    104, 139, 155, 168, 196, 211,
    216, 217, 229-41
University of Georgia
    drug problems in football program,
        157
    integration of African-American
        athletes, 62, 127, 205, 206
    integration of women in athletics,
        64, 65, 154, 155, 159, 206.
        See also Title IX
    Jan Kemp crisis, 130-34, 156, 164
    Jim Harrick crisis, 173-75
    national championship in football,
        2, 6, 13, 23, 28, 31, 34, 37, 62,
        66, 68, 83-88, 91, 104, 108,
        117, 119, 129, 154, 196, 211,
        212, 217
    NCAA investigation into football
        program (see University of
        Georgia: Jan Kemp crisis)
    SEC championships, 6, 13, 14, 23,
        28, 32, 37, 57, 62, 70, 75, 76,
        77, 79, 80, 82, 86, 92, 93, 94,
        107, 114, 117, 125, 127, 128,
        158, 160, 161, 175, 185, 197,
        210, 211, 213, 215, 216
University of Georgia (UGA) Athletic
    Association, 47, 56, 158, 169,
    170
University of Georgia (UGA)
    Foundation, 24, 168, 169, 170,
    177, 182, 187, 189
University of Houston, 32, 78, 230,
    231, 234
University of Iowa, 111
University of Kansas, 140
University of Kentucky, 28, 67, 69, 70,
    94, 101, 137, 172, 194, 196,
    229-41
University of Maryland, 233
University of Memphis, 49, 52
University of Miami, 76, 115, 230, 234
University of Michigan, 93, 155, 216,
    229
University of Mississippi (Ole Miss), 26,
    43, 52, 81, 98, 230-41
University of Nebraska, 66, 89, 231
University of North Carolina, 43, 44,
    51, 61, 94, 96, 127, 140, 163,
    168, 205, 210, 211, 229, 230,
    232
University of Notre Dame, 20, 28, 35,
    49, 60, 86, 87, 115, 117, 160,
    172, 211, 217, 237
University of Oklahoma, 35, 116, 117,
    119, 140
University of Oregon, 91, 235
University of Pittsburgh, 3, 66, 83, 89,
    91, 98, 233, 234, 235, 237
University of Richmond, 98, 234, 235,
    240
University of South Carolina, 28, 45,
    60, 61, 77, 78, 84, 85, 211,
    229-41

University of Southern Mississippi, 239
University of Tennessee, 49, 66, 77, 78,
    84, 85, 139, 196, 231, 233, 237,
    241
University of Texas, 21, 23, 104, 105,
    151, 163, 205, 238
University of Virginia, 84, 91, 150, 160,
    236, 240
University of West Georgia, 102
University of Wyoming, 48

V

Valdosta State University, 14, 42
Vanderbilt University, 42, 49, 50, 66,
    100, 103, 135, 136, 137, 139,
    210, 229-41
Varnado, Jerry, 196
Vickers, Jimmy, 51, 52
Villanova University, 155
Vincent J. Dooley Library Endowment
    Fund, 157
Vincent J. Dooley Professorship in hor-
    ticulture, 198
Virginia Military Institute (VMI), 230,
    236
Virginia Tech, 44

W

Wake Forest, 44, 84, 236
Walker, DeLoss, 120, 122, 123
Walker, Herschel, 12, 14, 20, 24, 33,
    34, 58, 75, 84-92, 102, 129,
    135, 154, 196, 199, 211, 217,
    222, 223, 226
Walker, Larry, 139
Walker, Veronica, 154
Wallace, Jeff, 64, 65
Washington, Gene, 37, 67, 98-99, 100,
    221
Washington Redskins, 20
Watergate, 169

Waters, Greg, 223
Weaver, Eddie, 222, 223
Webster, Terrie, 224
Wesley Foundation, 196
Wheeler, Todd, 224, 241
Whittemore, Charlie, 24, 33, 52
Wilder, Hoke, 200
Wilkins, Dominique, 196
Wilkinson, Bud, 116
Williams, Ted, 72
Wilson, Barry, 52, 219, 229
Wilson, Jim, 17, 34, 194, 219, 224
Wilson, Mike, 221
Wilson, Mike "Moonpie," 15, 225
Wisdom, Chip, 52, 96, 220
Woerner, Scott, 34, 102, 194, 215, 217,
    222, 226
Worley, Tim, 35, 224, 227
Wright, Elmo, 78

Y

Yeoman, Bill, 32
Yoculan, Suzanne, 63
Young, Andrew, 130
Young, Steve, 91

Z

Zambiasi, Ben, 35, 36, 98, 221, 222,
    226, 235